In a day of compromise, apathy, and complacency, George Bloomer brings a breath of fresh air back into the American pulpit. His unique ministry style of hard hitting gospel preaching, combined with his keen sense of humor, is stirring up the anointing in the Body of Christ.

—*Reverend Ron Watts*
Pastor, Living Waters Christian Community
Durham, North Carolina

Witchcraft in the Pews is a most compelling topic. The response was great when this message was preached at the Praise Power Conference. It has been a blessing to the conference participants and thousands of others who have heard the cassettes or seen the videos. This topic is a must-read for pastors and church leaders interested in Satan-proofing their churches and equipping their congregations for true spiritual warfare.

—*Bishop Thomas Weeks*
President of Praise Power Conference
Pastor of Greater Bethel Apostolic Temple
Wilmington, Delaware

After perusing *Spiritual Warfare*, two things became very clear to me. First, it is very obvious that George Bloomer is on a divine assignment to lift the lid off the strategies of the enemy so that all believers can live a life of power and victory. Second, because of George Bloomer's faithfulness to this assignment, hell is turning over and Satan has been forced back to the drawing board. Every believer who is serious about canceling the agenda of Satan over his life ought to read this book.

—*Bishop Neil C. Ellis*
Senior Pastor
Mount Tabor Full Gospel Baptist Church
Nassau, Bahamas

Spiritual Warfare is a book that guarantees to expose the forces of the enemy and eliminate his agenda in the lives of those who believe and receive. George Bloomer's divine insight and lucid stratagems on defeating the enemy will impel readers to rise and fight the good fight of faith, war against the enemy, and intercept Satan's weapons of destruction. A book designed to impart and provoke positive reaction, *Spiritual Warfare* is the type of supernatural armament needed in the body of Christ to incapacitate Lucifer's armed forces!

—*Bishop Noel Jones*
Senior Pastor
Greater Bethany Community Church
Los Angeles, California

In *Spiritual Warfare*, Bishop George Bloomer has presented a balanced, reasoned approach to the often abused and controversial topic of spiritual warfare. He employs his considerable teaching gift to provide solid and substantive strategies for believers, that they might capably and intelligently "*contend for the faith which was once delivered unto the saints*" (Jude 1:3 KJV).

—*Pastor Jacqueline E. McCullough*
Senior Pastor
The Gathering at Beth Rapha
Pomona, New York

WITCHCRAFT
IN THE PEWS *and*
SPIRITUAL WARFARE

WITCHCRAFT
IN THE PEWS *and*
SPIRITUAL WARFARE

Best-selling Author
GEORGE BLOOMER

WHITAKER
HOUSE

Witchcraft in the Pews and Spiritual Warfare
Two-Books-in-One

George G. Bloomer
GG Bloomer Ministries
PO Box 3867
Durham, NC 27702
www.bishopbloomer.com

ISBN: 978-1-64123-759-8
eBook ISBN: 978-1-64123-758-1
Printed in the United States of America
Witchcraft in the Pews © 2008 by George G. Bloomer
Spiritual Warfare © 2004 by George G. Bloomer
Whitaker House compilation 2021

Whitaker House
1030 Hunt Valley Circle
New Kensington, PA 15068
www.whitakerhouse.com

1 2 3 4 5 6 7 8 9 10 11 ⊔⊔ 28 27 26 25 24 23 22 21

CONTENTS

WITCHCRAFT IN
THE PEWS

DEDICATION

This book is dedicated to my mother,
Georgia Bloomer,
and to my two lovely daughters,
Jessica and Jennifer.

CONTENTS

FOREWORD

The Lord Jesus Christ has endowed Bishop George G. Bloomer with insight into the spiritual realm. Brother Bloomer has engaged in direct warfare with the forces of darkness in foreign fields where he has traveled to preach the Gospel. However, let us not be deceived. As Brother Bloomer so poignantly points out, witchcraft is practiced in the United States of America as well. Brother Bloomer has remained humble as he continues to shed light on this overlooked or ignorantly dismissed topic.

This book is timely because many pastors, church leaders, and laymen, not knowing the truth, have been deceived by the enemy. The truth is simple: there is witchcraft in our pews.

Witchcraft is a true threat to the church of Jesus Christ. Only by accepting Him, the Son of God, as our Lord and Savior, and by knowing the truth as given to us in the Bible, can we confront such error. This book is mandatory reading if you want to be made aware of the devices that Satan uses to confuse and divide the body of Christ.

—*Dr. Ernestine Reems-Dickerson*
Center of Hope Community Church
Oakland, California

INTRODUCTION

Have you ever attended a church where the pastor was domineering, using fear to manipulate the members? Perhaps a faction in the church seemed excessively controlling and wanted to influence every decision. Whether these people knew it or not, they may have been practicing witchcraft.

Witchcraft is alive and well, and its influence is felt throughout American society and many of its institutions—including the church. Don't believe me? Far more than a harmless children's fable, witchcraft is found in Scripture and used by evil forces to deceive, divert, and discourage believers from seeking God and fulfilling Christ's calling for His bride, the church. Instead of serving and worshipping God, too many Christians have allowed themselves to become vulnerable to spiritual attack. Instead of ministering to the sick, the needy, and "the least of these," they have been led astray into human causes and demonic distraction.

In the first part of this book, I will define witchcraft, show its origin in Scripture, and describe the many forms in which it exists in the world today.

In the second part, I will provide actual examples of witchcraft in action today. I will expose such culture phenomena as *The Secret*, the Religious Right, the Don Imus controversy, the Jena Six, and the Million-Man March as specific efforts to manipulate the body of Christ for the cause of Satan.

Finally, in the third section, I will explain what Christians can do to protect their homes, churches, and lives from the insidious effects of witchcraft.

The Bible says, *"My people are destroyed from lack of knowledge"* (Hosea 4:6). My prayer is that this book might equip the men and women of God with the knowledge they need to effectively wage spiritual warfare against the enemy and drive him out of the pews.

Part I

WITCHCRAFT IS REAL

Chapter 1

WHAT IS WITCHCRAFT?

With the ever-increasing fad and fascination of mystical teachings and beliefs, those who are seeking a deeper understanding of the supernatural often ask, "Why do Christians refer to witchcraft as a sin?"

Many will suggest that witchcraft is simply the harmless worship of nature. They claim that both Christianity and witchcraft serve a higher power and that there is no significant difference between the two.

To this, I must strongly disagree. As Christians, we must be very clear concerning the source of the *power* we are serving. But who are we to believe? How are we to discern between harmless fun and actual evil spiritual realities?

Just as those who follow the principles and teachings of other beliefs have their manuals to lead and guide them to gain knowledge and deeper understanding, Christians too employ a guide whereby we are led, according to our beliefs—the Bible. Biblical teachings are not meant to invoke argumentative debates, but to serve as direction for those who believe and for others who are seeking a deeper, revelatory experience with God.

Many people may not be aware that witchcraft is mentioned several times in the Bible. In the Old Testament book of 1 Samuel, Saul is rejected as king for his rebellion against God.

> *For rebellion is as the sin of witchcraft, and stubbornness is as iniquity and idolatry. Because you have rejected the word of the LORD, He also has rejected you from being king.* (1 Samuel 15:23 NKJV)

Why are *rebellion* and *witchcraft* compared in this instance? To rebel against something is to defy its authority. Our authority, as believers, is Jesus Christ, and in rejecting Him, we replace His beloved power with impious sources—mysticism and powers that derive from areas other than the Father.

THE ESSENCE OF WITCHCRAFT

The word *witchcraft* comes from an Old English word, *wiccecraft*. At its most basic, those who practice witchcraft, witches, use it to manipulate the will of others. In practicing witchcraft, human beings are actually attempting to replicate the wonderful acts of God, either with natural products or with the aid of devils. Scripture gives us three words that describe the occult: *divination*, *sorcery*, and *witchcraft*. These are the three pillars of demonology. Let's look at these three words closely.

DIVINATION

Divination is the fortune-telling portion of the spirit realm. It often works through tarot cards, tea leaves, crystal balls, horoscopes, and palm reading. Tune into late night television and you will see "psychic hotlines" flooding the airwaves where desperate people consult with modern soothsayers who tell people what they think they want to hear, as their 900-numbers rack up a nifty $3.99 a minute. Promoted as amusement, these tools of Satan not only steal people's money, the callers are actually giving legal ground to the enemy, drawing them even deeper into the influence of the demonic.

Both the Old and New Testaments in the Bible make it very clear that we are to avoid divination of any sort:

> *Do not turn to mediums or seek out spiritists, for you will be defiled by them. I am the LORD your God.* (Leviticus 19:31)

> *I will set my face against the person who turns to mediums and spiritists to prostitute himself by following them, and I will cut him off from his people.* (Leviticus 20:6)

Let no one be found among you who sacrifices his son or daughter in the fire, who practices divination or sorcery, interprets omens, engages in witchcraft, or casts spells, or who is a medium or spiritist or who consults the dead. Anyone who does these things is detestable to the LORD, and because of these detestable practices the LORD your God will drive out those nations before you. (Deuteronomy 18:10–12)

The central issue in the prohibition of divination in the Old Testament was that it led people away from God and attempted to control future events through spells and evil spirits. Again, the result was separation from God.

The people of God were warned not to get involved in any way with those who did not serve God. They were to tear down and destroy the enemy pagan influences among them. We know from reading the rest of the Scriptures that the Israelites did not do so. The nations that God displaced for Israel to enter the Promised Land served false gods of every sort, and some of these occult practices crept unnoticed into the everyday lives of God's people. *"Even while these people were worshiping the LORD, they were serving their idols"* (2 Kings 17:41).

> *The people of God were warned not to get involved with those who did not serve God.*

In the New Testament, we read of a woman who was controlled by a spirit of divination.

Once when we were going to the place of prayer, we were met by a slave girl who had a spirit by which she predicted the future. She earned a great deal of money for her owners by fortune-telling. This girl followed Paul and the rest of us, shouting, "These men are servants of the Most High God, who are telling you the way to be saved." She kept this up for many days. Finally Paul became so troubled that he turned around and said to the spirit, "In the name of Jesus Christ I command you to come out of her!" At that moment the spirit left her. When the owners

*of the slave girl realized that their hope of making money was gone, they
seized Paul and Silas and dragged them into the marketplace to face
the authorities.*   (Acts 16:16–19)

Notice that this spirit began its harassment as Paul and the others
went to prayer, that place of fellowship with God. The slave girl followed
them proclaiming the truth, but in a mocking manner. Finally Paul "dispossessed" the demonic spirit in the name of Jesus Christ.

We see in the next verse that not only did the spirit influence the girl,
but it also brought her masters under the influence of a spirit of greed as
they profited by her lying divination. In this way, one spirit opened the way
for the other. All, however, were living under the influence of witchcraft.

In Acts 13, Paul had another encounter with a sorcerer named
Elymas.

*But Elymas the sorcerer (for that is what his name means) opposed
them and tried to turn the proconsul from the faith. Then Saul, who
was also called Paul, filled with the Holy Spirit, looked straight at
Elymas and said, "You are a child of the devil and an enemy of everything that is right! You are full of all kinds of deceit and trickery. Will
you never stop perverting the right ways of the Lord?" (Acts 13:8–10)*

Note that the man was guilty of diverting others from *"the faith."* He
was employing Satan's old habit of seeking to deflect and distort the true
worship of God. Paul also called him a *"child of the devil"*—literally, one
who does what the devil does.

In an even earlier account, Peter encountered a sorcerer named Simon
who amazed a city of seventy thousand people through the power of
Satan. But when the people came to Christ, Simon's powers were no longer
impressive and he became a believer as well. But did he really? Later, when
Simon witnessed the true power of God flowing through Peter, he offered
to pay the apostles so that he could have this same power.

*When Simon saw that the Spirit was given at the laying on of the
apostles' hands, he offered them money and said, "Give me also this
ability so that everyone on whom I lay my hands may receive the Holy
Spirit."*   (Acts 8:18–19)

What was it that Simon offered to purchase? It was power, pure and simple. He had no desire to see the Holy Spirit come upon people to empower them and set them free. It was all about control. Nothing had changed in him; he still wanted to influence and impress.

SORCERY

Sorcery works through drugs, alcohol, suggestive dancing, charms, and even the wearing of ritual makeup. But, just as with divination, the ultimate goal is control, and to lure people away from worship of God.

> *Now the works of the flesh are evident, which are: adultery, fornication, uncleanness, lewdness, idolatry, **sorcery**, hatred, contentions, jealousies, outbursts of wrath, selfish ambitions, dissensions, heresies, envy, murders, drunkenness, revelries, and the like; of which I tell you beforehand, just as I also told you in time past, that those who practice such things will not inherit the kingdom of God.*
>
> (Galatians 5:19–21 NKJV, emphasis added)

This passage of Scripture lists *"sorcery"*—*"witchcraft"* in the King James Version and *New International Version*—among the deeds of the flesh. The Greek word there is *pharmakeia*, from which we get the word *pharmacy*, the place where prescription drugs are available. In ancient times the pharmacist was one who mixed potions and poisons with which to influence or kill people. Today, illegal drugs enslave us and make us dependent upon them. They waste our lives and our money.

Young addicts never get a chance to experience the joys of life because of their dependence on drugs. Each day, scores of young people leave their families for life on the streets. Some become members of gangs, an ever-increasing threat to society that encourages crime and acts of violence. In an effort to protect their "turf," gang members engage in violence, and innocent bystanders are often caught in the crossfire resulting in needless deaths.

Young addicts never get a chance to experience the joys of life.

According to the National Center for the Victims of Crime, the percentage of state prison inmates who reported being under the influence of drugs at the time of their offense was almost 33 percent (Bureau of Justice Statistics, 1997). In Albuquerque, New Mexico, and Chicago, Illinois, close to 30 percent of males and 40 percent of females arrested in 1999 tested positive for more than one drug at the time of arrest (National Institute of Justice, 2000). This intense craving for the next fix can even turn addicts against their own family members.

Drugs become the tool to gain dominion over users and enslave them.

In one city in the South, a young man was so desperate that he broke into the home of his two elderly aunts and killed them to get money to buy drugs. Another woman gave her preteen daughter over to prostitution to supply the money needed to fund her habit. Drug addiction affects the rich and poor alike. News outlets and magazines love to print headlines screaming about the latest famous athlete, actor, or musician with a huge salary who loses millions of dollars because he cannot refrain from using drugs and is subsequently suspended or released by his employers.

How do drugs cause people to behave in such a way? Using sorcery, people attempt to control with drugs and evil spirits those things which God controls supernaturally by His love.

Cocaine, for instance, affects the area of the brain where the pleasure center is located. This pleasure center controls our sex drive and experiences pain inflicted on the body. Our bodies naturally produce a drug called dopamine, which brings pleasure to the body during sexual intercourse or helps mask the pain of an injury. For the addict, the drive to satisfy a drug craving is similar to the sexual desires within a drug-free person. While the rest of us can satisfy our sexual desires within the bonds of marriage, there is no easy or legal way out for the addict. Enslaved by the addiction, a drug user must obey his or her craving, whatever the cost. This is an example of the control that sorcery can have over people. Drugs become the tool to gain dominion over users and enslave them. In other words, your local drug dealer is a type of sorcerer.

Not all drug use is bad. When properly administered, they can bring about healing as God intended or help people to endure severe pain. When abused by drug addicts and sorcerers, however, so-called "recreational" drugs bring nothing but destruction.

But even as illegal drugs plague our neighborhoods and families, we must realize that we are also the most legally medicated people on earth. Never have so many people used prescription drugs. We have drugs to bring us out of depression, to help us sleep, to aid our sex lives, and to manage weight, stress, and anxiety.

Antidepressant drugs are prescribed almost automatically today. While, in some cases, these prescription drugs can be helpful in correcting such things as chemical imbalances in the brain, there are other causes of depression. Depression also can be the result of demonic influence. In such cases, drugs may treat the symptoms, but they will never be able to address the spiritual source of the depression.

WITCHCRAFT

Normally, when we think of witchcraft, we envision black cats and old hags dressed in robes with pointy hats and riding on broomsticks. In reality, however, witchcraft is the calling forth of spiritual influences with the goal of controlling the will of another person and putting him or her in subjection to your own will. Witchcraft is the realm of the spirit dealing in *domination*. It works primarily through encouraging disobedience, which then opens the door to intimidation, manipulation, and control.

Paul asked an interesting question in Galatians. Many in the Galatian church were falling back into a mind-set of works and rituals to please leaders who sought to bind them to religion once again. Paul said,

> *O foolish Galatians! Who has bewitched you that you should not obey the truth, before whose eyes Jesus Christ was clearly portrayed among you as crucified?* (Galatians 3:1 NKJV)

Believe it or not, religion itself can be an influencing factor to instill fear into the lives of believers and separate them from the true and living God.

What do I mean by *religion?* Religion, in the broadest sense, refers to a *system* of beliefs about God. But religion itself can become an obstacle if we begin to relate to the system of beliefs or doctrine and forget about our personal relationship with God. For the ancient Jewish people, religion became a mechanical following of rules, done by rote, rather than a personal relationship with their God. In the Old Testament, God Himself had told His people that while they practiced religion, their hearts were not in it.

> The Lord says: *"These people come near to me with their mouth and honor me with their lips, but their hearts are far from me. Their worship of me is made up only of rules taught by men."* (Isaiah 29:13)

Anything that tries to dominate, control, or manipulate is a form of witchcraft.

The Galatians had begun to fall back into that religious pattern. They put aside the truth of the Gospel of grace through Jesus Christ and began trying to earn their way to fellowship with God through legalistic religion. If it were possible for us to save ourselves, who would be in control? We would! Man would then *be like God.* That is the oldest lie in the cosmos. God is God, and He alone saves through His Son Jesus Christ.

Throughout the history of the church, various leaders have tried to exert control over the people they were called to serve. In the Middle Ages, a hierarchy of church leaders evolved that took control of every aspect of the people's lives. The church became a political force with the power of life or death. The result was corruption throughout the church to the point of selling forgiveness to those who had enough money. Again, leaders in the church assumed a place that was not theirs. They took their eyes off of God and said to themselves, *We can be like God and issue forgiveness.* Thankfully,

Martin Luther and other reformers came along, and the church was redirected to its original purpose: worship of God, not a form of religion.

Anything that tries to dominate, control, or manipulate is a form of witchcraft. It is still a fact that, from time to time, movements and individuals rise up and assume a place of influence in an attempt to control a crowd—be it a handful of people or thousands. That is why it is crucial for those whom God has called into leadership to remain diligent in examining their own hearts. Leaders serve the Lord by caring for those they lead—not dominating them. Jesus talked about this issue:

> Jesus called them together and said, "You know that the rulers of the Gentiles lord it over them, and their high officials exercise authority over them. Not so with you. Instead, whoever wants to become great among you must be your servant."   (Matthew 20:25–26)

Unfortunately, witchcraft continues to work its way, not only into our church pews, but also into our pulpits. The sad truth is, far more witchcraft exists within our churches today than many of us are willing to admit.

Chapter 2

WITCHCRAFT WITHIN

Raised as a Seventh-Day Adventist, I encountered many new and strange worship experiences when I converted to Pentecostalism through my born-again confession. Though I was not spiritually mature enough to recognize what to call it, I sensed that my minister was a very controlling person. Ours was a very dogmatic and legalistic church. The pastor's preaching focused primarily on things we were forbidden to do. We were not allowed to play sports like other young men. We were not allowed to date. During the summer we did not go to the beach, nor were we allowed to participate in outings that public school students attended. Later, I discovered that this man even arranged and dissolved marriages. He was in control, and to him, everything beyond the church doors was satanic.

Later I was able to realize that *he* was satanic.

In the two years I worshipped at this church, I witnessed the worst type of witchcraft in operation. This same minister preached at every service. We never held any revivals; we never discussed opposing opinions of theology; we heard no other messages from visiting preachers. Our spiritual diet consisted solely of things this one man wanted us to hear and know. Each Sunday his message dealt primarily with fire and brimstone. By instilling fear in our hearts, he was able to control his congregation.

What prompted me to leave this church? One day the pastor told a story about a group of church members holding a conversation about him in their home. Although he was not present at the gathering, he said that the Lord allowed him to sit in on private meetings of members of the church "in the spirit." He claimed to know what everyone in the church was doing and discussing that pertained to him and to the church. I now assume that someone was slipping him some inside information because on several occasions he hit the nail on the head, striking even greater fear in our hearts.

> *Many of God's people have not been exposed to the incredible joy of true freedom in Christ.*

I began to wonder why God would reveal my personal thoughts, prayers, and conversations to this man. I realized that I feared my pastor more than I feared God. When I fell short and sinned, my prayer was not "Lord, forgive me" but, "Lord, don't let my pastor find out."

Shortly after this pastor passed away, God took me through a season of purging. The Holy Spirit gave me three dreams. In one dream this minister was still alive. I had been invited to preach at his church. When he stepped on the platform, however, all the lights went out. When he finished preaching and stepped off the platform, the lights came back on. God revealed to me that the church was in darkness. God also revealed that He was calling me to enlighten His people regarding the awful, dreadful myths about witchcraft. There is nothing harmless about it.

How many churchgoing people today are presently under this type of witchcraft? Why do so many stay in these controlling, manipulative churches? In many cases, a blinding spirit prevents them from seeing the truth of God, and many of them willingly accept the lie.

While most preachers today are God-fearing servants dedicated to laying down their lives for the sake of the Gospel, there are, unfortunately, far too many preachers operating as nothing more than witches and warlocks in their practice. They manipulate the people of God and profit off of them by plundering their finances and resources. They control through fear, intimidation, and false prophecies. Many of God's people have not been exposed to the incredible joy of true freedom in Christ. Unfortunately, many of these people sought refuge in the church from the world of sin only to enter into the bondage of witchcraft.

Don't be naïve. Satan often uses ministers as his taskmasters. He arms them with whips formed from twisted interpretations of Scripture to control the people of God. The result is great deception, immorality, and perversion.

In one horrific example, a young girl shared with her pastor how she had been abused by her uncles and by a brother. This young girl went to the church and asked her pastor for help. How did he counsel and care for her? He had sex with her for six months. Eventually, she lost touch with reality and was placed into a mental health institution. You might suggest that this was an unfortunate but isolated incident with one bad pastor. If only that were the case. Today's headlines are too often filled with reports of cases similar to this one. The church is under attack from within.

> *Many Christians have been exposed to doctrine but not to the person of Christ Jesus.*

I am not on a witch hunt, but I do want to shed a light on the church in order to expose the devil and his deceptions. A major problem facing the church today is that far too many Christians have not been exposed to real Christianity. Many have come into the church based on a culture, religious affiliation, or denominational background, but have not been truly introduced to Jesus.

What a frightening thought to know that many of us who repented ten years ago are just now discovering and establishing a relationship with the true Jesus Christ. We have been exposed to doctrine and church order but not to the person of Christ Jesus.

CAN YOU SEE JESUS?

The prophet Isaiah said, *"In the year that King Uzziah died, I saw the Lord seated on a throne, high and exalted, and the train of his robe filled the* temple" (Isaiah 6:1). Unfortunately, for many in the church, there are some people who are preventing them from seeing the Lord.

I love the story of one man and his friends who would not be prevented from seeing Jesus:

> *A few days later, when Jesus again entered Capernaum, the people heard that he had come home. So many gathered that there was no room left, not even outside the door, and he preached the word to them. Some men came, bringing to him a paralytic, carried by four of them. Since they could not get him to Jesus because of the crowd, they made an opening in the roof above Jesus and, after digging through it, lowered the mat the paralyzed man was lying on. When Jesus saw their faith, he said...."I tell you, get up, take your mat and go home." He got up, took his mat and walked out in full view of them all. This amazed everyone and they praised God, saying, "We have never seen anything like this!"* (Mark 2:1–5,11–12)

These men carried their sick friend to the roof because the people there were too focused on themselves to move out of the way and let them enter. The sick man was unable to see Jesus because others stood in his way. Not to be denied, his friends removed tiles on the roof and lowered the sick man to Jesus. Hopefully, that is what this book is doing—removing the obstacles to seeing Jesus that have been put in place by the powers of darkness and witchcraft. After exposing the deceptions of Satan, we must break up his strongholds so that the hurting, sick, and wounded may come to Jesus.

In the same way that Jesus taught the crowd, we need teaching to expose the forces of evil. The Bible says, *"Do your best to present yourself to God as one approved, a workman who does not need to be ashamed and who correctly handles the word of truth"* (2 Timothy 2:15).

Satan wants to deceive us. If he has to, he will even use an evangelist to attract crowds and attempt to trick people into worshipping him. How do I know this? I experienced it myself.

MADNESS AT MIDNIGHT

As a missionary, I was excited to be in the evangelistic field. Finally I had a chance to share the Gospel, cast out devils, and proclaim the acceptable year of the Lord. My missionary journey took me to a remote section of Jamaica, in the West Indies. I was invited to speak at a church that held two hundred people.

On one particular night, however, the crowd swelled to more than five hundred people. I grew excited at the opportunity to minister to such a throng.

I found one thing unusual, however. This church had scheduled me to speak at midnight. The darkness was even more intense because this church, which was located in the jungle, had no electricity and used candles to light the building. As I sat in the pulpit, it appeared that we would later celebrate the Lord's Supper. A communion table was draped in white linen with black tassels and white lace hanging from it. Coconuts, bananas, star apples, jack fruit, and a bottle of water sat on the table. Two women standing at the door were wearing white dresses with a red ribbon sachet around their waist and blue and red ribbons on both legs. We were in a different culture so I assumed this was their unique style of worship. Besides, I had certainly seen much stranger dress in some churches in the United States.

> *After exposing the deceptions of Satan, we must break up his strongholds.*

The service proceeded without incident. Suddenly, I heard a loud scream that sent chills up my spine. Instead of fading, it seemed to increase in volume. This screaming provoked others to join in. My experience as a young evangelist had not prepared me for what was about to occur.

A man whom I didn't know was sharing the pulpit with me. He stood up and announced that I would be speaking after the "raising of the dead service." Instantly, every bit of Holy Spirit boldness drained from my body. Lazarus had already been raised by Jesus Christ, and I did not know of any other candidates for resurrection.

Suddenly, a drum cadence began to pound out as the two women at the door produced machetes and began to jump to the beat. Two men came down the center aisle, overturned the communion table, and poured boiled rice on it. By now the whole congregation had joined in with screaming and hollering. The coconut that had been sitting on the table popped open by itself.

Frantically, I prayed to God for deliverance out of this place. But the situation only grew worse. The men beat the drums violently. Another man started convulsing and frothed at the mouth. This was no strange version of Christian worship. Witchcraft was in the pews. While everyone focused on the action on the floor, I ran out of the church as quickly as I could.

Later I discovered that I had been used as a drawing card for this witchcraft service. Often, when an American evangelist preaches in Jamaica, he attracts a large crowd. Even though many of the people there were acting in ignorance, they were, nonetheless, practicing a form of witchcraft. Perhaps they did not know that witchcraft and Christianity are opposed to each other. This experience, however frightening, gave me great insight into how witchcraft can seep into the church.

OPENING THE DOOR TO EVIL

Today, Catholicism is the primary form of Christianity in Latin America. Before the Catholics arrived on their shores, however, many of these Latin American countries engaged in pagan religions. As the military might of the European powers enabled explorers to subdue these countries, the Roman Catholic Church was able to convert the native population to Christianity. Eventually, Catholicism, with its many rituals and symbolism, combined with the native practices, serving as a catalyst for their followers to drift into heresy and witchcraft.

In many parts of the Caribbean, as well as South and Central America, the religion of Santeria is an example of heresy resulting from the fusion of Christianity with West African religions brought to the New World by slaves. This cult is devoted to certain African divinities which, over time, became identified with Catholic saints. Thus, though they may say the name Saint Peter, they are actually referring to one of their African deities.

HEALED OF OPPRESSION

Because many churches do not believe in spiritual warfare or are not equipped to overcome the power of evil, many of those who need and seek spiritual deliverance are unable to get it.

My involvement in Young Witnesses for Christ Ministries takes me all over the world. We try to minister to the whole person—spirit, soul, and body. This occasionally means providing food, basic personal hygiene products, and medical supplies. On one occasion, we were holding a healing service at the National Sports Hall in the South American city of Georgetown, Guyana. Blackouts occur frequently in this country. Sure enough, as I was praying for people, the lights went out. As we continued to cast out evil spirits in the name of Jesus Christ by candlelight, I could hear howling and screaming all around us.

During the service, a young girl with a disfigured face came up to me. She had the scars from third-degree burns on her mouth. Apparently, because she had confessed faith in Jesus Christ, the local witch doctors had seared her mouth shut at the corners with hot irons to prevent her from witnessing. Before coming to me, she had gone to various churches in the area to gain deliverance from the demonic oppression placed upon her by the witch doctors. The local pastors had tried to console her, but they could not help her.

> *Witchcraft is as prevalent in the churches of the United States as in those of any other country.*

Because the pastors could not help her, she then opted for some local cults that promised to communicate with the spirit world. How did they try to drive out the evil spirits? They inflicted third-degree burns over most of the rest of her body.

As this poor child stood before me, the Holy Spirit instructed me to have her stand up. After she stood up, I rebuked the spirit of perversion, witchcraft, doubt, and fear, ministering the healing power of Christ Jesus.

This girl, who had been tormented and oppressed by the devil, began to renounce the hidden works of Satan. As she did, her mouth popped open, no longer seared shut at the corners. The arena lights came back on and I ministered there for another three hours. This scheduled one-week revival lasted an entire month.

We must not, however, live under the misguided impression that witchcraft is practiced exclusively in Latin America. Such practices are just as prevalent in the United States. Just as it is disguised in the Santeria cult, witchcraft is also disguised in our churches today. In fact, I believe that witchcraft is as prevalent in the churches of the United States as in the churches of any other country.

INFILTRATING THE CHURCH

I was once invited to preach a revival for a church in the U.S. that had been through nine pastors in five years. Five women controlled this church based on their ownership of the land on which the church was built. For three days I preached on spiritual warfare. On the fourth night of the revival, the five women came to church dressed in black. They walked around the walls of the church as the congregation joyously jumped and shouted their praises to God.

The following night, the pastor told me to shut down the revival. It turns out that those five women were demanding that I close the meetings and were relaying their sentiments through the pastor. Deciding not to leave the city, I continued the revival at a nearby motel. A tremendous outpouring of God's Holy Spirit put the seal of approval on the revival that had begun in the church.

On one of the nights, I fell asleep in my clothes because the revival had exhausted me. As I slept, I dreamed that little gremlins undressed me. When I awoke, I was wearing only my undergarments and my tie was wrapped around my neck. Instead of shying away, I took this unusual incident was a sign that my message of spiritual warfare was stirring the evil spirits in the area.

On another occasion, after preaching the Word of God at a revival in New York City, I proceeded to minister to the needs of people who came forward for prayer. One man for whom I prayed did not respond to the deliverance message. Instead, he reached out, grabbed me by the neck, and began choking me. One of the sisters in the church cried out, "It's a demon!"

The entire church immediately moved to one side. I pleaded the blood of Jesus over the man, but it seemed to no avail. His hold on my throat only tightened. The old George Bloomer who grew up in the Red Hook projects of New York City emerged. I raised both my hands, put them on his neck, and choked him right back. I didn't let up until he loosened his grip on my neck. Once he returned to his senses, I cast the evil spirit out of this man in the name of Jesus Christ. This man is now a devoted servant of Jesus Christ our Lord and works faithfully in the church.

HOW SATAN WORKS

To understand witchcraft we must understand the order of Satan's kingdom.

> *Put on the whole armor of God, that you may be able to stand against the wiles of the devil. For we do not wrestle against flesh and blood, but against principalities, against powers, against the rulers of the darkness of this age, against spiritual hosts of wickedness in the heavenly places.*
> (Ephesians 6:11–12 NKJV)

According to this passage, Satan's kingdom has four divisions. First, we find *"principalities,"* or the domain of evil spirits. The word *principalities* is a combination of the words *princes* and *in the palace.* In other words, evil spirits are territorial.

In the Old Testament, Daniel prayed, fasted, and mourned before God for three full weeks, but there was no answer. Had God turned a deaf ear to his cry? Finally, the angel Gabriel spoke these words to Daniel:

> *Do not be afraid, Daniel. Since the first day that you set your mind to gain understanding and to humble yourself before your God, your words were heard, and I have come in response to them. But the prince of the Persian kingdom resisted me twenty-one days. Then Michael, one of the chief princes, came to help me, because I was detained there with the king of Persia.*
> (Daniel 10:12–13)

During those three weeks, the angel Gabriel could not give Daniel the answer because he was held up by a spirit assigned to Persia. It wasn't until the archangel Michael came to Gabriel's assistance that he was even able to contact Daniel with God's answer.

The second of Satan's divisions are *"powers,"* the evil spirits representing the power of the unseen kingdom: demons, fallen angels, and seducing spirits.

Third are the *"rulers of the darkness of this age"* which refer to such phenomena as psychic hotlines, enchanters, witches, warlocks, and prognosticators.

Finally, we find *"spiritual hosts of wickedness in the heavenly places."* These are actually pastors and teachers who preach against God in the name of God. This is where Satan's power embeds itself within the church. Today, false teaching and blatant heresy run rampant throughout much of the church. Some churches in this country are ordaining homosexuals, sanctioning adultery and mental telepathy, and "tickling ears" with a "name it and claim it" theology. These teachings are tactics aimed more at placating the desires of the flesh than pleasing and honoring God.

This form of witchcraft practiced in the United States is far more insidious than the form practiced by the witch doctors in Guyana. There, at least the battle lines are clearly drawn. The enemy is clearly recognized. But the form of witchcraft being practiced in the United States is much more subtle and deceptive. Many a well-meaning soul has sought the protection of a local church as means of escaping the grip of Satan. Little do they know that condoning certain sexual behavior, teaching doctrines of devils, and holding services based on the needs and desires of the flesh constitute the practice of witchcraft.

BREAKING THE CURSE

As we were dismissed from church one Sunday, a young man approached me. He looked as if he hadn't slept in a few days. I could smell alcohol on his breath and noticed his ragged clothes. Seeing a mild shaking in his body, I thought he might be having a nervous breakdown.

He told me that I had invited him to church a few years ago. He decided to look me up because he was going through a difficult time in which he was losing control. His girlfriend had left him and he did not know what to do because he really loved her. He admitted that he was hearing voices that were urging him to commit suicide. These voices were so persistent and relentless that he was considering the idea just to be free of their torment. He also revealed that he was addicted to alcohol, cocaine, and cigarettes.

I immediately took him into the church where a few other members and I began praying for his deliverance. First, I led him in accepting Jesus Christ as Lord and Savior of his life. Then we confessed the Word of God over him in prayer. *"Greater is he that is in you, than he that is in the world"* (1 John 4:4 KJV). *"For this purpose the Son of God was manifested, that He might destroy the works of the devil"* (1 John 3:8 NKJV).

We were not there long when the young man stood up from prayer; he had stopped shaking. The drunken look had disappeared, and he confessed that he had been delivered.

The form of witchcraft practiced in the United States is extremely subtle and deceptive.

After his deliverance, this young brother often accompanied me when I witnessed to others. His testimony stirred many hearts toward the Lord. One day we knocked on the door of a young woman who was in graduate school studying to become a dietetic clinician. When the young man explained how he had been delivered from alcohol, cocaine, and cigarettes, the young woman was in utter disbelief. She had learned that those three substances were the most addictive drugs known to mankind.

"Did you have any withdrawal symptoms?" she asked.

"Never," he replied.

What an amazing act of God. But it only happened because we believed the Word of God rather than the words of man. Jesus Christ said, *"If the Son sets you free, you will be free indeed"* (John 8:36). The world tells us that alcoholism is a disease and cocaine addiction is a sickness. God did not say this; man said it—and too many of us will believe man before we will believe God.

How can you break the curse of witchcraft? First, you must accept Jesus Christ as Lord and Savior. Then, you must also confess and acknowledge the Word of God in your life. God's promises are powerful and they can be trusted.

YOUR LEGAL DELIVERANCE

What took place on Golgotha's hill is the basis for our salvation and deliverance. Jesus became a curse that we might be the recipients of the blessing. He was our sin substitute. Scripture says, *"The law requires that nearly everything be cleansed with blood, and without the shedding of blood there is no forgiveness"* (Hebrews 9:22). The blood of the risen Lamb of Calvary did not merely *cover* our sin; it took our sin away.

We must understand that God is just, and therefore He is a legalist. He cannot do anything illegal. The cross is the basis of our salvation. Faith appropriates what God has done for us. We must understand this as we pull down strongholds. *"The weapons we fight with are not the weapons of the world. On the contrary, they have divine power to demolish strongholds"* (2 Corinthians 10:4).

Satan is also a legalist. He goes by the book. Our adversary comes with legal papers concerning our bondage. The kingdom of heaven is likened to a courthouse where God is the Judge, Jesus is our defense attorney, Satan is the accuser of the brethren or the prosecuting attorney, the blood is the jury, the demons are Satan's police officers, and our case is before God in glory.

The Holy Spirit is the paralegal who prepares our case for litigation. What Satan accuses us of is true. We are guilty as charged. Because of the blood that has been applied to us, however, we are released because of time already served. Because our penalty has been paid, God no longer sees us in our sin. He sees us through the blood. The blood of a common man convicts, but the blood of Jesus justifies.

We must apply the blood of Jesus. The work which was done on the cross of Calvary defeats the work of the enemy. Satan is rendered powerless when we apply the blood. We are no longer subject to his snares.

God promises healing and deliverance to His children, the curse is broken, but that doesn't stop our adversary from attacking our lives. Since the beginning of time, Satan has plotted to skillfully mislead people and draw them away from a relationship with God and into bondage. Unfortunately, he even is able to do this from within the church itself.

Chapter 3

OPENING THE DOOR TO THE OCCULT

Without realizing it, many Christians possess or use articles of evil in all aspects of life. Perhaps they wear historically occult jewelry, or bring "Christmas Spirit" boxes into their homes, or display spiritual artwork on their bodies and in homes. Some innocently purchase eerie, demonically suggestive action figures as toys for their children, not realizing that many of them derive from African religions, rituals, and even voodoo. Even though they are unknowingly embracing the spirit of witchcraft, believers are not exempt from the curses that these articles bring.

The Bible says we are to bring no *"accursed things"* (Joshua 6:18 NKJV) into our homes. Many consider such everyday items to be harmless, thinking they have nothing to do with witchcraft. But the spirits that have possessed these articles throughout history have never left them and are just as strong today. Voodoo, witchcraft, and sorcery are very much alive and thriving, and new curses are being exacted in people's lives by the practitioners of these ancient religions and cults.

We go on vacations and visit the ancient ruins of pagan temples and we send the relics of King Tut to museums around the country. We purchase trinkets in the gift stores and bring items representing these empires into our homes. We must be careful when bringing such souvenirs, symbolic stones, and other memorabilia into our lives and the private spaces where we live. Once an accursed item crosses the threshold of our homes, we have inadvertently invited the devil in for a permanent visit.

SIX "HARMLESS" LITTLE MEN

A young woman in our church told me that when she was in grade school, she received a Christmas gift that had remained in her house ever since. Knowing my teachings on current-day witchcraft, she thought it was something that I should see. One day, she presented me with what looked like a little gift box. Light and small enough to fit in the palm of my hand, the box was made of bamboo and was covered with colorful markings made with berry dye. The brightly colored stripes on the box were painted in such a way as to make it look almost like a woven basket.

The box was very delicate, almost fragile in construction, and was covered by a lid that lifted off. I removed the lid, revealing six tiny human figurines constructed of a thin, brown fiber laying inside, stacked one upon another. All of these little men had ink markings on their heads to illustrate eyes and hair, and they were dressed in strong, colorful weaving thread.

When an accursed item enters our home, we have invited the devil in for a permanent visit.

As I tilted the box, the six tiny figures tumbled into my hand. There was no doubt in my mind—these cute little figurines were actually satanic voodoo dolls. Not only was this obvious by simply looking at the dolls, but there was a tiny, printed note inside the box, which revealed their true purpose:

> The children of Guatemala are told that these dolls are available to hear and take care of their worries. Each night before going to sleep, the children pray to the dolls with their concerns. But they can only have six worries each night.

I asked the young woman where the dolls had come from, how long they had been in her home, and whether she had ever consulted or prayed to them. She told me the box had been innocently given by a relative and had been in her home for over a decade. And, yes, on several occasions, she had taken the dolls out of the box, held them in her hands, and prayed to them.

I took immediate action to bind the curse that had undoubtedly been placed on her life by these demonic characters that now sat before me. I led this young woman in a prayer of repentance and denounced any satanic attack and influence. We broke the spiritual curse and wicked stronghold of the enemy in her life. Today, she is growing and walking in the knowledge of the truth.

In the meantime, I started researching the history, meaning, power, and mystery of the six little men in the tiny box through a specialist in matters of the occult. According to the specialist, it was no coincidence that the box contained six little men, because there were six people in the household of this young woman—each had a specific demon in one of the figurines. The spirits of the figures in such boxes control the inhabitants of the house where they dwell through their dreams and imaginations. If there weren't little men in the little bamboo boxes, then often symbolic animals would be used, such as a bird, cat, or dog. Each of these animal spirits would have a specific mission and purpose to exact on an individual's life. According to the specialist, the spirits were awarded their power through the action of the individual who placed them there. When these little dolls are taken out of the box and held in the hand, or even when the top of the box that contains them is lifted off, their spirits are released into the house to work their demonic magic.

The sign outside may say "church," but the practices within may say "paganism."

The young woman who showed me the strange box said she believed the spirit of the six men had affected the lives of her family members. Several unusual and unnatural events had occurred during the thirteen years in which she owned the box. For example, the family had been unable to stay in one place of residence for more than a year at a time. During a nine-year period the family lived in at least twelve residences. In addition to this lack of stability, the family had also experienced stunting financial instability; they never seemed to be able to break free from the spirit of poverty. A final unusual occurrence was an unnatural swelling of the left ankle of each female family member (except for the youngest, who just happened to have moved from the household).

It is not always easy to determine where an evil influence in the life of an individual originates. But in the case of this young lady and her family, the mystery was revealed. The demonic presence of these accursed dolls—these "innocent," "harmless," "meaningless" figurines—caused them much turmoil. Nevertheless, through the demon-binding power of the Holy Spirit, the shackles of poverty, sickness, and instability that plagued them for years is now being eradicated, slowly but surely.

PAGAN RELIGIONS

Any religion that is not Christ-centered and in obedience to His Word is witchcraft. All pagan religions are based in witchcraft. Therefore, even though the sign outside a building may say "church," the practices within may say "paganism."

> *The sacrifices of pagans are offered to demons, not to God, and I do not want you to be participants with demons.* (1 Corinthians 10:20)

Who are the spiritual heads of the occult or pagan religions? According to the apostle Paul, they are demons.

The church, once considered the place to learn about moral behavior and put it into practice, is under attack. This attack is not from without but from within. Clergy and lay members alike are being seduced by carnal pleasures.

> *The Spirit clearly says that in later times some will abandon the faith and follow deceiving spirits and things taught by demons.*
> (1 Timothy 4:1)

This seduction is already taking root within the church.

POLITICALLY CORRECT, SPIRITUALLY CORRUPT

A wedding is taking place in a traditional church in the United States. The wedding ceremony has an ordained pastor, a best man, ushers, seating for the bride, and seating for the groom. What's so unusual about this wedding? Two men are being joined together in "holy matrimony."

How could this happen in a traditionally conservative Christian denomination that has long been noted for its stance against homosexuality? How could it happen in a part of the country where the Gospel is preached incessantly on television and radio? This is an area where Bible verses are memorized and quoted as freely as lines from movies or sports statistics.

What is taking place in the church is not unique. God has given us Scripture as an example so that we do not fall into the same condemnation of the disobedient men recorded in the Bible. (See 1 Corinthians 10:11.) Let's look at Israel in the Old Testament to better understand some of the ungodly compromises foisted upon us.

FALSE WORSHIP

Because of Solomon's sins, God split the nation of Israel into two kingdoms after his death. The northern kingdom was called Israel and the southern kingdom was called Judah. Jeroboam, a servant of Solomon, was called by God to rule the northern kingdom. God told Jeroboam that He would bless Israel as long as the nation obeyed Him.

> However, as for you, I will take you, and you will rule over all that your heart desires; you will be king over Israel. If you do whatever I command you and walk in my ways and do what is right in my eyes by keeping my statutes and commands, as David my servant did, I will be with you. I will build you a dynasty as enduring as the one I built for David and will give Israel to you. (1 Kings 11:37–38)

Jeroboam, however, fell into some of the same traps that church leaders are falling into today. God instructed both the northern and southern kingdoms to continue to offer their sacrifices and attend designated feasts at the temple—which was located in the southern kingdom. Instead of trusting God's promise, however, Jeroboam feared that his people would desert the northern kingdom and remain in the southern kingdom. In his irrational fear, Jeroboam listened to the foolish counsel of men and set up a counterfeit place of worship in order to keep his people in the northern kingdom.

Thus, the Israelites now had two temples—one in Judah, and one in Israel. They appointed prophets and priests to minister in the temples. They also had their holy days set aside. What was missing? They had replaced Jehovah with false gods. Because of this, God pronounced judgment on the northern kingdom and the Assyrians invaded, carrying them off into exile. Ever since, Jeroboam's name has been spoken of derisively by the Jews for the role he played in leading the northern kingdom astray.

> *Why is the church so easily seduced?*
> *We love the world more than we love God.*

Just as Jeroboam instituted a false copy of Israel's worship of God, so have many churches and church leaders today. They have pastors, teachers, and deacons. They sing inspirational songs. Just as in Jeroboam's northern kingdom, everything appears to be right on the outside. However, they are not worshipping God *"in spirit and truth"* (John 4:23).

Just as with Jeroboam, many churches today are trying to retain their people by catering to the whims and affections of the world of popular culture. This misplaced devotion causes the church to drift into false worship. The church then loses its first love and replaces it with a love of the world.

> *Do not love the world or anything in the world. If anyone loves the world, the love of the Father is not in him. For everything in the world—the cravings of sinful man, the lust of his eyes and the boasting of what he has and does—comes not from the Father but from the world.*　　　　(1 John 2:15–16)

Why is the church so easily seduced? We love the world more than we love God.

DEFILED BY SEXUAL SIN

Homosexuality is not the only sexual sin that has taken root within the church. God warned the Israelites that indulging in any type of sexual sin, as the heathen nations that surrounded them did, would defile them.

> The LORD said to Moses, "Speak to the Israelites and say to them: 'I am the LORD your God. You must not do as they do in Egypt, where you used to live, and you must not do as they do in the land of Canaan, where I am bringing you. Do not follow their practices....No one is to approach any close relative to have sexual relations....Do not have sexual relations with your neighbor's wife and defile yourself with her..... Do not lie with a man as one lies with a woman; that is detestable....Do not have sexual relations with an animal and defile yourself with it.... Do not defile yourselves in any of these ways, because this is how the nations that I am going to drive out before you became defiled.'"
>
> (Leviticus 18:1–3, 6, 20, 22–24)

This list of sexual sins in Leviticus 18, expressly forbidden by God, are pervasive in our culture today. These include incest, adultery, homosexuality, and bestiality. Pagan nations served their idol gods by indulging in such deviant practices. The Lord graphically revealed the condition of people who do not know Him. In other words: your sexual lifestyle reflects your relationship to God.

HOMOSEXUALITY

The word *homosexuality* is not used in the Bible, but certain terms are used to refer to this practice. Genesis shows us the origin of the word *sodomite* and how its meaning was derived.

> Before they had gone to bed, all the men from every part of the city of Sodom—both young and old—surrounded the house. They called to Lot, "Where are the men who came to you tonight? Bring them out to us so that we can have sex with them." Lot went outside to meet them and shut the door behind him and said, "No, my friends. Don't do this wicked thing. Look, I have two daughters who have never slept with a man. Let me bring them out to you, and you can do what you like with them. But don't do anything to these men, for they have come under

the protection of my roof." "Get out of our way," they replied. And they said, "This fellow came here as an alien, and now he wants to play the judge! We'll treat you worse than them." They kept bringing pressure on Lot and moved forward to break down the door. But the men inside reached out and pulled Lot back into the house and shut the door.

(Genesis 19:4–10)

The men of Sodom were seeking to have sexual intercourse with Lot's guests, who happened to be angels of God. This is how the term "sodomite" came about—by men having sexual intercourse with other men. This act was so reprehensible that God strictly forbade the admittance of a sodomite into the congregation of the Lord.

He that is wounded in the stones, or hath his privy member cut off, shall not enter into the congregation of the Lord....There shall be no whore of the daughters of Israel, nor a sodomite of the sons of Israel. Thou shalt not bring the hire of a whore, or the price of a dog, into the house of the Lord thy God for any vow: for even both these are abomination unto the Lord thy God. (Deuteronomy 23:1, 17–18 KJV)

What does the New Testament have to say about these sexual practices?

Therefore God gave them over in the sinful desires of their hearts to sexual impurity for the degrading of their bodies with one another. They exchanged the truth of God for a lie, and worshipped and served created things rather than the Creator....Because of this, God gave them over to shameful lusts. Even their women exchanged natural relations for unnatural ones. In the same way the men also abandoned natural relations with women and were inflamed with lust for one another. Men committed indecent acts with other men, and received in themselves the due penalty for their perversion. Furthermore, since they did not think it worthwhile to retain the knowledge of God, he gave them over to a depraved mind, to do what ought not to be done.

(Romans 1:24–28)

The apostle Paul, the writer of Romans, stated that when someone enters into homosexuality and other sexual perversions, he has turned from God. Many believe that sexual perversion starts the downward spiral from God. Notice the words *"did not think it worthwhile to retain the knowl-edge of God"* and *"because your hearts were hard."* These are the conditions of a person who has rejected God. Therefore, according to Scripture, God leaves him to his own devices.

THE WRONG FOCUS

As the things of this world have encroached upon the church, some ministers have become people-counters. They could not care less about the destiny of a person's soul as long as others in the community, and those among their peers, perceive their church as successful based on the number of people sitting in the pews and the amount of money collected in the plates.

Too many ministers shy away from addressing sinful, destructive behavior with their flocks.

Jesus declared, *"No one comes to the Father except through me"* (John 14:6). He stood resolutely on His ministry and did not waver, and because of that, some refused to walk with Him. Jesus even turned to the twelve disciples and asked, *"You do not want to leave too, do you?"* (John 6:67). He showed His disciples that it was not the great crowds following Him that constituted righteousness, but those who were willing to do the will of His Father—even if it meant that no one else followed Him. Jesus demon-strated that *quality* is more important than *quantity*.

Too many ministers have fallen into a trap: they believe that they cannot financially support the kingdom of God without turning a blind eye to sinful behavior among the believers so as not to chase away faithful givers to the ministry. They shy away from addressing sinful, destructive habits within their flocks. Their desperation for money leads them to forget the words of the apostle Paul: *"My God will meet all your needs according to his glorious riches in Christ Jesus"* (Philippians 4:19). It is God's church, His ministry, and His gifts. If God cannot sustain the ministry through righ-teousness, who can?

> *God's patience and love should lead us to repentance, not to an unholy lifestyle.*

Many believe that God tolerates or overlooks sin and does not condemn it because of His love for us.

Do you show contempt for the riches of his kindness, tolerance and patience, not realizing that God's kindness leads you toward repentance?   (Romans 2:4)

God's patience and love should lead us to repentance, not to an unholy lifestyle that is contrary to His Word. When pastors and ministers soft-sell the Gospel, they end up destroying the faith of many who come seeking truth. Instead of correcting sinners, they condone their behavior, making them *"twice as much a son of hell"* (Matthew 23:15) as themselves.

MIRACLES ARE NO PROOF

Many of the attractions of Spirit-filled churches are the miracles and wonders of God being performed. Many will leave their home church to attend a crusade or revival if they hear a prophet or healer is across town. Don't get me wrong, I fully believe that miracles are still being performed in the church today. However, Satan is no stranger to miracles, and charlatans who do not flow in the power of God are creeping into the church unnoticed.

Turn on the television and you will see mind-readers and illusionists claiming to reveal the future or defy the laws of time and space. False prophets go to churches "in the name of God" in an attempt to read the futures of the congregation before passing the offering plates. Not only are the television audiences deceived, but so are many church members.

Remember the sorcerer named Simon in Acts who tried to purchase the gifts of God from the apostles. (See Acts 8:19–24.) Today, we still have the word *simony*, which means "the purchase and sale of ecclesiastical powers." Whenever a prophet comes to your church or town but will only "minister" for a specified amount of money, he is selling his gift and therefore practicing a form of witchcraft.

> *The gifts of God were never meant to*
> *be hired out to the highest bidder.*

Jesus said, *"Freely you have received, freely give"* (Matthew 10:8). In other words, the gifts of God were never meant to be hired out to the highest bidder. Instead, the gifts of God are given freely that the body of Christ may be perfected. (See Ephesians 4:11–13.)

All gifts find their origin in the Holy Spirit, who directs you to Jesus Christ.

> *When he, the Spirit of truth, comes, he will guide you into all truth. He will not speak on his own; he will speak only what he hears, and he will tell you what is yet to come. He will bring glory to me by taking from what is mine and making it known to you.*　　　(John 16:13–14)

If someone is glorifying what he can do and how wonderful he is, this is a form of witchcraft. God shares His glory with no one. Remember what happened to Herod when he did not correct the people who thought his voice was that of a god:

> *Immediately, because Herod did not give praise to God, an angel of the Lord struck him down, and he was eaten by worms and died.*
> 　　　　　　　　　　　　　　　　　　　　　　　　(Acts 12:23)

We cannot and must not be deceived by every supernatural event, believing it is from God. Just as the magicians in Pharaoh's court duplicated almost all of the miracles that God performed by the hands of Moses, so also the devil can perform miracles to astound the masses. But just as Pharaoh's snake was swallowed up by the snake that God had Moses form, the devil is powerless against the children of God because we have the Spirit of Christ living inside us. That is why the devil seeks to deceive us. He knows that he cannot overpower us because Jesus Christ fights our battles for us. If we allow ourselves to become deceived, however, we provide an opening for the devil to enter in and wreak havoc. We can protect ourselves if we simply obey God's Word.

Jesus told His disciples, *"Thus, by their fruit you will recognize them"* (Matthew 7:20). If those who come to you in the name of God live a life of immorality, do not acknowledge Jesus as Lord and Savior, and seek only monetary gain, you will know that they are not of God. Do not follow them! If they are unable to give glory to the Father through Jesus Christ His Son, that's a good indication that they are practicing witchcraft.

Chapter 4

PROPHETS AND PROGNOSTICATORS

Interest and involvement in the things of the spirit realm—but not necessarily in the Holy Spirit—is growing at an alarming rate, attracting everyone from respected celebrities and athletes to occult and religious groups around the globe; from government officials and high-ranking professionals to the next-door neighbor. It is no surprise that parapsychology is a multimillion-dollar industry, or that the ancient seer Nostradamus and his predictions have experienced a resurgence in popularity. What is surprising is how many Christians—believers, Christ-followers—have fallen prey to demonic practice and participation as well.

This being the case, it is imperative for us to study the satanic spirits, powers, and forces that are leading so many astray. The truth-telling is long overdue. The Bible tells us that the practices of necromancy and sorcery are abominable, and that the doers thereof will receive eternal damnation. (See Galatians 5:20–21). Those who believe in and receive the services of such ungodly spiritualists are displeasing to God and will in no way enter into His kingdom.

Due to the spiritual urgency of this issue, and the need to properly identify and powerfully eradicate these demonic forces, we will investigate, define, expound upon, and use true testimony to illustrate the biblical origins of foretelling, fortune-telling, and prophetic utterance. We will compare these godly concepts to Satan's powerful, but weaker, imitation and reveal how to distinguish between the two.

PROPHECY

The apostle Paul described the biblical gift of prophecy as a gift of the Holy Spirit to be desired and even coveted by the saints:

> *And in the church God has appointed first of all apostles, second prophets, third teachers, then workers of miracles....eagerly desire the greater gifts.* (1 Corinthians 12:28, 31)

Technically defined, true biblical prophecy is declaring and predicting future events as guided by the influence of the Holy Spirit. Such spiritual foretelling extends from the anointed tongue of the prophet. The prophet, according to biblical tradition, was a man handpicked by God to speak truth into the lives of God's people. The words spoken by the prophet included those of salvation, damnation, binding, and deliverance, and were given expressly and exclusively to individuals of all walks of life—kings and commoners, countries and communities, and other groups of people.

The prophets of old were generally well-revered men in their time, respected for their privileged communion with God and the sanctity of their spiritual profession, not to mention the accuracy of the words they spoke and events they foretold. Particularly in the Old Testament, incidents of prophetic utterance and biographies of the prophets themselves are most prevalent. The fame and renown of certain of prophets—Isaiah, Elijah, and Elisha—are retained even to this day. The prophet was God's mouthpiece, His messenger to the masses. The prophet would translate God's words, be they blessing or curse, to His people. On occasion, the prophet risked persecution as well as his or her very life by bringing unpopular and threatening words to God's people—or even His enemies.

PARAPSYCHOLOGY

Satan's twisted version of God's anointed prophet is none other than the false prophet, or prognosticator. Several Bible stories give accounts of false prophets wielding their deadly, ungodly words or practicing the sin of witchcraft. (See, for example, 1 Kings 13.)

Modern-day prognosticators practice in the same demonic vein as did those mediums of old. Astrologers, fortune-tellers, palm readers, psychics, spiritualists, mediums, wizards, warlocks, witches, and mind controllers are in the business of rendering evil-based "prognoses," or foretelling. In all of the lives they touch, these prognosticators bring a spiritual curse along with their message, even when the results of their prognoses appear to be accurate and beneficial to those who employ them. This is because the source of their prophetic gift is not godly, and no authentic, long-lasting good can come of it.

An anointed prophet is God's mouthpiece, His messenger to the masses.

The power and spirit of prognosticators are thoroughly satanic for they offer their natural talent and gift to the prince of this world, Satan, to be used for worldly, perverted purpose and profit. In reality, it is a form of satanic worship, and the only possible outcome of such a practice is evil and division. I know this from personal experience.

Hung by the Tongue

When the church I now pastor was in its infancy, a most peculiar woman joined our membership. This woman was there even before the church was actually born. She became a regular at the powerful, inner-city revivalist tent meetings we held in the southern city where the church now stands. These popular, highly anointed tent meetings were a prelude to the formation of the church.

Prior to the tent meetings and our introduction to this woman, we saw several forewarnings of the satanic attacks to come upon us. For example, before each revival, our leadership team would meet at the tent site for three days of intense prayer. On the final evening of our three-day prayer meeting, a few of us were talking as we walked across the five-acre field when a black van suddenly appeared on the street. Rap music blared as it drove around the field where we stood. Then, the music stopped, and two young men jumped out, armed with shotguns. They aimed and fired their weapons at another young man who was running through the field, hitting him in the heel. As quickly as it appeared, the black van sped away. The young man who had been the target continued to run across the field with blood gushing from his badly wounded foot. It was obvious to us that the devil had a foothold in this neighborhood. Our prayer group turned to one another, and in unison we agreed, "This is the place."

The next evening, a tent was erected, and the revival began. While standing in a trailer at the front of the tent I spotted one peculiar woman. She sat in the audience wearing a straw hat, sandals, and a T-shirt that bore a written message: "Don't be hung by your tongue." Looking back on that evening much later, those of us who saw the strange woman recognize the prophetic poignancy that the saying on her shirt would have regarding her own life.

The power and spirit of prognosticators are thoroughly satanic.

After the first service, this woman approached me at the front of the tent and handed me an odd-looking piece of fruit. It was a red apple with strange, colored streaks running through it. According to the woman, red was symbolic of perfection, and the green spots symbolized youth. Receiving the apple from the woman, I immediately disposed of it by flushing it down the commode.

Not long after she began attending our church, we discovered this woman to be a manipulating, controlling woman who dabbled in the occult. She burned ceremonial candles, performed rituals that attempted to place curses on certain church members, and tried to exert power and control in the actual running of the church.

On one occasion, she prayed for a certain young woman in the church. As a result, this young woman experienced nights of sleeplessness and stomach sickness. Another time, she gave a young woman in the church some articles of clothing to wear. Before the young woman ever got to try them on, however, the Lord revealed to me exactly who this woman was and where she was coming from. In the middle of the night, I was awakened by the Holy Spirit, who spoke to me of this woman's evil spirit and demonic involvement—He confirmed that she was indeed a witch.

> *Satan's tactics will only give you temporal relief, but God is concerned with seeing you set free completely.*

I warned the young woman who received the accursed clothing not to wear it. Not long thereafter, we asked the demonic woman to leave our congregation based on a decision by a general consensus of the people. Angrily, and after much protest, she eventually left. She took a few members who had fallen prey to her witching spell with her. Nevertheless, if this woman and her crew had not left and taken their evil, satanic influences with them, there's no telling what damage might have been inflicted upon our newborn church.

Scripture tells us that *"all things God works for the good of those who love him, who have been called according to his purpose"* (Romans 8:28). I now know that our church's encounter with this evil woman was one that produced a greater good: the Lord used her to initiate us and educate us about the divisive, confrontational realm of spiritual warfare.

REACHING THE DEAD

Another fascination in popular culture today is communicating with the dead. This has become so popular that there are entire television programs preying on the grieving emotions of their audience by promoting the possibility of contacting a deceased loved one. Regardless of their high ratings, however, the Word of God is clear:

> *Let no one be found among you who sacrifices his son or daughter in the fire, who practices divination or sorcery, interprets omens, engages in witchcraft, or casts spells, or who is a medium or spiritist or who*

consults the dead. Anyone who does these things is detestable to the
Lord.   (Deuteronomy 18:10–12)

In this passage of Scripture, God is giving the priests proper instructions on how to remain pure before Him, and to refrain from partaking in the abominations of Canaan. He reminds them that, instead of having to rely on the demonic manifestations of evil spirits, He would send them prophets to foretell the times and speak a Word. (See Deuteronomy 18:15–22.)

This same Word remains relevant today. Those who profess Jesus Christ as Lord are to rely upon His voice for enlightenment and direction, and resist the temptation of dabbling in evil spirits. When you desire answers to life's crises, seek God first. The enemy's tactics will only give you temporal relief, but God is concerned with seeing you set free completely. He cares about your needs, but you must trust Him enough to rely on Him to bring resolution to what concerns you the most.

*Cast all your anxiety on him because he cares for you. **Be self-controlled** and **alert**. Your enemy the devil prowls around like a roaring lion looking **for someone to devour**.*
(1 Peter 5:7–8, emphasis added)

+ Be *"self-controlled"*: do not allow yourself to become intoxicated by the rising demonic trends of spiritism. Remain clear about whom you consult for guidance—the Lord Jesus Christ.

+ Be *"alert"*: Remain watchful, and guard yourself against the devices that come to distract your attention away from God.

+ Notice that the devil looks *"for someone to devour"* (1 Peter 5:8). As he roams about, don't open the door for him by dabbling in things that God has warned are detrimental to your spiritual health. He may seek you out, but by remaining steadfast in your beliefs and exercising godly vigilance, he will be forbidden to consume you.

WHEN MESSENGERS DILUTE THE MESSAGE

What goes wrong when men and women of God who were once doctrinally sound suddenly begin preaching with *"a form of godliness but denying its power"* (2 Timothy 3:5)? Disguised as messengers of God, many false teachers with vast platforms are popping up throughout the nation, scattering their demonic propaganda. For some, the name of Jesus is rarely mentioned or discussed. Instead, many churches simply refer to "a higher power." These organizations attract followers who are seeking God, but are unsure of His existence and power. Hence, presenting a *"form of godliness"* becomes a safer and more convenient alternative. The characteristics of those who dilute the Word of God and use it to pull others into their deception are outlined in 2 Timothy:

> People will be lovers of themselves, lovers of money, boastful, proud, abusive, disobedient to their parents, ungrateful, unholy, without love, unforgiving, slanderous, without self-control, brutal, not lovers of the good, treacherous, rash, conceited, lovers of pleasure rather than lovers of God. (2 Timothy 3:2–4)

1. *"Lovers of themselves"*: this refers to excessive self-love that trickles into narcissism.

2. *"Lovers of money"*: ungodly materialism is driven by the need to acquire things that society uses to measure individuals' success.

3. *"Boastful"*: have you ever been around individuals who annoy you with constant boasting? They inflate their accomplishments and never give others a chance to praise them before patting themselves on the back.

4. *"Proud"*: the proud continually exaggerate their worth and status, portraying a pompous aura to all who come in contact with them.

5. *"Abusive"*: they will resort to controlling and manipulative methods in order to get their way.

6. *"Disobedient to their parents"*: I am convinced that much of an individual's blessing is tied to how that person treats his or her parents. While we may not always be able to have close relationships with our parents, we should exercise care and much thoughtfulness before purposefully disrespecting them.

7. *"Ungrateful"*: the most heartbreaking thing is to give to someone out of the abundance of your heart and in return have that person

act with ungratefulness. These are individuals who feel that the world owes them. They exude a characteristic of entitlement and believe that they are deserving of all the things they are given. It is out of this attitude that they conclude they should not have to show gratitude or appreciation.

8. *"Unholy"*: holiness refers to the sanctity of God. Unholy individuals have little or no reverence for Him—a defiant state of mind, which is reflected in their actions and behavior.

9. *"Without love"*: there is a complete lack of tenderness. When individuals are without a natural affection toward humankind, they come across as bitter persons who invoke difficulty and strife in whatever environment they find themselves.

10. *"Unforgiving"*: there are certain types of people who are enemies of peace. No matter how much energy has been expended creating a peaceful resolution to a volatile situation, they will find a way to retract from its serenity.

11. *"Slanderous"*: Proverbs 17:4 says, *"A wicked man listens to evil lips; a liar pays attention to a malicious tongue."* Those who cause strife and accuse others falsely are wicked individuals who have become accustomed to not only diluting the truth, but destroying truth altogether.

12. *"Without self-control"*: *"incontinent"* in the King James Version, this refers to those with unrestrained passions and out of control immorality.

13. *"Brutal"*: the cut-throat mentality our society now exhibits is just another reflection of the time in which we live. Lack of compassion and dogmatism have become dominant character traits of those seeking power at any cost.

14. *"Not lovers of the good"*: perilous times expose the true nature and intentions of wicked individuals. They despise the good in everyone and never have anything positive to say regarding the benevolent acts of others.

15. *"Treacherous"*: traitors are true to no one. Their disloyalty is without prejudice and they will stoop to the lowest level in order to get what they want.

16. *"Rash"*: rash individuals can not be counseled or given direction. Even when they are found to be in error, they make excuses for their wrongdoings and stubbornly continue to stand their ground.

17. *"Conceited"*: conceit is the fastest route to self-destructive behavior. *"Pride goes before destruction, a haughty spirit before a fall"* (Proverbs 16:18).

18. *"Lovers of pleasure rather than lovers of God"*: Jesus exposed this better than anyone ever will when He said, *"No one can serve two masters. Either he will hate the one and love the other, or he will be devoted to the one and despise the other"* (Matthew 6:24).

Regarding people who exhibit these characteristics, the next verse warns, *"Have nothing to do with them"* (2 Timothy 3:5).

A DEMONIC COUP D'ÉTAT

There is one common thread that runs through all of these destructive behaviors. It is what I call "me-ology." People who are only concerned about themselves make no room or consideration for others. Their negativity is contagious. It infects anyone nearby and spreads when you least expect it. This is because demons are constantly looking for a place to dwell. They seek out vulnerabilities and weaknesses, and use those frailties as an opportunity to control.

> *Though unsuccessful in defeating God, the devil still attempts to defeat His children.*

This does not mean that if you are currently struggling with a weakness you are being controlled by the devil. To those warring with weaknesses, the Bible says, *"let the weak say, 'I am strong'"* (Joel 3:10 NKJV). That's not to imply that we are to ignore our weaknesses, but instead, we must keep our eyes on God as we work through them to receive our deliverance.

Never lose your focus and allow yourself to be swayed or manipulated into engaging in behavior or acts that contradict your God-given beliefs. When the will of God becomes contaminated by demonic influences, your attention is diverted from God's voice and may become consumed with attaining the pleasures of this world. This is when deception can entice you to put God in the backseat as your drive for material things drives your faith into the ground.

We must realize that nothing the devil does is by happenstance. His demonic kingdom is highly systematic in its administration of a *coup d'état* against the kingdom of God. Though unsuccessful in defeating God, the devil still attempts to defeat His children. This is why we are admonished in Ephesians 6:10 to *"be strong in the Lord and in his mighty power."*

> *The trick of the devil is to deceive us into thinking that every battle we fight is against natural forces.*

Because we are battling unseen forces, we must draw from the strength of God and the power of His might, and not our own, if we expect to be victorious. The trick of the devil is to deceive us into thinking that every battle we fight is against natural forces, thereby exhausting ourselves in a fight that cannot be won with physical strength.

Our opponents do not fight fairly. They are evil forces ruled by the tyranny of a demonic ruler whose goal is to spread his ungodly agenda. That is why not all attacks are self-inflicted. Some of the most well-intentioned and selfless children of God are inflicted by some of the most hideous attacks. Often, when I am being attacked by people in the natural world, I can immediately tell when it is a demonic attack as opposed to an innocent misunderstanding. Refrain from going on physical rampages when anger erupts. That is what the devil wants you to do in order to fulfill the remainder to his plan. If he can get your eyes off God long enough to get you to listen to him, he knows that he has won half the battle already. Lend your ear to him long enough and you will find yourself engaged in all out war, using physical means against an unseen adversary—a losing battle.

The weapons that we use to defeat the devices of Satan are spiritual. This does not mean, however, that amidst adversity, we just pray and wait for the war that is waging against us to magically disappear. On the contrary, we must take proactive steps to gain victory. How do we know what steps to take and how to strategize against the devil? We must be tuned-in to the voice of God so that, as we are taking the proper steps to attain victory, the steps are ordained of God. *"The steps of a good man are ordered by the LORD"* (Psalm 37:23 NKJV).

A good man is not a man without flaws,
but someone who actively seeks the face of God.

A good man is not an individual who is without flaws, but someone who actively seeks the face of God so that, even in his or her imperfections, God might use those flaws to invoke His perfect will through invaluable learning experiences. Have you ever gone through something that you thought would definitely defeat you, but as you began to overcome the traumatic experience you realize strength that you have never experienced before? Certain things that once frustrated and antagonized you no longer move you. You are able to see the growth that has taken place in your life, which was needed to propel you into certain areas about which you'd been diligently seeking the Lord.

Often, we go through certain things so that God becomes the predominant voice in our lives. The more you seek Him and learn of Him, the less likely you are to become manipulated by controlling voices disguised as the voice of God. No one's voice should hold more power in your life than the voice of God. Though the voice of reasoning for humankind fluctuates relevant to moods and stages of life, the voice of God is unwavering. Many false doctrines have emerged out of mood swings, bad teachings, and the uncertainties of individuals whose opinions, unfortunately, invoked great followings. Deception is a brutal beast that nibbles ever so subtly at the core of our faith until we turn to what's killing us for replenishment, instead of turning to God for renewed strength. The worst deceptions are religious traditions that keep us from God. A classic example is given in Matthew:

> Then they brought him a demon-possessed man who was blind and mute, and Jesus healed him, so that he could both talk and see. All the people were astonished and said, "Could this be the Son of David?" But when the Pharisees heard this, they said, "It is only by Beelzebub, the prince of demons, that this fellow drives out demons."
>
> (Matthew 12:22–24)

The Pharisees, who were already looking for an excuse to discount Jesus (see verse 14), jumped on the opportunity of discounting His ministry—even to the point of accusing him of conspiring with Beelzebub to cast out devils. They were so intoxicated by their own selfish motives that they refused to celebrate with the crowd the miracles of God—the God they claimed to confess.

Normally, it is not what people say that reveals their deceptive practices, but what they do. For when God shows up, everything that does not reflect His image is revealed as an imposter to His cause and purpose. In an accuser's accusation he always reveals the source of his deception.

The Pharisees accused Jesus of casting out devils by the devil. Perhaps this is because that is who they were being influenced by at the time. Have you ever been around an individual whose total concern is physical appearance, money, and everything else besides the spirit of God? This is an individual whose motives are being revealed by the god whom he or she serves. Though the mouth confesses servitude to God, it is ultimately one's actions that reveal the solidity of that confession. For when God shows up, those who know Him, or seek to do so, embrace Him, while those who *claim* to know Him, but do not, hurl malicious accusations.

> Jesus knew their thoughts and said to them, "Every kingdom divided against itself will be ruined, and every city or household divided against itself will not stand. If Satan drives out Satan, he is divided against himself. How then can his kingdom stand? And if I drive out demons

by Beelzebub, by whom do your people drive them out? So then, they will be your judges. But if I drive out demons by the Spirit of God, then the kingdom of God has come upon you. (Matthew 12:25–28)

Jesus knows those who are His, and He knows those who are not. (See 2 Timothy 2:19.) Without ever hearing the Pharisees say a word, Jesus knew their ungodly thoughts and brought a very interesting fact to their attention, saying in effect, "Even Satan knows that the strength of his kingdom is unity, so why would Satan cast out himself? And if I cast out the devil by the devil, then by whom are your children casting them out?"

Or again, how can anyone enter a strong man's house and carry off his possessions unless he first ties up the strong man? Then he can rob his house. "He who is not with me is against me, and he who does not gather with me scatters. (Matthew 12:29–30)

Jesus draws the line between following Him versus rebellion against Him: *"He who is not with me is against me."* There is no in-between. This relevant point is restated in Revelation 3:15–16: *"I know your deeds, that you are neither cold nor hot. I wish you were either one or the other! So, because you are lukewarm—neither hot nor cold—I am about to spit you out of my mouth."* You cannot bind the strong man in Jesus' name if you are not following Jesus wholeheartedly and with a sincere heart. Before you even say a word, Jesus already knows the intent of the heart, and those who earnestly seek Him become one with Him in spirit, endowed with power and authority to spoil the kingdom of darkness and bind the forces of Satan's domain.

Jesus knows those who are His, and He knows those who are not.

The devil is after those who profess Jesus as Lord because he knows that if he can get them to fall, then those who are watching God's followers will become less prone to submit to God. From the beginning of time he has sought to discount the word of Truth and to manipulate the word of God. When you find yourself being lured back into the acts of your past, make no mistake about it, seducing spirits are at work, using whatever tactics they deem necessary to get you to bow to temptation.

The Spirit clearly says that in later times some will abandon the faith and follow deceiving spirits and things taught by demons.

(1 Timothy 4:1)

What causes us to "*follow deceiving spirits*"? We are lured by our own hidden desires. The devil makes sure that whatever he is using to lure you is going to be appealing to your desire. Otherwise, the object of your enticement would not be temptation. In order to "*follow*" something, you must give it serious and thoughtful consideration. The best way to keep from departing from the faith is to cast down every imagination that is attempting to seduce you away from God. (See 2 Corinthians 10:5.) Don't dwell on it or daydream about it. Simply cast it down immediately; otherwise, you will begin to think of ingenious ways of committing sinful acts. The devil always presents the pleasures of committing the acts without revealing their consequences: "*after desire has conceived, it gives birth to sin; and sin, when it is full-grown, gives birth to death*" (James 1:15). Of course, "*death*" does not always mean physical death, but there is a part of you that dies whenever you commit acts that contradict what you know to be acceptable behavior.

> *The devil always presents the pleasures of committing sinful acts without revealing their consequences.*

Disciplining the mind takes practice, but the more you do it, the easier it becomes to think on things that are true, honest, just, pure, lovely, and of good report. (See Philippians 4:8.) So, how do we begin training our minds and thoughts to overcome instead of giving in to ungodly desires?

1. Resist the temptation of daydreaming about committing sinful acts. Instead, replace those thoughts with more positive images.

2. As tempting as it sometimes is, don't experiment with immoral behavior, and you won't become addicted to it.

3. When you find yourself overcome by the urge to engage in acts of immorality, pray and ask a trustworthy individual to agree with you in prayer as well.

4. Figure out what is being used to invoke the temptation, and flee from it. *"Resist the devil, and he will flee from you"* (James 4:7).

Chapter 5

POWER IS NOTHING WITHOUT CONTROL

W e all want to love and be loved; to know and be known; and, strangely enough, to control and be controlled. Therein lies the key to the plot of the following story.

FRAUDULENT FRIENDSHIP

Some years ago I met a young man whom I will call John Doe. It was not uncommon for John's housemate, whom I will call Kyle, to invite someone to stay with them—these guests were often complete strangers to John, and their visits were a complete surprise.

John came home from work one night and sat down with a group of friends gathered there. As John sat down and joined their conversation, Kyle formally introduced John to someone I will call Elder Phillip.

As they talked, Phillip told John the story of his life. "The Lord delivered me from a life of drugs and gang violence. God healed my body from all the trauma I put it through. When I gave my life to God, my family wronged me and tried to destroy my ministry. But I turned the other cheek; I refused to do to them what they did to me. I left it in the hands of the Lord."

John told Phillip about his father who pastored a church in another state. John explained how he was sending his tithes home to help support his father's ministry. John also disclosed that he was an aspiring minister himself.

Phillip smiled and responded, "First of all, John, before you can pursue your calling into the ministry, you have to line yourself up with the Word. Scripture makes it clear that you are to give to the ministry that is supporting you spiritually. You have to be in the will of God before He can bless you."

John thought that Phillip's story and teaching was compelling. Having sized up John well, Phillip had successfully gained the respect of this younger apprentice.

Kyle brought Phillip to church and reintroduced him to his pastor, for they had known each other before. As was customary, she allowed this visiting minister to share a few words. Phillip seized this opportunity to expand his ministry in this new venue, and in two minutes he proceeded to "go to town." But the pastor was more discerning than the congregation. She told Kyle, "If you love me as your pastor, and if you believe that I am a woman of God, you will get that man out of your house."

Presented with such a compelling assessment from someone he trusted, Kyle accepted her counsel and proceeded to severe his ties with Phillip.

No Respect

John, on the other hand, continued to spend time with Phillip. On one particular occasion they were to meet at a local mall. Two hours passed, however, and Phillip didn't show up or call. John was angry that Phillip failed to value his time—a sure sign of disrespect.

When the two men met again, John expressed his disappointment. Phillip responded, "You know, John, I'm getting tired of you 'rising up' on me. One of these days I am going to knock you back down."

Completely confused, John said, "Let me get this straight. What do you expect me to say when you 'rise up' on me?"

Phillip responded harshly, "Nothing! I expect you to take it. When I was a young minister, I couldn't even *talk* around my elders."

And so the discussion ended.

Kyle never shared the advice of his pastor with John. Heeding her warning, Kyle continued to distance himself from Phillip. However, thoroughly blind to the whole situation and not discerning the man's character, John only saw that Phillip was stuck in a new city with no support and no counsel, and volunteered to be his advocate.

THE DECEPTION BEGINS

Seeing Phillip's need to become established, as well as the personal benefits he might reap from their friendship, John agreed to help Phillip rent a house in the country. The bi-level home was filled with expensive designer furniture. A sliding glass door led to a patio and backyard overlooking lush, rolling hills.

Next, John helped Phillip purchase a green Lexus coupe and a fully loaded Honda Accord with a wooden dashboard, leather seats, moon roof, tinted windows, spoiler, rims, and gold trim. Because Phillip lacked credit, John agreed to cosign for a loan and was approved. The final kiss of death was in providing Phillip with a brand-new American Express gold card. John was truly setting himself up for a fall!

After Phillip was settled, John decided it might be best to see less of him. John was beginning to think that perhaps he had made a mistake. He decided that he would attend some of Phillip's preaching engagements, talk to him on the phone once a week, and only meet with him outside of church twice a month or so.

Then, one day, John got an unexpected phone call at work.

"Hello. Is this Mr. Doe?" asked the voice.

"Yes," said John.

"This is American Express."

"Yes. What can I do for you?"

"Our records show that your account is past due."

"By how much?"

"The full amount of your balance is due. That's $3,500. Although there is an additional cardholder on this account, the payments are your responsibility."

"I am well aware of that. I'll have to call you back."

John hung up the phone and called Phillip right away.

"What's going on, sir?"

Phillip replied in a monotone voice, "Nothing much."

"American Express just called me."

"I guess I forgot to send the payment in," Phillip sighed with an embarrassed voice.

"I wish you would have told me sooner. When will you be able to send it in?"

"In two weeks."

John hung up the phone, but the conversation continued to play in his mind. He knew he had made a mistake. He bowed his head and prayed.

"Father, give me strength."

The Plot Unravels

Phillip paid this bill on time, and everything seemed okay. The next month, however, he wasn't so conscientious. In fact, he skipped payments for the next three months and never called American Express. John called him every time the credit card company contacted him. Then John began to receive letters from the bank as well, and he called Phillip.

How did this "minister" respond?

"John, I'm going through a very trying time and I need to know that you're with me."

"Of course I'm with you," John replied, feeling offended. "What does that have to do with anything?"

Mankind has wanted to be in control since the beginning of time.

"Well, if you tell them where I live they are going to take the car."

"Don't worry. If they take the car, that would show up as a repossession on *my* credit file. I'm trying to save it, not lose it."

John was true to his word. He did not tell the bank where Phillip lived.

Suddenly Phillip stopped returning John's calls and stopped answering his phone all together. The reality of the situation hit John hard. He knew he was in trouble. Desperate, John did all that he possibly could to save himself. He and Kyle went to Phillip's place of work and repossessed the car. John was devastated. Now he was thirty-two thousand dollars in debt, had two cars to maintain, and had a very angry American Express representative to deal with.

John finally summoned the courage to tell his friends what had happened. How did they respond to him?

"How could you be so naive?"

"I can't believe you were so gullible."

"Why would you do something so stupid?"

Phillip was one of the most controlling people I have ever met. But this story is not just about money. It is not even about Mr. John Doe and Elder Phillip. It is about the fraud, the manipulation, and the controlling spirit of witchcraft that conceives and breeds more fraud, manipulation, and control.

WHO'S IN CONTROL?

Unfortunately, mankind has wanted to be in control since the beginning of time. Instead of obeying God's only command, Adam and Eve chose to *"be like God, knowing good and evil"* (Genesis 3:5).

Even after God devastated the earth with a flood, the enduring civilizations tried to build a tower that would reach to the heavens.

> *Now the whole world had one language and a common speech....Then they said, "Come, let us build ourselves a city, with a tower that reaches to the heavens, so that we may make a name for ourselves and not be scattered over the face of the whole earth"....The* LORD *said, "If as one people speaking the same language they have begun to do this, then nothing they plan to do will be impossible for them. Come, let us go down and confuse their language so they will not understand each other."* (Genesis 11:1, 4, 6–7)

Men want to exercise control over the work of their hands, over their families, and over their futures. Because we don't have all the facts and don't see life from God's perspective, our desire to control is often doomed to failure and a curse.

We think, *But if we don't control things, then who will?*

God has our lives in the palm of His hand. He is able to providentially guide us in every area of life, if we will only trust Him to bless us as He sees fit. But, like a three-year-old in a parking lot, we yank our hand from his and race perilously out ahead and into danger.

What happens when men decide they won't allow God to reign over them?

WE KNOW WHAT'S BEST

God exercised control over the nation of Israel by raising up judges to settle disputes and lead the people. This period of the judges began after the death of Joshua and continued until Samuel. The judges served a twofold purpose. First, God anointed the judges to provide deliverance to Israel from their oppressive enemies. Second, He appointed them to rule and administer government in the name of God. Scripture says, *"For dominion belongs to the LORD and he rules over the nations"* (Psalm 22:28).

Israel accepted this form of control until the time of Samuel, when the people of Israel believed they could control their daily affairs better than God. They wanted a king like the other nations around them had. They wanted to take control from the hands of God and place it in the hands of a king. They didn't understand that with control comes power. Control can be good when properly administered, as the judges did. But it can also cause hardship for the recipients if not administered properly, as some of their kings did.

> *So all the elders of Israel gathered together and came to Samuel at Ramah. They said to him, "You are old, and your sons do not walk in your ways; now appoint a king to lead us, such as all the other nations have." But when they said, "Give us a king to lead us," this displeased Samuel; so he prayed to the LORD. And the LORD told him: "Listen to all that the people are saying to you; it is not you they have rejected, but they have rejected me as their king. As they have done from the day I brought them up out of Egypt until this day, forsaking me and serving other gods, so they are doing to you. Now listen to them; but warn them solemnly and let them know what the king who will reign over them will do."* (1 Samuel 8:4–9)

God warned the nation of Israel of the consequences awaiting them if they rejected Him, but they refused to heed what God spoke through the prophet. The result was a series of corrupt, greedy, and power hungry kings that left the nation of Israel divided and conquered.

IS ALL CONTROL BAD?

A little girl wanted to cross a very busy street to go to a candy store. Her parents refused to let her go because they knew the dangers awaiting their little girl. The parents exercised control for the good of the child. Moreover, this control was based on experience and knowledge of what could happen to their child if she wandered into the street. Not all control is bad, but all control should be based on godly principles.

Control is usually set in place by a person or small group of persons with oversight of a much larger group. Even though the black Africans outnumbered the white Africans in South Africa, they were still under the oppressive control of the apartheid government. Control has nothing to do with numbers; rather it has to do with influence.

CREATING A COMMON ENEMY

The person or group exerting control is usually very charismatic, a characteristic that enhances the ability to control. These charismatic people or groups will usually create an enemy on whom to focus the attention of the people they control. When people focus on a common adversary, they think less critically of the person or group exerting this influential control.

Creating a common enemy also mobilizes people around a common goal. As long as communism was perceived as a threat to the safety and security of the United States, there was little debate on the buildup of America's defense. Attention could be centered on this common enemy. Eventually, the major power brokers of communism dissolved. With no perceived enemy clawing at the door, the people started to clamor for reducing the defense budget.

If the person exercising control points us to an actual enemy, those actions are proper and right. If the desire is to turn brother against brother, race against race, denomination against denomination, or church against church, this control is evil.

As stated earlier, our struggle is in the spiritual realm. Those leaders wanting to exercise proper control must know how to address the spiritual problems facing all of us. If they allow the flesh to dictate this control, they are identical to Israel, who was ignorant about the benefits that result from serving a loving God and the destruction that can result from seeking another source of spiritual guidance.

God cannot relinquish control because He is our creator. If we refuse to acknowledge that He is in control, God will allow us to persist in our ignorance.

Romans 13:1 states,

> *Everyone must submit himself to the governing authorities, for there is no authority except that which God has established. The authorities that exist have been established by God.*

Whenever leaders exercise control without acknowledging God, who bestows control, they are practicing a form of witchcraft, an attempt to bend the will of someone to make it agree with the person exercising control. Unfortunately, corrupt leadership does not just happen in politics, business, and the church—it can also happen in the home.

Chapter 6

WITCHCRAFT IN THE HOME

When we hear the word "witchcraft," we often think of casting spells and blatant occult behavior. Seldom, however, do we look at those close to us as practitioners, bewitching those in their own home in an attempt to manipulates our movements. It is subtle and can be hard to detect because, instead of chants and incantations, the weapon of choice is mind control. It forces its way into relationships, raises havoc, and either destroys the object of its control or leaves the target of its deception stunned to the point of dysfunction.

THE CONTROLLING MARRIAGE

As I stated in the last chapter, those casting their "magic" have a need to control what they feel they cannot attain through practical means. They will use whatever is most important to someone else as a pawn in order to push their own self-gratifying agenda, sometimes even going so far as to twist Scriptures to defend their point.

> Let the husband render to his wife the affection due her, and likewise also the wife to her husband. (1 Corinthians 7:3 NKJV)

Unfortunately, this Scripture is often the manipulator's greatest weapon. Although this passage is referring to maintaining equal respect— the give-and-take equality that belongs in all relationships—it is all too often perverted by one individual to get his way through manipulative means. Therefore, let's dissect the first several verses of this chapter.

In verse 3, to *"render"* something is to give it away *willingly*, not under duress. In many relationships, the priceless commodity of intimacy has been lost, and rendering *"the affection due"* has become just another chore to be done in order to keep the other party happy. When things are forced instead of passionately initiated the relationship becomes so mechanical that it loses its fervor and lacks the vitality of compassion.

> *In a healthy relationship, both parties willingly give to one another.*

> *The wife does not have authority over her own body, but the husband does. And likewise the husband does not have authority over his own body, but the wife does.* (verse 4 NKJV)

In a healthy relationship, both parties willingly give to one another the affection they are entitled to receive. Both realize that they are no longer two individuals but one flesh. (See Matthew 19:6.) Flesh is constantly seeking self-gratification, so when you please your spouse, you are ultimately gratifying yourself.

> *Do not deprive one another except with consent for a time, that you may give yourselves to fasting and prayer; and come together again so that Satan does not tempt you because of your lack of self-control.*
> (1 Corinthians 7:5 NKJV)

In the King James Version, *"deprive"* is substituted with *"defraud."* To defraud someone of something is to deprive them through deceitful or manipulative means. In a proper relationship, one does not defraud another by using demands or ungodly abstinence as a means of control. Each person takes into consideration the needs of the other and willingly submits to please the individual to whom he or she has vowed, "'Til death do us part."

Why do spouses remain in a controlling marriage? For many, it is like the story of the frog in the pot. As the story goes, if you throw a frog into a pot of boiling water, it will jump out immediately. But if you put it in the pot with cold water and slowly increase the temperature, it will remain until it slowly boils to death.

Here is the story of one woman who experienced those slowly rising temperatures.

ERICA'S STORY

I grew up in a very small town. Although we had an old washer, there was no dryer, and my mother still hung the clothes out on the line to dry. I learned to cook by age twelve, and every Sunday I went to church. Life consisted of household chores, going to school, doing homework, and then more chores. As I grew older and began to date, I became enamored by a certain young man whom impressed me as one who had the potential of being "the perfect spouse." Even those around me revered him as "a great catch." After dating for only a few months, we were married. It was just after saying "I do" that I wondered, *What have I gotten myself into?*

My new husband began making irrational demands, such as forcing me to wear scantily-clad attire that was neither sensual or appealing, but instead made me feel like a prostitute. His bizarre behavior soon escalated into masochism and I ultimately became his sex slave. His insatiable sexual appetite could not be satisfied, and the more I tried, the more deviant became the demands of his twisted imagination. Just as washing the laundry, cooking, and cleaning were a way of life, taking care of his needs by being at his sexual "beck and call" became part of my daily duties as a wife.

By our eighth year of marriage, I'd had five children. My identity had been stripped from me as I had slowly become a woman of convenience rather than a wife. No matter where I was or what I was doing, on his command I was expected to drop everything and tend to his needs. Any refusal on my part subjected me to even more humiliation, as well as physical and mental abuse.

We attended a church where divorce was not an option. To even mention the word invoked rebuke and threats of being banished to an eternity of hell. I began confiding in John, a friend of mine at work, who could not believe that I was staying in such a degrading and abusive relationship. John was the ideal friend—never judgmental, scornful, or rude. He was a caring individual with whom I could share my most intimate thoughts, desires, and dreams. He became my outlet, my reason for going on, and I looked forward to going to work each day. We began having lunch together, and talking to each other over the phone on the weekends—having an emotional affair without the physical aspects of an actual union.

Because the teachings of my church were heavily ingrained within my psyche, and my conviction to God was still intact, I guess this was my rationalized way of having the man of my dreams without committing the physical act of fornication and adultery.

John became my rock, the one I could lean on after being subjected to the daily degradation that faced me at home. It seemed as if the more I was with him, talked to him, and listened to what he had to say, the stronger I became.

In truth, I had allowed my church and my marriage to distort my image of God. Surprisingly, however, it was John who encouraged me that God would never leave me or forsake me and that if I continued to seek the Lord, He would bless me with the understanding and direction that I so desired.

I soon gained the strength to end my marriage, moved to another state, and eventually began a new life with my best friend, John. The equality of the relationship sometimes seemed so surreal that I was scared I would eventually awaken from the dream. On those days, it was John who assured me that "'Til death do us part" was not a one-sided commitment, but a lasting union and a vow that he intended to keep forever.

While I in no way condone the act of turning to another member of the opposite sex for consolation while married, I would like to stress the fact that the story of Erica's rocky marriage is typical of those who become victims of mass deception within relationships. Perhaps if her church had been a safe harbor instead of a place of judgment and condemnation, she wouldn't have needed to seek affection from an outside source.

> *There will be times in all marriages when sin will erupt and one spouse will attempt to control the other.*

Unfortunately, not every situation concludes with a happy ending. The evening news is filled with horror stories of spouses who snap and harm themselves or others in order to flee from an unbearable situation. In most toxic relationships, the conflict is only intensified by the meddling influence of outsiders whose opinions do nothing to extinguish the fire, but only add fuel to an already volatile situation.

You can always tell when manipulation is at the forefront of a relationship, simply by noticing the obvious, and sometimes not so obvious, signs:

1. One partner is always belittled by the other in public.

2. One partner lives as if he or she is still single while the other remains secluded at home.

3. Affection in the relationship consists of one person doing all the giving while the other does all the taking.

4. One partner is "brainwashed" to the point of quoting the manipulating partner's distorted versions of Scripture.

5. One partner always seems on edge, unhappy, and defeated while the other maintains a happy-go-lucky attitude and visage.

No one should be expected to remain in a situation where physical or emotional abuse has gotten to the place where a person's well-being feels threatened. In such cases, separation is the only remedy for the safety of all parties.

HEALING A CONTROLLING MARRIAGE

All relationships are made up of two sinful, imperfect human beings, and there will inevitably be times in all marriages when that sin will erupt and one spouse will attempt to control the other. At such times, action must be taken so that God can work to bring healing and forgiveness into the situation.

THE CONTROLLING WIFE

A wife may seek to control her husband by crying, threatening to leave the home, using children as pawns, or withholding affection. She knows that she could never be more physical or vocal than her husband, so she seeks to exert control in ways that empower her. She tries to manipulate her husband so that she has the advantage. A man may be unaware that he is being controlled in such a subtle way.

If a husband approaches his wife about misguided control without the right prescription for correction, he, too, risks practicing a form of control that could damage the relationship. The Bible says for men to *"dwell with [their wives] with understanding"* (1 Peter 3:7 NKJV). Before he corrects her, therefore, a loving husband should make the effort to discover why his wife is going to such extremes to manipulate the situation. In such cases, a husband will often find a hurting woman who has become embittered because of her inability to express suppressed feelings.

Once he discovers the basis for her hurt, he can then more aptly apply the Word of God in a consoling, healing manner. Sometimes a woman may reject healing because her pain may have been festering for years. Anything that takes years to surface is not going to be easily smoothed over. Therefore a husband should be patient when administering healing to a nonresponsive wife.

THE CONTROLLING HUSBAND

A man tends to control by what comes naturally to him—his physical strength and powerful voice. The degree of force a man uses has a lot to do with what he believes he can get away with. This is why it is important for a woman to state in no uncertain terms that she will not tolerate abuse from her husband. Often, such men do not realize that such aggression is misplaced. God intended for a husband to provide and protect. Those big hands were never meant to punish his wife or his children, but rather to hold and care for them.

When a husband finds that his wife has been hurt by his aggression, first, he must openly confess and apologize to her. Even if a man confesses his wrongdoing, however, it does not guarantee that the woman will forgive him right away. In such a case, he should be careful not to compound his error by getting upset with her again for not immediately forgiving him. Should forgiveness not be given initially by the woman, the man must be willing to prove he is truly repentant for any wrong he has done by patiently demonstrating good works toward her.

> *God intended for a husband to provide for and protect his wife and children.*

Eventually, a wife must admit that love and forgiveness are attributes every Christian should have. The same thing holds true for the woman as for the man. If the woman feels she can maintain control by withholding forgiveness and love, she may not naturally wish to relinquish such control. To combat this, the man must state in no uncertain terms the boundaries in the relationship and what he will and will not accept.

The inability to forgive removes a person from the forgiveness of God. Forgiveness not only allows God's grace to be manifested in a person's life, but it also releases people to love once again. Many marriages have broken down because of the inability of one spouse to forgive the other. Jesus said, *"if you do not forgive men* [or women] *their sins, your Father will not forgive your sins"* (Matthew 6:15). Therefore, if we do not forgive, we are in danger of hell's fire.

THE ASSAULT AGAINST MEN

God has ordained that the man should be the head of his household.

Wives, submit to your husbands as to the Lord. For the husband is the head of the wife as Christ is the head of the church, his body, of which he is the Savior. (Ephesians 5:22–23)

Why do men suffer more violence, a higher rate of prison incarceration, a greater incidence of sickness, and a higher mortality rate than women? I believe it is because the devil is aggressively pursuing his goal to destroy the head. Man's only hope, therefore, is to accept Jesus Christ in order to thwart the plans of Satan.

In battle, every army knows the quickest way to turn a battle when they are outnumbered: shoot the enemy commander. Without their leader, the enemy will fall into disarray and eventually retreat. This is why most commanders in the field during wartime remove the officer stripes from their uniforms so they won't be targeted by the enemy.

Satan uses the same strategy against men today. His efforts have been somewhat successful in keeping many men out of church. Building contractors know that any church construction project will need more bathroom facilities for women than for men, as approximately 60 percent of any church population is female. In some churches the ratio of women to men is even more pronounced. These numbers testify to the assault that Satan has made upon men.

If Satan can destroy the man, he destroys the family. The decadence present in today's society is directly attributable to the diminished role of men. Statistic after statistic shows the greatest perpetrators of crime are young men who have no father in the home.

> *If Satan can destroy the man,*
> *he destroys the family.*

MEN'S CHANGING ROLE

Little by little, today's society has effectively stripped away the authority that God invested in men. God told Adam in the garden of Eden *"to work it and take care of it"* (Genesis 2:15). God meant for man to be the protector, but today's culture has changed the role of man. From biblical times through the Industrial Revolution, we had an agrarian society where people made their living primarily off the land. Because of men's physical strength, families depended upon them to plow the ground, sow the seed, and harvest the crops. Because of the remote location of most farms, a man often had to defend his family and land against intruders—both man and beast. Today, we have the local police serve as our protectors.

The apostle Paul also spoke to the role of the man. *"If anyone does not provide for his relatives, and especially for his immediate family, he has denied the faith and is worse than an unbeliever"* (1 Timothy 5:8). In Scripture, the man was the main provider for his family. Inasmuch as economics and skills determine a man's ability to provide for his family, they also determine his *in*ability to provide for his family.

If he does not provide, what happens? The government dispenses food stamps, housing allowance, welfare checks, and medical assistance, if needed. In other words, the government becomes the provider.

I believe this is the reason so many women walk away from their marriages today. There is no incentive to make the marriage work—or even to get married in the first place—because of the illusion painted by the government.

> *Satan uses the government to advance his agenda.*

Satan inspired this deceit, and many women have fallen for it. Just as the woman was deceived in the garden of Eden, women are being deceived today. The government has come in and enticed women to either abort their babies, or to have illegitimate children whom they have difficulty in disciplining morally, especially with no father in the home.

God intended for children to be raised by a father and a mother. Nowhere in the Bible does it say that a parent's ability to raise a child is based on income, intelligence, or social status. The most important quality that parents can have is the ability to teach their children the Word of God. It is far more important for a child to know his Lord and Savior than to graduate from the finest school or wear the most expensive clothes.

Ephesians 6:4 tells us it is the father's responsibility to bring up his children *"in the training and instruction of the Lord."* Since Satan is opposed to the teaching of God's Word, he plots to separate church and state, and eliminate the influence of Christianity in our nation. Satan, *"the god of this age"* (2 Corinthians 4:4), uses the government to advance his agenda.

THE CONTROLLING PARENT

There is an even more subtle form of witchcraft being practiced in many family households—including many Christian homes. The witchcraft I speak of here is that of domineering, manipulative parental control.

UNABLE TO LET GO

Early on in Scripture, we see the picture of a healthy rite of passage: *"For this reason a man will leave his father and mother and be united to his wife, and they will become one flesh"* (Genesis 2:24).

In controlling households, however, the growth-stunting strongholds of mothers and fathers who refuse to let go wreak nothing but havoc and dysfunction in the relationships and marriages of their grown children. It is not the will of God that grown children be unduly influenced and persuaded by their parents. These parents must learn, however difficult the lesson, to cut the emotional umbilical cords connecting them to their sons and daughters, allowing them to develop proper and healthy ties with their chosen spouses.

When mothers and fathers refuse to relinquish their grown child to a daughter- or son-in-law, it is often a direct carryover from the dictatorship and spirit of domination that governed the household when their child was still young.

SHOWING FAVORITISM

Another common sign of control is favoritism shown to a specific child. A parent's preference of a particular child usually means indifference to or the emotional neglect of other offspring. Quite often, such favoritism can have a tragic effect on the favored child as well as the neglected.

As children, those who are not "the favorite" are often too weak to fend for themselves or demand what is rightfully theirs. The nurture and protection they are due is given to someone else. The effects of this unbalanced love on the neglected may result in drug addiction, emotional instability, psychological disorders, alienation, inferiority complexes, hostility, crime, extreme character flaws, and even physical seizures.

A parent who loves unequally risks sowing emotional ruin into the neglected child.

At the same time, the favored child may develop equally disturbing qualities, such as arrogance, vanity, weakness of character, overconfidence, selfishness, and the need to dominate others. All of these exaggerated qualities of the spoiled, "special" child are unclean spirits, which only serve to sicken other members of the family, turning them against this particular child.

The parent who loves unequally risks sowing emotional ruin into the neglected child and spiritual rancidness in the favored child. Fortunately, God, who is just and fair, can fully redeem the damaged souls of both of these children and will not hesitate to fairly judge and punish the unsuitable parent as well.

TRUE STORY OF WITCHCRAFT IN THE HOME

The following is a testimony from a woman who witnessed first-hand the spiritual, emotional, and psychological damage by a parent's dominance and misdirected love:

> My mother-in-law was a witch. Not a witch who practiced sorcery or who was into the occult, per se, but one who practiced a form of witchcraft much more subtle. Instead of creating magic potions and performing satanic rituals, her craft manifested itself in manipulation, domination, and control.

This woman had given birth to eight children. Over the years, she successfully built them into a fiercely united army, which no one could divide, infiltrate, or join without first getting the approval of their commanding officer—Mom. Even though her husband lived in the household, there was no doubt that she was the commanding officer in charge.

As soon as we were married, it became apparent that my every action had to be geared toward pleasing my husband's mother. For all eight children, every decision required her stamp of approval. Not only did everyone need to remain on Mom's good side, but her approval and acceptance guaranteed that the rest of the family would be in agreement as well. For any of these children, including my husband, to go against their mother's opinion was to cut their own throats.

On the outside, my mother-in-law seemed a normal mother—caring, observant, nurturing, and gentle—so much so that, in the beginning, I had great respect for her for rearing her children almost single-handedly, as their father was not actively involved. They were a churchgoing family. Their father was an official in the church, and their mother was also a church leader. Sadly, the picture inside this dysfunctional household was much different from the one presented in public.

Inevitably, the day came when I, her newest daughter-in-law, was targeted for a knockout. Her control and manipulation were so cunning it began to look as though I was the one at fault. To the family, I was perceived as the unwelcome intruder for the express purpose of taking her son (my husband) from his innocent, victimized mother. Through it all, she claimed that she only wanted to "keep peace in the family."

This entire episode came about when my husband decided he wanted to leave the family's church—his mother's church—to join me at my place of worship. I had nothing to do with my husband's decision; it was a choice he made on his own. But, of course, this type of action went directly against one of the major, unspoken rules of the household: the family must stay together. In the mind of his mother, if her children did not all abide in the same house, the least they could do was attend the same church.

So strong was this woman's domination and control that it soon spilled over into their marriages as well. Instead of allowing marital issues to be handled and mended within the private confounds of their homes, they were either taken to my mother-in-law or she would sift them out. Once the issue was exposed, she would give orders on how to address the situation. As a result of her inordinate involvement, many of their marriages were broken as divorce and promiscuity soon ran rampant.

I am convinced that the spirit of Jezebel possessed this woman. (See 1 Kings 21.) In fact, the only difference between this woman and Jezebel is that Jezebel always sent a messenger to let her victims know that she was going to kill them; with my mother-in-law, there was no forewarning. Indeed, my husband's mother was even more dangerous because she used her witchcraft in more cunning and subtle ways than Jezebel. It surfaced anytime when she was challenged or confronted head-on, or when she went on a personal mission to exercise control in some facet of her family members' lives.

Needless to say, her controlling influence bred incredible instability, mental and emotional turmoil, and breakdowns in the lives of her children. These character flaws opened the door to drug and alcohol abuse among many of them. A spirit of favoritism also existed in the household. As a result, many of them went through their adult lives seeking approval from men and women in incredibly damaging ways in a misguided attempt to abate their feelings of inferiority.

Early on, the children learned to compete to win the love of both parents. During the holidays, the race was on to see who could give Dad, and more importantly, Mom, the better gift in order to win the most parental approval points. One Christmas, I remember my heart breaking as I watched one of the least favorite sons proudly hand his mother a gift as his father mercilessly mocked him. His mother kindly thanked him for the gift, though it was obvious she couldn't have cared less. Throwing the gift on the bed, she rushed to open a gift from one of her daughters, and another from her oldest son, both of whom were obviously favored over the others. Upon opening these gifts, Mom screamed with excitement. The rest of the family rushed into the room and soon joined in her enthusiasm. Meanwhile, the unpopular son sat in the corner, looking heartbroken. He stared at his forsaken gift lying on the bed as if to say, "Why did I even bother?"

It wasn't unusual for several of the male children to establish multiple relationships with women inside and outside the church. As soon as they became bored, the relationship was immediately abandoned and another one was pursued. Their mother seemed to have no problem with this rampant promiscuity. As long as her "boys" were happy and kept coming to church, nothing else mattered. But if one of the women involved with her sons challenged or crossed one of them, Mom would step in and establish control.

While the males tended to be passive and introverted, the female children were incredibly strong-willed women. They refused to relent, even when the Word of God disputed their claims. These girls developed extremely masculine traits and were always looking for a fight. They, too, experienced many broken relationships. They made it a sport to see who could belittle their man the most in front of the family. It was all about openly rebelling against the authority of their husbands and convincing themselves that they were in charge—just like Mom.

Because she was a crafty, subtle witch, my mother-in-law kept her family in a kind of protective box mentally, spiritually, and psychologically. For years, their only nourishment was her narrow-minded wisdom. Her daughters were cold and selfish; her sons were weak and unassertive.

The majority of these children went through life experiencing one traumatic experience after another. As trial after painful trial came and shook their lives, they began to break from within, becoming steadily loosened from their mother's vise-like grip. Inevitably, as they learned lessons the hard way, their independence grew. Their mother slowly began to lose her controlling influence. Her children were getting married, moving away, and no longer consulting her for advice. As they ventured out on their own, God began to heal them from years of witchcraft and bondage to this woman. Despite the change, it was up to her to accept this natural rite of passage and develop some peace of mind. If she had continued to try to hold on, I believe she would have permanently driven away and lost her children, and possibly her own sanity as well.

The story of my mother-in-law actually has a rather positive ending. The bonds of control have crumbled, and deliverance and healing are now in store for both the children and their mother. Likewise, we all need to guard our hearts from all spirits of control, domination, manipulation, and witchcraft that may rage within and learn the more comely art of submission. In doing so, the lives of our children, as well as the lives of others we try to control, will begin to heal. And at the same time, God is faithful to fill our every emotional and spiritual void.

SATAN'S DOMAIN

Satan may control the things of this world, but he can't touch the things of God. Just what does Satan control? We get a glimpse through Scripture's account of what Satan offered Jesus:

The devil led him up to a high place and showed him in an instant all the kingdoms of the world. And he said to him, "I will give you all their authority and splendor, for it has been given to me, and I can give it to anyone I want to. So if you worship me, it will all be yours."

(Luke 4:5–7)

Satan may control the things of this world, but he can't touch the things of God.

If we have not submitted our families, jobs, schools, and communities to God, they are controlled by Satan. The devil uses control in these areas to destroy his greatest threat: a born-again man. Any man filled with the Holy Spirit and trusting in Jesus Christ assumes his rightful position in God and makes the church stronger.

The devil is a lot like we are. He only controls what he thinks he can get away with. Knowing he cannot control a Spirit-filled person, he seeks those who are not Spirit-filled. The Bible warns us,

> *Be self-controlled and alert. Your enemy the devil prowls around like a roaring lion looking for someone to devour.*　　　(1 Peter 5:8)

Wherever he sees a weakness, Satan tries to exert influence and exploit that weakness for control. God seeks those who willfully submit to His loving authority but it is never forced. Any control that is not based on the righteous Word of God is a form of witchcraft.

Part II

WITCHCRAFT
IN ACTION TODAY

Chapter 7

MY ENCOUNTERS
WITH THE DEMONIC

Demonic possession has long been a popular theme in the films of Hollywood and in science fiction literature. *The Exorcist, The Omen, Rosemary's Baby,* Steven Spielberg's *Poltergeist,* and many of the novels of Stephen King all glorify the terrifying tales of the paranormal. Within the realm of popular media, however, the fascinating subjects of witchcraft, sorcery, magic, and the demonic are often intended to induce fear or make a scary spectacle of glamorizing the devil. To most of the world, evil spirits and their missions are merely the invention of fictional mythology and imagination, not that of reality. This is primarily because they are not treated as serious subjects and forces to be defensively explored and eradicated. Outside of the ranks of Christendom and the actual practicing circles of the occult, the satanic is nothing more than an amusement.

But the invisible *"rulers," "authorities," "powers of this dark world,"* and *"spiritual forces of evil in the heavenly realms"* mentioned in Ephesians 6:12 are all very real. In fact, because they are not treated as powerful, menacing entities of evil, witchcraft and all its satanic variants are able to exert their deadly influence with increasing popularity.

Evil spirits must be hosted by a living vessel in order to exert their influence. Just as we don't see the wind but only the effects of the wind, we don't often see demons with the naked eye, only the aftermath of damage done by the devil's delegates. Not only is the soul of the possessed human cursed when the enemy lives within, but the lives of others touched by the possessed individual can be damaged or destroyed as well.

> *Satan's army is nearly as skilled in the art of spiritual warfare as God's army.*

Satan's army is nearly as skilled in the art of spiritual warfare as God's army. The devil has a multitude of controlling commanders and manipulating men ready to attack not only vulnerable men and women of this world, but also the isolated believer as well. Satan has a host and hierarchy of strongmen attempting to destroy Christians' lives in an attempt to discourage them and make them doubt the soul-saving covenant they've made with their God.

Only through the power of prayer, fasting, and undying obedience to God are we able to shield ourselves from their daily attacks. However, when we are not spiritually strong and on guard, we become vulnerable to their satanic strategy and can be brought to our knees or to our graves through a number of indecent, unclean involvements, activities, and practices.

Demonic attacks may come to us in subtle ways, such as through other people or organizations, or they may strike us directly in their basic hellish forms. What follows are actual accounts of encounters that I have personally had with demonic attacks of the direct variety.

THE DEVIL'S SPAWN

The following is a story of one of the most extreme cases where sexual perversion led to the birth of the unthinkable: a spawn, or child, of the devil himself.

Perversion is one of the primary elements employed by the devil to bring down God's people. Sexual perversion, in particular, is one of the most prevalent forms of the spirit of perversion being practiced today. This is rarely acknowledged because of the shame and secrecy surrounding such abominable acts. Nevertheless, this ungodliness is very much alive and well in the church. If we don't point it out and take action to eliminate Christians' involvement in such deadly sexual persuasions (pornography, promiscuity, masturbation, adultery, pedophilia, and even intimate relations with demons), then the bride of Christ will remain defiled. Scripture implores Christians to remain pure and prepared for Jesus, her Heavenly Groom.

> *Husbands, love your wives, just as Christ loved the church and gave himself up for her to make her holy, cleansing her by the washing with water through the word, and to present her to himself as a radiant church, without stain or wrinkle or any other blemish, but holy and blameless.*   (Ephesians 5:25–27)

> *I saw the Holy City, the new Jerusalem, coming down out of heaven from God, prepared as a bride beautifully dressed for her husband.*
>   (Revelation 21:2)

Through counseling sessions, I've heard numerous accounts of demonic, satanic relationships from both men and women. Not long ago, however, I was involved in a Christian tent crusade here in the United States. One night, a powerful deliverance service took place. More than two thousand souls came to the altar, many being touched and released from whatever was binding them by the shackle-breaking power of the Holy Spirit.

Of those people at the altar, one individual in particular stood out. She was an attractive young woman, but it was apparent that she either had some kind of stomach tumor or she was several months pregnant. She approached me and the other presiding ministers and asked to be taken aside for a few moments to share some things and be ministered to individually.

Once taken aside, this young woman began an open confession. She admitted to having been involved in indecent sexual relations with demons. According to her, these unclean spirits would visit her in her bedroom at night, lay with her, and deposit their filthy residue into her spirit. She also admitted to involvement in the occult. It had all started innocently as she began reading daily inspirational New Age messages, depending upon them and taking them to heart almost as if they were daily horoscope predictions. This practice evolved into an investigation of New Age literature and then to consultations with mediums and witch doctors. Little did this woman know that one of the voodoo specialists she had hired to affect a curse on a boyfriend had turned on her and was now working for that same boyfriend against her!

The information this young woman shared shocked and disturbed me. It caught me off guard. It seemed impossible that such foul, damnable activities could be practiced by such a well-educated, articulate, beautiful young woman. She was not crazy or feebleminded. Satan, however, is no respecter of persons. Yet, despite her pleasant, presentable appearance, the proof of her tale was soon to be manifested in the flesh.

> *Don't allow the deadly, unclean spirit of perversion to lead you into sexual sin or addiction.*

Shortly after the woman shared her story, she became ill and went to a rest room in the building adjacent to our tent gathering. By the accounts of those who accompanied her there, what happened next was very much like the scene of a typical labor and delivery process during natural childbirth—almost.

According to witnesses, this woman travailed in labor in the rest room, and she eventually gave birth to the unimaginable—a ghastly, unspeakable, horrifying, nauseating demon. The woman birthed what appeared to be an egg. This "egg" had what looked like a strange type of hair growing out of it, along with indented spaces in its shell from which two little eyes looked out. I saw this incredible, indescribable creature with my very own eyes when it was brought to the sanctuary after the service. Needless to say, seeing this lifeless, hideous creature lying in a handkerchief was a most uncomfortable and sickening sight—one that would haunt me for many days to come. Those who witnessed it were completely distressed and even terrified. And yet there was more of the disturbing and unexplained to come.

The stillborn form that the young woman had passed was soon taken back to the rest room to be flushed down the commode. It appeared to be dead, and it was clearly demonic. There was no purpose in saving or making a spectacle of it. It had to be destroyed and the commode seemed to be the most convenient means of removing it from our presence. As it was dropped into the toilet, it suddenly sprang to life and began to move. Then, as if to beat us to the punch, it swam swiftly up the plumbing of the commode and vanished! Just like that, it was gone! In an instant, it disappeared with the express movement of one who knows the lights are about to be turned on. Or, perhaps more accurately, like the devil when he realizes that truth is about to expose him and call him by his foul name.

> *When Christians play in Satan's territory, they become subject to his poison and laws of consequence.*

To this day, I don't know what became of the young woman. The testimony of that night is terrifying and haunting, one that should frighten anyone out of any curiosity, experimentation, or actual practice in the realm of the occult.

Don't allow the deadly, unclean spirit of perversion to lead you into sexual sin or addiction. When Christians meddle and play in the territory of Satan, they become subject to his poison and the laws of consequence.

Even so, we have the blessed assurance that our Redeemer *"will keep in perfect peace him whose mind is steadfast"* (Isaiah 26:3). Likewise, Scripture tells us that *"no weapon forged against you will prevail"* (Isaiah 54:17). For those who remain faithful, there is nothing to fear. For all facets of this accursed spirit of fear are completely cast out by the liberating power of perfect love.

A DEMON IN MY BEDROOM

This is the story of a demonic curse aimed directly at me with the most deadly and hostile of intents—a curse that could have prevailed in its purpose had it not been for the protecting power of God on my side. The chilling effect of this incident has never left me, and every time I recall it, I am reminded of how crafty and cruel Satan and his demonic commissioners really are.

Some years ago, while on the road preaching, I ran into a young woman whom I'd met previously. As we reintroduced ourselves, she introduced me to another young woman standing with her. As soon as I shook this woman's hand, I immediately sensed the presence of a foul and unclean spirit. As soon as I was able, I warned my friend about this woman. "Noooo," she laughed, totally disbelieving my words. "It can't be." I told her in the most serious of tones that her friend was involved in ungodly activities.

My friend eventually told her acquaintance what I had said about her. I know this because of the demonic attack that soon came to exact certain revenge upon me. It happened a few days after I'd spoken those words of warning to my friend.

I was staying at a local guest house, a private residence where a few other ministers on the circuit were residing. On this particular night, I was awakened from a peaceful sleep to a nightmarish vision. At the foot of my bed stood what appeared to be a wrinkled old woman dressed in filthy rags. She didn't look at me, but hunched over in a crouched position. Reaching into a bag, her gnarled hands withdrew a dust-like substance and began to sprinkle it onto my feet. Horrified, I frantically began to pray and plead the blood of Jesus!

> *When I blurted out the single word,*
> *"JESUS!" at once the evil spirits fled.*

Then, a host of forceful, demonic black shadows appeared out of nowhere, binding me in a powerful attempt to restrain my cries to God. Covering my eyes, mouth, and nose, these angry, unholy spirits were cutting off my breath, draining the life out of me as I struggled against their powerful grip. In a fighting frenzy, I desperately tried to loose their hold of my face, but although I could feel them all over me as they engulfed me, I could not seem to pry them off. Thrashing my head from side to side to break free, I was finally able to loose my mouth for a split second, long enough to blurt out a single word: "JESUS!" At once, the spirits fled.

Traumatized and terrified, I jumped from the bed and began to pace the floor in frenzied confusion. Although my heart was pounding and I was sweating profusely, I still wasn't sure if it was all a nightmare, a terrifying vision, or if what I witnessed had actually happened. As I walked around the room, speaking in tongues and praying profusely, I began to notice an exceedingly foul smell pervading the room. It seemed to have started the moment the evil spirits had departed.

Soon, there was knocking at the door of my bedroom. The other guests in the house heard me calling upon the name of Jesus and had come to see what all the commotion was about. Eager for some familiar human company, I allowed those at the door to come into the room. As they entered the room, each one asked, "What is that awful smell?" Then, each one affirmed the fact that what had happened in that room had not been a dream, a nightmare, or a vision, but was an actual instance of spiritual, demonic attack. It was then that I knew the creepy old woman with the cursing dust and the suffocating shadows had not been a mere figment of my imagination!

Later that night, I acquired the telephone number of the acquaintance of my friend. I dialed her home phone number, and when she picked up, I immediately told her that I knew who she was and knew the evil she had just done. I proceeded to powerfully denounce the satanic spirit ruling and raging within her. She let out a piercing, high-pitched, demonic scream and hung up the phone. I believe that this vindictive young woman had commissioned these evil entities of hell to come and destroy me because I had revealed her to be a demon-possessed soul.

Ordinarily, such an attack on a child of God would not have happened so easily, but several occult and satanic articles in this house allowed the evil spirits to enter my room and harass me there. For this reason, I no longer stay at private homes when I travel. Of course, public lodging facilities have their histories as well, so even when staying in a hotel, I take the time to pray throughout the room to dismiss any ungodly spirits that may reside there.

KNOWING THE ENEMY

I share these stories not to instill fear, but rather to illustrate the power and reality of Satan's demonic realm of evil spirits. Christians may acknowledge the presence of the devil and his daily attack upon the lives of believers, but many do not fully believe in the actual existence of Satan's hellish host of fallen angels and demons. It is essential that we know our adversary in spiritual warfare. For if we don't recognize the enemy for who he really is, in all of his demonic variations, we cannot successfully fight him or win the spiritual war.

It is essential that we know our adversary in spiritual warfare.

Scripture tells us, *"Resist the devil, and he will flee from you"* (James 4:7). Christians are guaranteed victory over the forces of hell. On that night when I was violently targeted by demonic spirits, even though the artillery of spiritual warfare was fired at me in full force, I still possessed the most powerful and lethal of ammunition—the power of Jesus Christ. I resisted; the devil fled; I overcame! So can you.

Despite these bold and direct attacks of Satan, perhaps the most prevalent and damaging demonic strategy he uses is to subtly ply his witchcraft through popular culture, celebrity, and the media.

Chapter 8

THE SECRET

I learned about the principles behind *The Secret* long before its national spotlight on *The Oprah Winfrey Show,* or even before the documentary itself was created. I learned about it through the teachings of prominent preachers. Their teachings did not sound exactly like *The Secret,* but they fell under beliefs expressed in such books as *The Power of Possibility Thinking* by Dr. Robert Schuller or the writings of Norman Vincent Peale.

For those who don't know, *The Secret* is a documentary and subsequent book featuring a series of interviews with several self-help "experts," produced and written by Rhonda Byrne. The content is based on a concept called The Law of Attraction, which states that people's feelings and thoughts can attract real-world events into their lives, from the workings of the universe to interactions among regular people in their physical, emotional, and professional affairs. The film further claims that there has been a conspiracy by those in positions of power to keep this principle hidden from the public—hence, *The Secret.*

The film became somewhat of a phenomenon in 2007 after being featured on two episodes of Oprah's television program. The film and subsequent book rose to numbers one and two on the best-sellers' list for several months. The book's publisher, Simon & Schuster, ordered a second printing of two million books—the largest second printing in publishing history according to the *New York Post.*

I remember being in Los Angeles on February 8, 2007—the day *The Secret* made its appearance on Oprah Winfrey's program. I recall Oprah explaining that there is a secret to life. As I watched the program, something began to eat at me. Later, I decided to take the initiative to do my own research and find out why this program was tugging so harshly on my spirit.

While there may be some kernels of truth within The Secret, there are also some damaging teachings.

For twenty years, I had been watching Oprah on television. Although I had never met her personally, I felt that I had gotten to known her over the years. Just like her millions of faithful viewers, the Oprah I saw was accountable, honest, and a person of great gravity who valued experiencing life to its fullest. She put an emphasis on personal growth and accountability, and she was quite an inspiration to all generations. Due to her outstanding record of integrity, people listen very attentively to whatever she has to say. The mere mention of a film or book on her program usually means millions of dollars in sales.

As I delved into the origin of many of the teachings embraced by *The Secret*, I became very concerned, to say the least. I began to realize that Oprah's integrity had been manipulated and her influence had been usurped. Right there on national television, she had been subjected to witchcraft. In all her years on the small screen, Oprah had never before put her seal of approval on any religion—be it Christianity, Islam, Cabalism, Krishna, or anything else. I suspected that this was a dishonest thing that had happened to an honest woman.

Just as Rhonda Byrne, at a very low time in her life, found herself searching diligently for the secret to life's fulfillment, I too found myself searching to find everything that I possibly could find about *The Secret*. In my searching I found that it was not really a secret at all.

A Secret Revealed

Many people are building their lives around The Law of Attraction, but you must understand that it is just one of many laws that we live by in order to make up the well-being of our existence. There are several other laws that also define us as we exist upon this earth. For instance, there are the laws of transition, life and death, action, gravity, and reciprocity, to mention only a few. Our universe is filled with laws.

So, while there may be some kernels of truth within *The Secret*, there are also some very damaging teachings that can have detrimental and irreversible effects upon those who receive them as truth. I do not believe that you can just hope, wish, and dream for the universe to give you everything you need without working for it. Life is not totally positive, and life is not totally negative. Life is full of pain and joy, sorrow and rejoicing, fulfillment and loss.

Scripture states, *"The tongue has the power of life and death, and those who love it will eat its fruit"* (Proverbs 18:21), which means that we hold the power to speak both blessing and curse into existence. Still, there must be an element of reason and common sense that we apply in knowing that the grace of God prevents us from reaping all of the negative things we do and say.

In the case of *The Secret*, the plan was to have Oprah—someone accountable, someone with a huge following—introduce the concept. Fortunately, I was pleased to see that a few weeks after the airing of *The Secret* on her program, Oprah took the initiative to address some of the misconceptions that her audience gathered from this phenomenon. I was impressed that she was able to turn the lights back on in order to dispel the darkness of its underlined message.

Life is not totally positive,
and life is not totally negative.

On this particular show, she addressed some of the numerous e-mails and letters that she had received from her viewers. One disturbing letter caught her attention. In this letter, a woman explained that she had been diagnosed with breast cancer. Upon viewing Oprah's program, this woman decided to reject modern medical treatment and, instead, to concentrate her thoughts on healing herself. Oprah brought this woman on the show to confront her face-to-face. Sitting beside her on the couch, Oprah gently rebuked her for not allowing the gifts of medical technology to fulfill the purpose for which God had created them—to bring about healing.

While misleading teachings had attempted to replace hard work, education, doctors, nutrition, and common sense with one's own positive thinking, Oprah made it clear that we are not to irresponsibly leave the process of life and all of the things that God has given to us and to rely solely on our own thoughts in order to obtain whatever we want.

Oprah admitted that if she had cancer, she would make use of the accessibility of chemotherapy while continuing to think on things that are lovely, pure, kind, and of a good report. (See Philippians 4:8.) In the end, Oprah had presented both sides of the spectrum and left the decision up to the general public to base their individual decisions upon all the facts instead of a select few.

Reaping What You Think

One of the reasons we pray is because our own wisdom often fails us. Therefore, we seek a source higher than ourselves to fulfill our earthly needs. When we are constantly taught that everything we need comes from us, it brings many questions to mind regarding the Scriptures that God has given us as way of leading and guiding us into all truth.

It was he who gave some to be apostles, some to be prophets, some to be evangelists, and some to be pastors and teachers, to prepare God's people for works of service, so that the body of Christ may be built up.
(Ephesians 4:11–12)

Jesus replied, "What is impossible with men is possible with God."
(Luke 18:27)

Both of these Scriptures reveal that although God has given us dominion, we are always to acknowledge the fact that not only has God placed people around us to assist us in becoming who we are, but where mankind's finite wisdom fails to get the job done, nothing is impossible with God. In order to receive His impossibilities, therefore, we are to acknowledge Him in all of our ways.

> Delight yourself in the LORD and he will give you the desires of your
> heart.   (Psalm 37:4)

Suppose for a moment that everything that happened to us was due to the effect of our thoughts. Most likely, we would live our lives in a constant state of paranoia that any sort of negative thought would bring certain calamity. We would become our own puppeteers. What a nightmare! Fortunately, we have another source of blessing, wisdom, and healing beyond that of our own thoughts.

GOD'S SECRET

Before I had ever heard anything about *The Secret*, I had started to teach a series at my church entitled "Dominion." Since the beginning of time, subtle forces of deception have been able to dupe man into embracing half-truths. In doing so, lies become truth, and the truth, in turn, becomes a lie. In the garden of Eden, man and woman were given dominion over everything upon the face of the earth, including their own negative thought patterns. This dominion was a gift from God Himself.

I do not condone thinking negatively, or deny the possibility that negative thoughts can have a detrimental impact upon our lives. Rather, I think it imperative to point out the fact that throughout our time here on earth, life—both the good and bad—will happen. Therefore, we must learn to confront issues biblically, not attempt to avoid them by "thinking them away." Scripture teaches that *"There is a time for everything...a time to weep and a time to laugh, a time to mourn and a time to dance"* (Ecclesiastes 3:1, 4).

PAIN HAS ITS PURPOSE

What makes the witchcraft of *The Secret* so appealing is the hope that it gives to those who are stressed, angry, hurt, or simply searching for the realization of their goals and aspirations. I would agree that we *can* attract negative situations by stubbornly embracing a negative mind-set toward every situation. For example, many women continually find themselves trapped in toxic relationships by the low esteem that they are unknowingly feeling and projecting. Some people constantly start projects but never finish anything because they are projecting the incompetence they feel within. In the end, however, you simply cannot think your way out of every negative situation. Change requires action on the part of the person who is ready to experience positive results.

> *Fortunately, we have another source of blessing, wisdom, and healing beyond that of our own thoughts.*

In a day and time where so many are searching for joy, peace, and tranquility, we must point out that the cure-all cannot simply be summed up in a thought. Furthermore, many of the negative things that happen to you have nothing to do with you did or didn't do. Some of these events will serve to strengthen you so that you will be able to walk alongside of others who face similar traumatic events. The Lord will redeem your most painful moments in life in order to give someone else some much-needed encouragement.

Can you imagine what it would be like if you never went through trials, or had anything negative happen to you? You would probably have very little compassion for the struggles and trials of others. The Word of God encourages us to *"be strong in the Lord and in his mighty power"* (Ephesians 6:10). This means that the trials or negative things that happen do not always come to make us weak. On the contrary, they also serve to reveal just how strong we can be through Christ Jesus.

Chapter 9

IS AMERICA
A CHRISTIAN NATION?

We have learned that one of the ways in which witchcraft works is to distract us from our worship of God, and to place that worship elsewhere. Often, this type of worship does not take the form of prayers and song, but merely devotion and passion.

A tidal wave of conservatism swept the country in the last part of the twentieth century—a tidal wave called the Religious Right. It continues to gain strength today. With it come the traditions and values of a society many thought was dead. This wave of conservatism stands firmly opposed to the evils of society that are poised to destroy the traditional family—specifically the evils of legalized abortion and the homosexual agenda.

This wave of conservatism has as its underpinning the Bible, the Constitution of the United States of America, and the Declaration of Independence. These documents have proven to instill moral behavior; they turned a fledgling collection of independent colonies into a great country of united states and granted civil liberties to its citizens. The success and growth of our nation has served as an inspirational model for the rest of the world.

The Religious Right firmly believes that the United States was providentially founded by our forefathers of faith who composed the Declaration of Independence and the Constitution from within the mind-set of a

Christian culture. This being the case, it is widely believed that their tenets will only work in a decidedly Christian country. These staunch conservatives stand firmly against any secular humanists or liberal politicians who they believe have conspired to undermine the integrity of these documents, forming a threat not only to Christian America, but also to the traditional moral values that made this nation great.

The Religious Right wields the power of the ballot box to influence politicians and deliver its message. If they can control the political arena, or at least influence the political process, they believe they can mitigate or altogether negate laws and legal decisions that stand opposed to their conservative agenda. Any time a legislature vote or court decision is rendered that threatens these traditional values, the Religious Right springs into action, activating their substantial base of citizenry with great passion and fervor.

CULTURAL DECAY

To many in this country, the decades of the 1960s and 1970s were times of great moral decline. These periods caught conservative Christians quite unaware and unprepared. Because there was no "watchman on the wall," privileges Christians once took for granted were suddenly dismantled or outlawed as a new cultural climate set in. Prayer and the Ten Commandments were banned from public schools, where evolution was being taught instead of creationism. Parental rights were limited as deviant sexual practices were promoted to children in sex education classes or at Planned Parenthood. Because there was no Religious Right to serve as vigilante over matters of morals and righteousness, the new cultural climate seemed to be bent on destroying the importance of God and morality in public life.

Situational ethics became the rule of the day, suggesting that "if something feels good, do it." By the 1980s, such attitudes began to pit liberals against what political pundit Pat Buchanan called "The Silent Majority." This newly formed Religious Right believed they were engaged in a great spiritual war for the soul of their country. Any setback was seen as a betrayal of the cause of Jesus Christ that would plunge the nation into further degeneracy.

It's hard to refute. Consider the impact of the 1963 Supreme Court decision *Abingdon v. Schempp*, which essentially removed any expression of God from public schools. Within just a few years, public schools, lacking any kind of moral compass, quickly become like a police states with metal detectors to check for guns and knives. Teachers became fearful of physical abuse at the hands of their students. Hostile climates in the classroom created a vacuum devoid of learning, and test scores began to plunge as dropout rates soared. The decline in the public school system continues today and has motivated many to get politically involved. Within one generation, we have seen what the removal of God from the public setting can do.

> *Public schools, lacking any kind of moral compass, have quickly become police states with metal detectors.*

DEFENSE AND FISCAL POLICY

Conservative Christian activism quickly reached into other issues as well. Activists became concerned not only about the moral climate, but also about other interests affecting the country. During the 1980s, Communism, which preaches that the state is the ultimate authority, became enemy number one. President Ronald Reagan referred to the Soviet Union as "the evil empire." Quickly becoming the "poster boy" for the Religious Right, Reagan inspired conservatives to put pressure on their legislators to support increased defense spending. The Religious Right took the position that our survival as a nation was based on a strong defense. In this way, the Religious Right began to veer away from moral policy into such things as national defense, and eventually into fiscal policy.

THE PROTESTANT WORK ETHIC AND
THE WELFARE STATE

John Calvin is seen as the progenitor of the "Protestant work ethic." His doctrine of predestination taught that God had chosen, or elected, those who would be saved from the foundation of the world. Since salvation was out of his hands, man was to therefore show forth the righteousness of God by a dedication to his work.

This work ethic had a twofold purpose. Not only did it teach that God wants us to be good stewards of our time here on earth by working, but it also fueled the Industrial Revolution in the early 1900s. The agrarian population hesitated to leave the farm, where workers had security and the ability to provide for their families. Factory owners had the technology, but not the people to be productive. The influence of John Calvin's work ethic directly addressed the shortage of manpower the factories initially experienced.

This work ethic is dominant within the Religious Right. Their penchant for work and personal responsibility affects their perception of social programs. Deeply embedded within the Religious Right is the belief that everyone should work for whatever he receives, leading them to frequently demand the diminishment or complete obliteration of any kind of welfare system.

Within one generation, we have seen what the removal of God from the public setting can do.

Since the Religious Right has such an astounding, principled belief system, why do so many groups feel alienated by this new conservatism, often to the extent that they oppose it outright? To understand the opposition, let's look at some of the documents on which their belief system is based.

WHO IS NATURE'S GOD?

The Declaration of Independence, signed on July 4, 1776, is a document many say was written from a Christian viewpoint. In a country that cries out for separation of church and state, we see in this founding document not only the mention of God, but also direct references to Him as Creator:

When in the course of human events...the separate and equal station to which the Laws of Nature and of Nature's God entitle them....We hold these truths to be self-evident, that all men are created equal, that they are endowed by their Creator with certain unalienable Rights, that among these are Life, Liberty and the pursuit of Happiness.

Just who is this "Nature's God"? Greek mythology worships the deity Diana, the fertility goddess of the Ephesians. She was also called Mother Earth—a euphemism for nature. Mystic fraternal organizations such as the Freemasons included the worship of nature in their formulas for advancement. Is it a coincidence, therefore, that the Declaration of Independence mentions "Nature's God," given that several of the founding fathers were admittedly members of the Freemasons?

If we take a closer look at the Declaration of Independence, however, we will notice something missing. Nowhere in the document is the name of Jesus Christ mentioned. Before Jesus Christ was manifested in the flesh, all religions of the world had a belief in a god. When Jesus Christ came on the scene, the New Testament states, *"There is no other name under heaven given to men by which we must be saved"* (Acts 4:12). That name is Jesus.

Jesus said, *"If anyone is ashamed of me and my words in this adulterous and sinful generation, the Son of Man will be ashamed of him when he comes in his Father's glory with the holy angels"* (Mark 8:38). The apostle Paul cried out, *"I am not ashamed of the gospel, because it is the power of God for the salvation of everyone who believes"* (Romans 1:16).

Can you imagine the impact the founding document would have had if it instead said that Jesus Christ created us?

Giving thanks to the Father, who...has rescued us from the dominion of darkness and brought us into the kingdom of the Son he loves....For by him all things were created: things in heaven and on earth, visible and invisible, whether thrones or powers or rulers or authorities; all things were created by him and for him. (Colossians 1:12–13, 16)

If the authors were writing from within in a Christian culture, why were they not more specific in pronouncing Jesus as Lord? The generic form of God used in the declaration leads to a wide window of possible interpretations.

ABOUT THE FOUNDING FATHERS

As it turns out, many of our founding fathers were deists or Freemasons. Deists believe that God created the earth and then stepped away, as if winding up a clock and letting it run. A God who does not intercede in the affairs of men does not give revelation to men. In other words, deists believe men are self-sufficient, autonomous, and do not need God to meddle in their daily affairs.

The Bible says we are to call on the Lord daily. *"I call to you, O Lord, every day; I spread out my hands to you"* (Psalm 88:9). Therefore, if some of our founders were deists, their understanding of Scripture was corrupt, at best.

Worship not devoted to the true and living God is worship devoted to the devil.

Freemasonry, a fraternal organization with millions of members worldwide, had a strong influence on the founding documents due to several of the signers belonging to a Masonic order, including Benjamin Franklin. Freemasonry holds to a rule that the name of Jesus Christ is not to be invoked during their meetings. A Christian joining the order may choose whether or not he wants to believe that Jesus Christ is Lord and Savior, but it is not a position taught by the Masons. Nowhere in Masonic literature is Jesus referred to as God or portrayed as Savior. Instead, they teach that many gods lead to heaven. Masonry holds that Jesus was merely a man.

THE MASONIC AGENDA

George Washington, the first President of the United States, was a Mason. He warmly supported a plan for having the states form a convention for the purpose of writing the Constitution. This sheds further light on why the Constitution is not more dogmatic in its proclamation of who the Creator is. Masons have as their agenda a humanist society where everybody's god is god.

Today, Masons continue to hold positions of authority worldwide. If they continue to put key people in positions of leadership, they can bring about the one world rule that is spoken of in these apocalyptic verses:

> *The beast was given a mouth to utter proud words and blasphemies....*
> *He opened his mouth to blaspheme God, and to slander his name and*
> *his dwelling place and those who live in heaven. He was given power to*
> *make war against the saints and to conquer them. And he was given*
> *authority over every tribe, people, language and nation.*
>
> (Revelation 13:5–7)

The apostle Paul showed that any worship not devoted to the true and living God is worship devoted to the devil.

> *Do I mean then that a sacrifice offered to an idol is anything, or that an*
> *idol is anything? No, but the sacrifices of pagans are offered to demons,*
> *not to God, and I do not want you to be participants with demons.*
>
> (1 Corinthians 10:19–20)

Masons who do not worship the Father through His Son Jesus Christ, whether they know it or not, are worshipping devils. Just as Eve was duped by the serpent's enticing words, Masons are being duped with their idea of a grand utopia here on earth governed by man.

There's only one way to accomplish the goal of world domination: they need Masons in positions of influence to carry out their agenda. Throughout the history of this nation, Masonic influence has continued. Unless we wise up to the deceptions and witchcraft of Satan, we will continue to fall victim to its redirection of our worship.

Masonic author H. L. Haywood, in his book *The Great Teachings of Masonry*, sets forth this group's objectives:

> It is a world law, destined to change the earth into conformity with
> itself, and as a world power it is something superb, awe inspiring,
> godlike.

Mackey's Revised Encyclopedia of Freemasonry illustrates this goal with its disclosure of the mission of Masonry: "to banish from the world every source of enmity and hostility," "to destroy the pride of conquest and the pomp of war," and "to extend to nations the principles of Masonry." Over and over again world domination comes up.

Paul A. Fisher, who wrote *Behind the Lodge Door*, observed that the Masons dominated the U.S. Supreme Court from 1941 until 1971. This may explain many of their decisions that shifted our nation away from a God-fearing society to a more secular society in this century.

The apostle Paul warned,

For our struggle is not against flesh and blood, but against the rulers, against the authorities, against the powers of this dark world and against the spiritual forces of evil in the heavenly realms.

(Ephesians 6:12)

We see this being played out before our very eyes in many of the Supreme Court decisions in the past several decades.

I believe the Declaration of Independence had Masonic influence and therefore mitigated the influence God intended for this country through strong Christian leadership. Leaders and lay members alike within our churches must be admonished so that we are not a nation-worshipping church, but a God-fearing nation.

CONSERVATIVE CAUSES AND BLACK AMERICA

While the majority of African-Americans consider themselves to be conservative, why is it that the Religious Right consists of only around 5 percent African-Americans? When blacks hear that the Declaration of Independence and the Constitution are a call to return to "traditional values," warnings signs automatically go off.

When blacks hear the call to "traditional values," warning signs go off.

Blacks remember all too well America's racist past. The Thirteenth Amendment didn't abolish slavery until December 18, 1865. Even after the abolition of slavery, this new freedom for blacks had to be assured and their rights had to be guaranteed.

The Fourteenth Amendment in 1866 gave civil rights protection to all citizens of the United States. This happened because many southern states passed laws that restricted the rights of African-Americans. The Fifteenth Amendment gave African-Americans the right to vote in 1869. These amendments passed much to the consternation of Southerners.

Many will say that this shows how effective the Constitution is for allowing such drastic changes. But there are two other amendments that show the limitations of this document.

Jesus wasted none of His valuable time on earth in trying to enforce His message through government.

The Eighteenth Amendment prohibited the manufacture, sale, or transportation of intoxicating liquors on January 29, 1917. Then, in 1933, the Twenty-first Amendment repealed the Eighteenth Amendment. Because the Constitution is not a fixed document, many African-Americans are uneasy when they hear talk of returning to the "good old days." When black people hear "traditional values," some hear it as a return to restricted civil rights, no voting rights, "separate but equal" segregation laws, and even slavery, instead of a progressive future for all of God's children. The values of the past, while nostalgic to some whites, can be offensive and frightening to many blacks. Whites must learn to communicate their vision in a way that assures blacks that this is not the case.

RENDER UNTO CAESAR

We should refrain from speaking in terms of a Christian nation. While the Bible states that all *"authorities that exist have been established by God"*

(Romans 13:1), all governments are ultimately human-based institutions led by fallible men and women. They are to be respected, but not deified or worshipped.

Jesus wasted none of His valuable time on earth in trying to enforce His message through governmental authorities. He observed a healthy separation between God and government: *"Render therefore unto Caesar the things which are Caesar's; and unto God the things that are God's"* (Matthew 22:21).

Christians should not shy away from fully participating in the political process, as is their right. The kingdom of God, however, will not come from the top down through any government. God's kingdom has always advanced from the bottom up through His people.

The Constitution is changeable, but God's law is not. As Christians, we have a written text to guide us in making decisions. The Bible has stood the test of time. Other documents—including the Declaration of Independence, the Constitution, and all the amendments—take a second place to God's Word.

Chapter 10

MEDIA MANIPULATION

I was awakened one morning by the persistent ringing of my phone. It would ring and ring, and then stop. Then it would ring again. Exhausted and groggy from a speaking engagement I'd attended the night before, I thought to myself, *Who's calling back-to-back like that?* Finally, and against my better judgment, I reached over, picked up my cell phone, and realized that someone had left several messages—sixteen, to be exact—and all marked as urgent.

In checking the first message I heard a very deep and stern voice informing me, "Bloomer, call me back. He put his foot in his mouth, and—shock-jock or not—I don't think he's going to be able to talk his way out of this one." The person to whom this caller was referring was the very well-known and controversial radio personality, Don Imus.

There was an outcry for justice and demands for public apology over insensitive and racist remarks that Imus had blurted out on his national cable television and radio program about the Rutgers University women's basketball team. The topic was one of debate in offices and homes all across America, as well as on radio talk shows from coast-to-coast.

Did he have the right to say it? Should he be fired for saying it? If he were prevented from stating his own opinions, no matter how distasteful, wouldn't that be treading on the very thin ice of censorship?

Overcoming Ignorance

Remember, witchcraft strives to manipulate and control, and nothing seems to do that as powerfully as the combination of race and the media.

Prejudice is nothing new, and until the Lord's return, it will never completely cease. So what, if anything, are Christians of any race and color to do about it? While we should all take the time to do our part, we must not forget the teachings, sacrifices, and struggles of prominent leaders who paved the way for true civil rights in this country. People like Rosa Parks, Martin Luther King, and Thurgood Marshall placed great value on the causes for which they fought and did not take God's favor for granted, but rather depended upon it for their life, health, and strength. Their successes were engraved with their innate ability to prioritize—that is, to put God first and to seek Him in all things with the understanding that He was directing their paths. (See Proverbs 3:6.) That is ultimately the component that will continue to lead all of us to victory over the battles of injustice today.

Whether it's the fight against racial injustice, women's rights, the right to free speech, wiping out extreme poverty, or religious intolerance, we must never forget that hatred and ignorance will never be overcome through the toxicity of strife, malevolence, and bitterness.

> *Hatred and ignorance will never be overcome through strife, malevolence, and bitterness.*

Do we have the right to be upset over injustice? Of course we do. Nevertheless, we need to turn those frustrations into productive actions that lead to peace and equality. Choose wisely the battles that are worth fighting and those battles that serve no productive purpose.

One of the most profound statements in the Word of God is taken from Ecclesiastes: *"The words of a wise man's mouth are gracious, but the lips of a fool shall swallow him up"* (Ecclesiastes 10:12 NKJV). We will never be able to quiet the mouths of fools, whose ignorance runs so deep that they no longer receive wisdom and enlightenment. Forcing them to remain silent regarding how they feel only permits them the opportunity to become more cunning with their deceptive tactics and prejudiced agenda.

> By transgression an evil man is snared, but the righteous sings and rejoices. (Proverbs 29:6 NKJV)

That is why, especially as Christians, we should not rush to judgment, but base our decisions upon the intentions of the unjustifiable act while simultaneously considering its source.

> If a wise man contends with a foolish man, whether the fool rages or laughs, there is no peace. (Proverbs 29:9 NKJV)

In other words, don't waste valuable time trying to convince someone of something who has no intention of listening to your concerns. Instead, take positive action. If only this combination of race and media were an isolated incident.

THE JENA SIX

In 2006, a dispute at Jena High School in Louisiana would soon turn the country upside down and shake the core of its hidden beliefs. It all began when a black student asked the administration for permission to sit beneath a tree that was considered for whites only. The next day, three white students hung several nooses from the tree. Several confrontations and fights followed leading to the arrest of six black teens—the Jena Six.

Most of the controversy stemmed from the fact that the six black youths were charged with attempted murder, while the white teens involved were basically sent home with a "slap on the wrist." To many, the charges seemed disproportionate and racially motivated.

By the time the story of the "Jena Six" reached national exposure in 2007, the opinions dividing races, classes, and even families had already begun to stir the country into a frenzy of anger and outrage. Some were shocked that judicial prejudice could be so bold as to rear its head in the "enlightenment" of the twenty-first century.

POINT-COUNTERPOINT

The media is motivated by conflict. Watch any cable news program. They get a person on one side of an issue and a person on the other side. Then, they throw the two together and allow America to watch the sparks fly. Their only motivations are ratings, conflict, and controversy—not peace and understanding.

If peace is to be attained, it must be preached, and it must be activated. Regulations and laws are set to maintain guidelines and barriers, but the ultimate solution to racial equality and the end of legalized victimization is in combating ignorance. Hate is a learned behavior.

Never is this more evident than by viewing the actions of young children. They play together and eventually disagree or even physically fight, but as long as adults allow them the opportunity to mend their disagreements, peace becomes evident—not in days, months, or even years, but in simply a matter of minutes. Children are the most tolerant and intelligent creatures when it comes to equality. It isn't until their parents or other authority figures teach them otherwise that hate becomes a part of who they are. Then the media shows up and, literally, all *hell* breaks loose.

> *If peace is to be attained, it must be preached, and it must be activated.*

In the case of the Jena Six, at the time of this writing, some of the charges against the black students have been reduced, but the authorities have succeeded in getting one of the boys to testify against the others and the litigation promises to continue for quite some time. Meanwhile, protestors on both sides of the issue continue to descend upon this little town with petitions, rallies, and, of course, TV cameras.

As adults, we must keep in mind that the purpose for which we fight is not a personal agenda, but a life-or-death struggle with spiritual forces who intend to sow the seeds of dissent and hate for generations to come. And to that purpose, we must make decisions which hold the power to protect, invoke peace, and pave the way for those who will become our future leaders. We must not fuel the fire that sets our children against each other, setting back generations the heartfelt labor of those who stood for change.

> *The church has fallen victim to the deceptive witchcraft of the media, while neglecting the business of the kingdom.*

The greatest trick of the devil is enticing one group of people to scream at another group across the street while no growth or understanding takes place—only the wildfires of conflict and contention. Protestors hold the power to either make viable statements that invoke positive change or incite wars that birth further injustice. There must come a time, if you are going to be used as an instrument for instituting equality, when you make the transformation from a foot soldier to a true activist.

Foot soldiers are followers. Activists "activate" and lead the process of equality. They set a plan in motion, they know how to call upon the proper resources to achieve it, and their mission becomes a success. You must not allow yourself to become so enraged and aroused by a "cause" that, in your righteous anger, you forget to invoke a positive change.

It's all too easy for the media to take an isolated incident and cry, "Race!" What's harder is to care about the issues that Jesus cared about, as well as the people He cared about. For far too long, the church has fallen victim to the deceptive witchcraft of the media, while neglecting the business of the kingdom.

THE BUSINESS OF POVERTY

Currently, one of the least discussed injustices in America is the fact that poverty is big business. Take a ride through any community plagued by economic decay and degradation, and there you will find certain industries on nearly every street corner where business is booming: liquor stores, lottery agents, and gun shops. Meanwhile, the educational system budgets pennies for these children, supplying them with minimal resources with which to learn and get out of their predicament. It's almost as if someone wants them to stay right where they are.

And where is the church in this crisis? It largely fled the cities for the affluent suburbs decades ago, leaving these blighted neighborhoods to charitable agencies such as the Salvation Army. Today, the church loves to take a stand on hot-button issues like abortion and same-sex marriages, but remains silent on issues of race and extreme poverty. For all its good intentions, Sunday morning in America remains the most segregated hour of the week.

The decade of the sixties ushered in the move of God and Word of Faith. Somewhere, however, between being saved and increasing one's faith, a "prosperity message" crept in and began competing with the anointing of God. The result has been an obsession with *getting more things* while neglecting the true purpose and call of God that has been placed on the life of the believer.

Upon leaving this earth in the flesh, Jesus promised,

> *Most assuredly, I say to you, he who believes in Me, the works that I do he will do also; and greater works than these he will do, because I go to My Father. And whatever you ask in My name, that I will do, that the Father may be glorified in the Son. If you ask anything in My name, I will do it. If you love Me, keep My commandments.*
>
> (John 14:12–15 NKJV)

Jesus left us here as an active witness of His majesty and power, and intended us not just to study Him, but to actively effect a change upon the earth. The *"works"* of Jesus are the guide by which we are to live in order to make a positive impact upon the society in which we live. If we are to do *"greater works,"* then just what were the works of Jesus anyway?

> *The Spirit of the LORD is upon Me, because He has anointed Me to preach the gospel to the poor; He has sent Me to heal the brokenhearted, to proclaim liberty to the captives and recovery of sight to the blind, to set at liberty those who are oppressed; to proclaim the acceptable year of the LORD.*
>
> (Luke 4:18–19 NKJV)

Jesus didn't leave it much of a mystery. We are to:

1. preach the Gospel to the poor,
2. heal the brokenhearted,
3. proclaim liberty to the captives,
4. recover sight to the blind,
5. set the oppressed free,
6. and proclaim the acceptable year of the Lord.

Unfortunately, the church has, for the most part, farmed out these *"works"* to others. While the church may occasionally write a check, it seems to generally prefer for others to actually get their hands dirty in the prisons, ghettos, shelters, and recovery clinics.

Meanwhile, the media parades Christian leaders on the cable channels parroting "family values," the right to life, and decrying the homosexual agenda, because these are the themes that "play" to the suburban church. These are the themes that open up the wallets of Christians.

Jesus left us here not just to study Him, but to actively effect change upon the earth.

SATAN STIRS THE POT

Whenever you find an unruly mob, there is one way to ensure that things will deteriorate: turn on the lights and the cameras. Media attention never seems to lead to cool heads and compassion. It always seems to lead to conflict and strife. And who benefits? The media, of course, with skyrocketing ratings. The media is not interested in resolution. Their job is to stir the pot and then move on to the next story.

The media knows that race is our biggest hot button and it will stop at nothing to take a simple isolated incident and blow it up into a bona fide racial divide. Their main commodity is fear and they sell it each and every night. One night it's the Jena Six, Don Imus, or O. J. Simpson; the next night it's shark attacks, toys made in China, or terror alerts. The media keeps us afraid and enraged because they know it will keep us tuned in. That's witchcraft in its most classic form: manipulate and control.

As Christians, we should know better—but we don't. As Christians we should focus on what we are *for*: love, compassion, justice, and liberation. Instead, too often we focus on what we are *against*: homosexuality, abortion, R-rated movies, rap music, and the list goes on. By focusing on what we are against, we draw a line and see the world as the enemy, as we huddle together with other Christians, safe and secure behind our church walls. Instead of being a light in the darkness, we hide with people just like ourselves within the light.

WHERE ARE THEY?

Many Christians point to a particular verse in Scripture as the reason why they don't do more for the poor. In Matthew 26:11, the apostles protested as a woman poured expensive perfume on the feet of Jesus, who replied, *"The poor you will always have with you."* For many, this was an admission by God Himself that the problem of poverty is impossible.

What if that's not what Jesus meant? What if He was actually telling His church, "I assume you will always have the poor with you, feeding them, sheltering them, and caring for their needs. I assume they will always be there in My church."

What if Jesus never intended that verse to be an excuse for Christians to ignore the poor and suffering?

Jesus rejected the pridefully religious and went out to seek another crowd.

Look around most suburban churches on a Sunday morning. Are the poor any where in sight? Perhaps the *"greater works"* that Jesus mentioned would be possible if the church stopped listening to Christian leaders in the media and paid more attention to the actual words of Jesus in the Gospels.

In the Gospels, Jesus rejected the pridefully religious and went out to seek another crowd.

> Now the tax collectors and "sinners" were all gathering around to hear him. But the Pharisees and the teachers of the law muttered, "This man welcomes sinners and eats with them." (Luke 15:1–2)

Jesus sought the sinners, lepers, and disenfranchised. He ate with tax collectors. He drank water with an adulteress. He befriended prostitutes and thieves. The Pharisees refused to allow these people to enter the temple in order to worship and hear God's Word but these were the people in Jesus' church. Are they in ours? Who are the lepers and tax collectors in our church?

Are we becoming like the Pharisees? Do we welcome and encourage black, white, and brown in our pews? Do we welcome and embrace the homosexual, the young couple living together, the addict, and the homeless? They were there in Jesus' day. They should be there in our church and in our pew. Look around; where are they?

Let's resist the fear and division that comes into our homes each night via the media. Let's stand *for* something and not *against* it. Let's not fall victim to Satan's witchcraft of control and manipulation. If only the church were immune. Alas, it's not just the white church that allows witchcraft in its pews. I've seen it in the black church as well.

Chapter 11

MARCHING TO A DIFFERENT DRUMMER

In 1995, the call went out. Old men, young men, and little boys gathered together. Professionals, tradesmen, clergy, and gang members pooled their resources for a great moment in history. They came from the northern, southern, eastern, and western parts of the United States. Baptists, Methodists, Pentecostals, Catholics, and Muslims, united for what some called a great spiritual awakening. Fathers walked proudly with their sons to form a sea of blackness in numbers greater than during the days of Martin Luther King, Jr. They gathered in Washington, D.C., for the Million Man March.

Although this event is more than a decade past, it still stands as a seminal moment in black history. What caused this unprecedented outpouring of black brotherhood? What important message did the marchers unify to convey? Was their message black determination, political empowerment, moral rectitude, or the ability of the black man to economically sustain himself? This event remains important because it shows how the church can be deceived by a bewitching ruse designed to build the reputation of one man.

A LEADERSHIP CRISIS

From the beginning, many African-American leaders and organizations were opposed to the march. Their problem was not so much the message as the messenger. The Honorable Minister Louis Farrakhan, leader of the Black Muslim sect in the United States, proclaimed that God had inspired him to call for one million black men to march on Washington, D.C. Yet, his religious beliefs, anti-Semitic attitude, and racial separatist views alienated many of those whom he was trying to attract.

Others within the African-American community, however, strongly supported this adventure. These were people who had become dissatisfied with the state of black America. Slavery may have ended in 1863, but many still believed that black men and women only existed to remain in servitude to white men.

Anger and frustration based on racial discrimination, a conservative Congress considered by many to be anti-black, and a continued lack of economic advancement were the conditions that caused people to begin to support the march. After years of the white Republican leadership of Ronald Reagan and George H. W. Bush that seemed to pander only to a white majority, the time for turning the other cheek was over. African-Americans needed a new direction and bold new leadership, and they believed this was the moment to make a statement, demonstrate their strength, and let their voices be heard.

> *The African-American community had sustained itself during the tumultuous twentieth century with its faith.*

This new leadership had to be visionary. It could not be someone with an old formula. The majority of the current leadership would not do because of their ties to the 1960s Christian civil rights movement, which many believed had not gone far enough in bringing about equality in ethnic groups and economic classes. This indictment also stretched to American Christianity, which many believed turned its back to bringing about the needed change.

Even though prominent Christians such as Jesse Jackson, Al Sharpton, and Joseph Lowery were perceived as leaders, they were not seen as men with strong convictions. African-Americans have a history of being very religious, even to the point of suffering persecution for their faith. (During the Civil Rights movement, Christian ministers and churches persevered through the lynchings, church bombings, and police abuse spawned by racial hatred.) Fair or not, these leaders were viewed as "sell-outs"— exchanging their faith for political and personal gain.

The African-American community had sustained itself during the tumultuous twentieth century with its faith in the Bible and the Gospel of Jesus Christ as the standards for all men to abide by. The black community believed that their clergy should be shining examples of righteousness and fortitude. Unfortunately, some of these leaders did not exhibit the same morality. Because there was no one else palatable to lead the charge toward vision and morality, the African-American community turned to the immoral message of leaders who were out of touch with their constituents.

Throughout history, men with enough conviction have always been able to stir the hearts and minds of their people—sometimes for good, but also for evil. Consider the carnage that Hitler, Mussolini, Stalin, the Crusades, the Inquisition, and holy wars have wrought on mankind. These episodes were precipitated by strong-willed leaders who stubbornly stayed the course even though history proved that their methods and ideas were misguided.

The populace looks for any leader who seems to embody their pain regardless of the message.

Many of today's leaders have learned the power of a good soundbite or photo opportunity. Most of the public masses are not economic experts, history buffs, or religious scholars who can comprehend long speeches or intricate social problems. Most will follow a leader who can communicate that he or she is truly concerned about their constituents. Therefore the populace looks for any leader who they think embodies their pain and disillusionment regardless of his or her true message.

Louis Farrakhan initially played the part of the reluctant leader. When the march was first called—a march to support him and his racist views—many leaders cried foul. In order to mollify those opposed to his leading the march, Farrakhan maintained that the march was not about him, but about economic and political empowerment for the black man in America. He was only a messenger giving the call. In this way, it seemed that Farrakhan humbly embodied the pain an disillusionment of black America.

As it turned out, not only was the march a success (attendance estimates of the event range from eight hundred thousand to 1.2 million), but the media was all too eager to assign the credit for the overwhelming turnout to Louis Farrakhan. In his speech to the marchers, he stated, "You cannot separate the message from the messenger," implying that the success of the march was a result of his leadership.

What was the message of Louis Farrakhan? Was he a modern-day Moses leading the black people out of bondage in Egypt, or was he Pharaoh, taking away their straw and telling them to continue to make bricks?

THE MAN AND HIS MESSAGE

Black Muslims base their teachings on the Koran, a collection of writings attributed to the Prophet Mohammed approximately six centuries after the birth of our Lord and Savior Jesus Christ. Mohammed's teaching birthed the faith of Islam, and his followers became Muslims.

Islam teaches that there is one god, Allah, and all must submit to His will. Muslims believe it is the will of God that the whole world be subjected to Islam. Furthermore, it teaches that the Prophet Mohammed is the chief and last prophet.

The central doctrine that separates Christianity from any other religion, whether it be Islam or any animist religion, is the person and work of Jesus Christ. Although Muslims view Jesus as a prophet, the Koran denies crucial elements of His life and death:

And for their saying: "We killed the Messiah, Jesus, the son of Mary, the Messenger of Allah." They did not kill him, nor did they crucify him, but [they crucified] he [Judas].   (Koran, Sura 4:158)

The Bible, however, contradicts this:

Then he released Barabbas to them. But he had Jesus flogged, and handed him over to be crucified....The angel said to the women, "Do not be afraid, for I know that you are looking for Jesus, who was crucified."
(Matthew 27:26; 28:5)

Christian faith is based on the crucifixion, death, and resurrection of Jesus Christ. This fundamental difference stands opposed to the Muslim faith. For Christians to support someone who does not believe in the crucifixion of Christ is completely offensive.

Farrakhan and Muslims also believe that we are not to worship Jesus as the Son of God.

Verily, the Messiah, Jesus, son of Mary, was only a Messenger of Allah and a fulfillment of His word which He sent down to Mary, and a mercy from Him. So believe in Allah and His Messengers, and say not "They are three." Desist, it will be better for you. Verily, Allah is the only One God. Far is it from His Holiness that He should have a son.
(Koran, Sura 4:172)

Jesus went up to Jerusalem to a feast of the Jews. During the feast, which occurred on a Sabbath day, Jesus met a man who had an infirmity for thirty-eight years. Demonstrating compassion, Jesus healed the man. The Jews, however, rebuked Jesus for performing this work of power on the Sabbath. Jesus claimed God was His Father when He said,

That all may honor the Son just as they honor the Father. He who does not honor the Son does not honor the Father, who sent him.
(John 5:23)

The Jews knew that this claim made Jesus equal with God. Jesus was emphatic, however, ascribing to Himself the same honor that the Father received. If we reject the words of Jesus Christ, which were written before

Mohammed was born and the Koran was written, we deny the foundation of our faith.

Even though Muslims selectively quote from the New Testament, they reject the Gospel. Jesus Himself clearly made the case for His own divinity when He said,

> I came out from thee, and they have believed that thou didst send me....
> That they all may be one; as thou, Father, art in me, and I in thee, that
> they also may be one in us: that the world may believe that thou hast
> sent me. (John 17:8, 21 KJV)

The apostle John further declared that Jesus was with the Father from the very beginning.

> In the beginning was the Word, and the Word was with God, and
> the Word was God....The Word became flesh and made his dwelling
> among us. We have seen his glory, the glory of the One and Only, who
> came from the Father, full of grace and truth. (John 1:1, 14)

"The Word" as translated in John 1:1 is the Greek word *logos* as opposed to *lego* or *lallia*, which are Greek words having to do with speech and language. Logos refers to the mind and intellect of God. In other words, logos is the deliberate thoughts of God made flesh.

We can understand the logos and the mystery of the Godhead by using a tape recorder as an example. If you record your voice, you can send the recording to someone in Swaziland who knows you and that person will recognize the voice as yours. You can be in one place and the tape can be elsewhere, leaving instructions or giving directions without compromising the credibility of the sender of the message.

In this analogy, God is the one speaking into the tape recorder, and Jesus is the cassette tape. The casing for the cassette tape represents the fact that "God was manifested in the flesh" (1 Timothy 3:16 NKJV). When Jesus said, "I and the Father are one" (John 10:30), he was referring to the impossibility of separating the recorded word from the person who spoke it.

Jesus gave them this answer: "I tell you the truth, the Son can do noth-
ing by himself; he can do only what he sees his Father doing, because
whatever the Father does the Son also does."   (John 5:19)

Even though the Father and Son are one, they are still separate. The cassette tape is in Swaziland, but you are in the United States. Just as the casing is inferior to the one who recorded it, so is the flesh inferior to God. The message on the tape lets you know who it is. Likewise God the Father, being in Christ Jesus, lets us know who He is.

Even though the Koran states that Jesus never said He was God or the Son of God, the Bible clearly shows us otherwise.

RACISM AND HYPOCRISY

Elijah Poole, who later changed his name to Elijah Muhammad, founded the Black Muslims in the United States in 1934 during the segregationist Jim Crow era. Through espousing racist views, Elijah Muhammad believed that he could raise the black man's consciousness to the point where he could achieve independence from the white man, whom he called the devil. To Elijah Poole, all the world's evils could be traced to the white man. Poole's way of eradicating the injustices of the past was to call for black people to separate themselves from white people.

This is not a view taught by the Word of God.

There is neither Jew nor Greek, slave nor free, male nor female, for you
are all one in Christ Jesus.   (Galatians 3:28)

From one man [God] made every nation of men, that they should
inhabit the whole earth; and he determined the times set for them and
the exact places where they should live.   (Acts 17:26)

Those who espouse racist views are not being led by God. It does not matter if they are white or black.

Louis Farrakhan has not repudiated the teachings of Prophet Mohammed or Elijah Muhammad; therefore, Christians should reject him as a spiritual leader. Revealing himself as the opportunist that he is, Farrakhan went to the Sudan where black Africans continue to be oppressed and even enslaved. Farrakhan, however, did not speak out against this inhumane treatment of our black African brothers. In refusing to do so, he betrayed the very teachings of his mentor, Elijah Muhammad, who was against the enslaving of Africans.

How can Farrakhan lead the black man out of his so-called bondage when he himself is a liar in bondage because of his rejection of Jesus Christ as Lord and Savior? Furthermore, Scripture states that anyone who believes that Christ has not come in the flesh is an antichrist.

> *Who is the liar? It is the man who denies that Jesus is the Christ. Such a man is the antichrist—he denies the Father and the Son.*
>
> (1 John 2:22)

> *They are blind guides. If a blind man leads a blind man, both will fall into a pit.* (Matthew 15:14)

During his sixteen-nation tour after the Million Man March, Louis Farrakhan stopped in South Africa, where one of the directors of Islam, as was commonly reported in the worldwide press, said that "Christianity had failed the black man. The black man needs Louis Farrakhan to restore him." In one of the Arab countries, Farrakhan is reported to have said that he wants to spread Islam throughout the west, especially in the United States.

A RETURN TO BONDAGE?

How have so many Christians been deceived by this man who is trying to replace Christianity with Islam? Have the black men in America become so enraged at the perceived injustices that they are willing to turn their backs on the true God and follow a liar?

Persecution is nothing new to a believer in Jesus Christ. The Donatists, a group of African Christians that arose in the fourth century A.D., survived until the Prophet Mohammed came on the scene. They were willing to lose their lives at the hands of the Muslims rather than compromise their belief in the Lord Jesus Christ. We are not under the threat of losing our lives, but we seem to be willing to compromise our Christian faith by following such an antichrist.

Egypt was never meant to be Israel's final destination. Some Israelites, however, became comfortable in Egyptian slavery, lost sight of the true God, and began serving false gods.

Ignorance creates a vacuum that can be filled with evil.

The same thing is happening to too many African-Americans. Too many of us have lost sight of the promises of God and have accepted a false god instead. We have embraced teachings and lifestyles that promise deliverance but are not godly.

Hosea 4:6 says, *"My people are destroyed from lack of knowledge."* This ignorance creates a vacuum that can be filled with evil. No matter how well-meaning a leader's intentions, if he is willing to subjugate God's Word and proceed without repentance, the end result will always be destruction. God pronounces judgment on a people only when they refuse to repent and yield to His authority.

WHO IS YOUR LEADER?

Look at the leaders who willingly followed Louis Farrakhan's march. Marion Barry, the former mayor of Washington, D.C., was caught on video smoking crack cocaine. Yet he jumped at the chance to once again to be seen as the leader of a cause, any cause.

Ben Chavis, touted as one of the principals behind the march, was later jettisoned as leader of the National Association for the Advancement of Colored People (NAACP) for indiscretions related to money and sex.

During his run for the presidency, the Reverend Jesse Jackson eagerly endorsed the homosexual and abortion rights agenda because it helped him in the polls. Today, he is seen more as an antagonist, one who jumps in front of any news camera to provoke discussion rather than as a man who can lead. Jackson was originally opposed to the Million Man March until he sensed a groundswell of support for the event. Then he changed his mind and became a part of it.

Many well-known African-American ministers who spoke at the event did not once invoke the name of Jesus Christ. Jesus said, "*If anyone is ashamed of me and my words in this adulterous and sinful generation, the Son of Man will be ashamed of him*" (Mark 8:38). These ministers prayed and spoke in the generic form of religion so as not to offend their Muslim brothers.

The black church was bewitched by sweet sounding words. The time has come for us to rise up and tell the "emperor" he has no clothes. We must refuse to fall for any more deception. Our allegiance is to God the Father and His Son Jesus Christ.

> *God has destined the black church to bring healing—not division—into the world.*

It is time for us to turn to the true and living God and to reject these so-called black leaders whose main concern is ill-gotten financial gain and media attention. God is the One who sustains. He is the One who gives us strength. Let us move on in the power of God and do great and wonderful things in the name of His Son Jesus Christ.

I believe that God has destined the black church to bring healing—not division—into the world. Why us? Because true love can only be shown by the persecution you are willing to endure from the one who hates you. Jesus Christ went to the cross as an innocent man so that the world, those who put Him there, would know the meaning of true love. If we really want to see God move, if we really want to experience deliverance, let us reject all hypocrisy and stand steadfastly on the Word of God no matter what persecution we may face.

Part III

GETTING FREE

Chapter 12

DO NOT BE DECEIVED

The men who wrote the Holy Scriptures were divinely inspired by the hand of God Himself. These men were literally overshadowed by the Holy Spirit, who guided their words to record and convey God's message. In light of this fact, how would it seem possible for some believers—men and women who have experienced the power of God with signs and wonders following—to stray from believing in the infallible Word of God? How could they possibly come to view the Bible as simply a compilation of theories or fictions scripted by senile old men?

Our contemporary society is constantly bombarded with an innumerable array of teachings, theories, and beliefs, making it easier to become susceptible to satanic witchcraft and false doctrines of unbelief. Make no mistake about it, the devil is strategically placing his philosophies and ideologies in all the right places at just the right moment to infiltrate the masses with his demonic agenda. Disguised as intellectual teachings that simply challenge certain beliefs and tickle the curiosity of those who are searching for godly answers, these subtle satanic traps entice people by simply asking, "What's the harm in weighing your options by opening your mind to alternative ways of thinking?"

In an instant, doubt and unbelief can be planted into the minds of those who are searching for God. Ungodly doctrines know exactly which buttons to push to infuse the inquisitive mind with the desire to hear more.

With so many messages, images, and other distractions so readily available at our fingertips via the Internet, media, and other avenues, Jesus does not want us to lose our focus. It is not enough to just hear the Word of God, but you must hear it and keep it. (See Luke 11:28.) We must hide the Word of God in our hearts and keep it with all diligence. While I do advocate being knowledgeable about different religious beliefs, such study should only be done as a means of becoming a more effective witness for Jesus Christ.

> *The devil wants us to begin questioning our faith and turning to alternative methods of spiritual well-being.*

We are housed in flesh that has its own will—a will often driven by personal passions. These passions can sometimes be detrimental to our physical, spiritual, and mental well-being. They can be overcome, however, by the love and grace of Jesus Christ. I was driven solely by my own passions at one time in life. I know without a doubt that if I had not accepted Jesus, I would not be alive today.

People have many personal reasons for serving the Lord. It is what we call their testimony—proof that God is who He says He is, and that He will do what He has promised. Therefore, it is no coincidence that the first thing the devil comes to steal is our testimony. He wants us to begin questioning our faith and turning to alternative methods of spiritual well-being and rejuvenation. That is why you should not only serve God for what He does, but more importantly, for who He is.

HEAVEN AND HELL

Some argue that there is no heaven or hell. Although I do believe in both destinations, I have never been to either place. You cannot, however, tell me that there is no Jesus, because He lives in me. For every crisis that I encounter in life, Jesus has not only left me His Holy Spirit, but also the sixty-six books that make up the Bible to remind me of His words. In those sixty-six books of the Bible can be found wisdom and strength for every question and challenge in this life. So, with all of this vital information so readily available to us, what makes a man stop believing in God? In my experience, it can only happen after an encounter with demons.

THE CYCLE OF DECEPTION AND THE
DEPTHS OF DECEIT

> *The Spirit clearly says that in later times some will abandon the faith and follow deceiving spirits and things taught by demons.*
>
> (1 Timothy 4:1)

HEEDING OTHER TEACHINGS

What causes an individual to depart from the faith? One cause is that he or she begins to heed to or seriously consider the enticing doctrines of devils that are now rampant in our society's beliefs. In the same way that jurors may acquit the guilty by becoming swayed by the eloquent speech of a gifted attorney, the devil attempts to play similar tricks on our minds. The evidence of God's glory, power, majesty, and might can be before our very eyes, but if we listen to the wrong voice for too long we begin to give heed to such erroneous doctrine. Scripture warns us to be equipped with knowledge and not to be ashamed of standing up for God's truth:

> *Do your best to present yourself to God as one approved, a workman who does not need to be ashamed and who correctly handles the word of truth. Avoid godless chatter, because those who indulge in it will become more and more ungodly. Their teaching will spread like gangrene.*
>
> (2 Timothy 2:15–17)

Lending your ear to profane babblings for too long will eat at your faith like gangrene and you *"will become more and more ungodly."*

INCORPORATING OTHER TEACHINGS

> *Such teachings come through hypocritical liars, whose consciences have been seared as with a hot iron.* (1 Timothy 4:2)

The conscience is *"seared as with a hot iron"* as you begin to receive lies as truth and incorporate those ungodly beliefs as a way of life. With no guilt or thought to the consequences, you now freely engage in things that once convicted you and caused you to feel uneasy. The morality that once measured how far you would go and the things you would and would not do quickly becomes a thing of the past. You live in the moment and do not think twice about the standards which you have now compromised by giving heed to these seducing spirits.

> *Lending your ear to profane babblings*
> *for too long will eat at your faith.*

IGNORING GOD'S TEACHINGS

They forbid people to marry and order them to abstain from certain foods, which God created to be received with thanksgiving by those who believe and who know the truth. (1 Timothy 4:3)

The days of sanctity through marriage are a thing of the past. Couples young and old are opting to "shack up" as opposed to entering lifelong marriage commitments.

Another way in which we are ignoring God's teachings is in the area of our diets. While I am an advocate of better health and taking care of the body, I also know that vain agendas for quick weight loss are pushing dangerous habits upon many young people, especially young women, inducing them to sacrifice their health for physical beauty. Statistics show that eating disorders such as anorexia nervosa and bulimia are wreaking havoc in the lives of many American teens.

Anything done to excess can have dire consequences. Eating too little is just as damaging to an individual's health as eating too much.

For every creature of God is good, and nothing to be refused, if it be received with thanksgiving: for it is sanctified by the word of God and prayer. (1 Timothy 4:4–5)

COMPLETE RELIANCE UPON GOD

The doctrines of witchcraft will attack at your most vulnerable moment in an attempt to overpower your faith. This is why God has promised to surround us with His angels. He wants us to remain focused on His truth in spite of all the satanic dogma that tries to shroud our way of thinking.

For he will command his angels concerning you to guard you in all your ways. (Psalm 91:11)

Even if you stray, the angels of the Lord are around you to bring you back on course.

I often tell the story of how I strayed as a young man, struggling with my faith. Sent out in ministry too soon, I found myself preaching the Word of God as a young minister while struggling to break free of drug addiction. All that time, it was the grace of God, along with His goodness and mercy, that kept me from continuing the self-destructive path that the devil intended for my ruin. I made a conscious decision to no longer live my life predicated upon my own will, but to instead submit my passions to God and allow Him to steer my path. I know I could not have done it without Him and the angels He sent to protect me during this very difficult time. I could not and did not wait for my condition or its cure to be announced by some prophet. I was in need of an immediate physician, who came in the form of my Lord and Savior Jesus Christ.

Doctrines of witchcraft will attack at your most vulnerable moment.

So many times, we sit and wait for God to speak to us through someone else when He really wants us to come to Him directly. It is fine to have a prophetic word spoken in your life, but God wants you to come to Him personally so that He might use your condition to build your faith and confidence in Him. God wants to develop a relationship of trust that will build your faith for any future trials and tests that you must face.

In the past God spoke to our forefathers through the prophets at many times and in various ways, but in these last days he has spoken to us by his Son, whom he appointed heir of all things, and through whom he made the universe. The Son is the radiance of God's glory and the exact representation of his being, sustaining all things by his powerful word. After he had provided purification for sins, he sat down at the right hand of the Majesty in heaven. (Hebrews 1:1–3)

In times past, God spoke to us by His prophets, but now He speaks to us directly. If you insist on waiting for a prophet to speak directly to you before taking the initiative to change your condition by talking to God yourself, then you are unknowingly delaying your healing. We have been given direct access to the *"radiance of God's glory,"* which is Christ Jesus.

To which of the angels did God ever say, "Sit at my right hand until I make your enemies a footstool for your feet"? Are not all angels ministering spirits sent to serve those who will inherit salvation? (Hebrews 1:13–14)

When has God ever said to an angel, "Sit on My right hand, until I make your enemies a footstool for your feet?" Never. He did, however, say it to you and me. You are seated with Him in heavenly places in Christ Jesus. *"And God raised us up with Christ and seated us with him in the heavenly realms in Christ Jesus"* (Ephesians 2:6).

> *In times past, God spoke to us by His prophets, but now He speaks to us directly.*

In Romans, Scripture says we are *"heirs of God and co-heirs with Christ"* (verse 8:17). That means that we have 100 percent of the same rights that Jesus has. The angels in glory are assigned to help you get what you need out of the universe. The Bible says, *"Are not all angels ministering spirits sent to serve those who will inherit salvation?"* (Hebrews 1:14). We are the ones destined to *"inherit salvation."* We inherited salvation because Jesus *"chose us in Him before the foundation of the world"* (Ephesians 1:4).

God assigns angels to us but He does not want us to worship angels. They are His messengers and our protectors. Once you receive the revelation of God's power to provide and how He assigns angels to attend to your needs, then all things will become possible for you, through Christ Jesus.

GOD WILL MEET YOUR NEEDS

I remember when I first decided to start my church. I had been traveling for a number of years as an evangelist, but soon came to realize that my wife and children were in need of a stable place of worship. Knowing that the Lord had called me to the office of the pastor, I decided to step out in faith and begin a church. I pitched a tent in an open field in the heart of the city and began a thirty-day tent revival. After the final night of the revival, we moved into a small office complex where we would hold our church services for approximately a year.

As I searched the city to find a suitable permanent dwelling, I came across an historic elementary school building, which had been vacant so long that it had become an urban blight to the community. Miraculously, with only a few members, we purchased this historic site, but still could not move into it until we had raised enough funds to complete its much-needed renovation. We continued our services at the temporary location until one day we walked into the office complex and found that due to heavy rainfall, the building had been completely flooded. Once again, we were without a home. Nevertheless, we did not give up. Instead, we cleared a central area of the dilapidated building that we had recently purchased and used it for our worship services. Little by little, we made the necessary repairs, and today what was once an eyesore for the community has been renovated into a beautiful place of worship that exemplifies the miracle-working power of God.

I know it was the angels of the Lord that led me to this site. Hundreds of people had driven by this same building every day and could not see its potential, but by the grace of God I was able to envision its restored grandeur even as it sat in its dilapidated state. In times of prayer I would openly voice what I saw in my mind until it finally began to come to fruition.

What Are You Saying?

I discovered that you *can have* what you say and *receive* what you continue to confess, if it is according to God's will and the Bible. If you aren't saying anything, more than likely you are not receiving very much either— or you are receiving all the wrong things due to the power of your negative confessions. Now is the time to start speaking. When you face hardships, don't give in to the adversity. Instead, look adversity in the face and declare, "This is not going to happen to me. I know I am going through hell, but I am going to have victory because of God's promises!"

The one thing that allows you to continually excel in your job, at school, or in whatever capacity you seek to conquer, is the God factor. There comes a time when God will speak life-altering components into your existence. When He does, you must not linger, but immediately gravitate toward that Word. Allow nothing to snatch the Word that God has spoken. This is the season when demons will grow upset because they know that as we come into the full knowledge of our Lord and Savior, His mercy and grace, nothing will seem impossible for us. So just know that, even when it appears that nothing good is happening for you in the natural, God is still working on your behalf behind the scenes. The devil's trick, however, is to get you to alter your confession, to go back on your promise. This is the time to ask God to hone your spiritual sight and renew your faith. Do not be deceived; you can have supernatural angelic beings working on your behalf.

Chapter 13

WALKING WITH GOD

Storms that come into your life to make you strong will sometimes make you weak at first. There is no one alive whom the devil has not tried to attack. Although some of our attacks are self-inflicted, Satan latches onto our weaknesses—those self-destructive behaviors—to intensify the disaster from which we are attempting to recover.

Years ago I began studying eschatology—the study of final things—and found out that many people remain in shallow waters. This is because walking with God requires a whole new level of responsibility. I believe that lack of biblical study is one of the main reasons that those who are in the ministry of deliverance fall prey to false doctrines, strange teachings, and the effects of witchcraft. Ignorance is a weapon the devil uses against our personal prosperity and growth.

Today, many people know more about church than they know about God. Church is the place where you are supposed to be able to get your spiritual rejuvenation through the person of Jesus Christ. It is not where we go to discuss Jesus as simply a "theory." In church, Jesus Christ should be spoken of as the true and living God.

TAKE A STAND

In order to learn of God and the Savior that He truly is, it will require you to take a unique stand that goes against the grain of the crowd. When you are equipped with the knowledge of God, taking a stand for what you believe becomes less of a task and more of an opportunity, even in the face of opposition and scrutiny.

In Genesis chapter six, a man is shown to have saved his entire household due to the favor that he obtained from God. That man was Noah.

> The LORD saw how great man's wickedness on the earth had become, and that every inclination of the thoughts of his heart was only evil all the time. The LORD was grieved that he had made man on the earth, and his heart was filled with pain. So the LORD said, "I will wipe mankind, whom I have created, from the face of the earth—men and animals, and creatures that move along the ground, and birds of the air—for I am grieved that I have made them." But Noah found favor in the eyes of the LORD. (Genesis 6:5–8)

What set Noah apart from the world? The attributes that allowed Noah to find grace in the eyes of God are revealed in the next verse:

> This is the account of Noah. Noah was a righteous man, blameless among the people of his time, and he walked with God. (verse 9)

NOAH WAS A JUST MAN

Noah was morally upright. This means that he seriously considered his actions before responding to what was going on in his environment.

NOAH WAS PERFECT IN HIS GENERATIONS

He was faithful to the standards which God set. He remained an exemplary spiritual role model to all his generations.

NOAH WALKED WITH GOD

In order for you to walk "with" someone, you must remain in step with that person's pace. You do not linger behind or race ahead. You remain right beside that person with each step. The fact that Noah walked with God reveals the amount of time spent in His presence. Anytime you are in the presence of God, His words light a perfect path that leads you in the direction God intended for you to go: "Your word is a lamp to my feet and a light for my path" (Psalm 119:105).

It is said that majority rules, but where God is concerned, His majority is not measured in numbers, but in His authority as an all-knowing God. When you walk in God's authority, it does not matter what the rest of society is doing because you do not base your decisions solely upon human beliefs. If you are ever going to be successful, you have to be aware of who you are and to whom you belong to in the spirit realm.

When you are equipped with the knowledge of God, taking a stand for what you believe becomes less of a task.

I belong to God. He knows more about me than I know about myself, and I'm on a life's journey to find out more about myself through the eyes of God. God made a commitment to Himself that no weapon formed against me would prosper. (See Isaiah 54:17 NKJV.) God also made a commitment to you by assigning His angels charge over you to protect you in all your ways. (See Psalm 91:11 NKJV.) It does not matter where you are; the spirit of the Lord has no boundaries.

> *He who dwells in the shelter of the Most High will rest in the shadow of the Almighty.* (Psalm 91:1)

What is the shadow? A shadow is normally created when something stands in front of the light. God promises that His shadow will protect you when you stand in His presence.

The woman with the issue of blood saw Jesus when no one could see the depth of her pain and suffering. (See Matthew 9:20–22.) She did not touch the Savior, but simply something that was attached to Him—the hem of His garment. She understood a very powerful fact: whatever is attached to Jesus is connected to His anointing.

If you are touching Jesus and someone in need touches you, then he or she is going to be touched by God. In the realm of the spirit, an angel's hand is resting upon yours and empowering you with the anointing of God. It is the anointing of the Lord upon your life that draws those who are hurting, sick, or in need. They may not completely understand why they are drawn to you, but it is the Holy Spirit in you that attracts them to you.

> *If you are ever going to be successful, you have to be aware of who you are and to whom you belong.*

When the anointing of God comes upon you, it accelerates what you already have. If you are a gifted singer, then your voice is magnified by the anointing of God to set people free. If you are a minister, God anoints you with the right words at the right time to help shape the destinies of His people. If you are a parent, God grants you wisdom and understanding to lead your children in the path of righteousness and to pray for them accordingly. God, through His Word, has already supplied an answer for every need we have.

A TRIP TO HEAVEN

Imagine being able to travel into space, beyond the various national and ethnic barriers, past the clouds, leaving behind all the cares of this world. Finally, you arrive at your destination: the gates of heaven.

As the gates open, you begin to hear the great multitude of angels crying out in worship, *"Salvation belongs to our God, who sits on the throne, and to the Lamb"* (Revelation 7:10). You are struck by the purity and peace of the aura of heaven. The streets are pure gold.

As you continue, you journey to the place of tears. Here, you discover that every tear you ever cried has been stored by angels with your name on it. *"You number my wanderings; put my tears into Your bottle; are they not in Your book?"* (Psalm 56:8 NKJV).

You learn that all your prayers have not been wasted as you may have feared.

The four living creatures and the twenty-four elders fell down before the Lamb. Each one had a harp and they were holding golden bowls full of incense, which are the prayers of the saints. (Revelation 5:8)

Each one of your prayers have been stored in heaven within golden bowls of incense upon the altar. These prayers ascend out of the hands of the angels toward the nostrils of God as a sweet-smelling savor.

> *God has already supplied an answer for every need we have.*

You then notice thousands of worshipping angels flying around the throne, saying with a loud voice, *"Worthy is the Lamb, who was slain, to receive power and wealth and wisdom and strength and honor and glory and praise!"* (Revelation 5:12). You realize that all those times when you asked, "God, how long? I don't think I can take these trials any longer," He sent another angel to strengthen you. You remember all those times when you suddenly felt the overwhelming power and presence of God. He'd given you a new song and new confession right at the time that you felt as if He had forsaken you. As you travel through the streets, you see loved ones reunited and mothers meeting up with the children who preceded them in death. The most enigmatic mysteries of earth are all answered here because you are in the chambers of the all-knowing God.

In the face of all the false worship on earth, He reminds you that you are still blessed because you have kept your heart steadfast. As you travel back to earth, you remind yourself of the gift you have been given in the form of His presence and peace. Just as He was available to you on your journey to heaven, Jesus is available to you right now, right here on earth.

But the Counselor, the Holy Spirit, whom the Father will send in my name, will teach you all things and will remind you of everything I have said to you. Peace I leave with you; my peace I give you. I do not give to you as the world gives. Do not let your hearts be troubled and do not be afraid. (John 14:26–27)

WORSHIP AND PRAISE

How do you get close enough to God to see Jesus? Through worship and praise.

What is worship? You must learn to talk to God in a way that moves Him from where He is to where you are. To worship something is to cherish it, to place great value on it. When you worship God, it reveals how you feel about Him and that you esteem Him highly.

Worship can also be defined as, "asking God for something."

In Matthew's gospel account, a man referred to as a centurion realizes that his great riches and position are not enough to heal his servant who lies dying at home. He hears about Jesus and immediately seeks His healing power:

> "Lord," he said, "my servant lies at home paralyzed and in terrible suffering." Jesus said to him, "I will go and heal him." The centurion replied, "Lord, I do not deserve to have you come under my roof. But just say the word, and my servant will be healed. For I myself am a man under authority, with soldiers under me. I tell this one, 'Go,' and he goes; and that one, 'Come,' and he comes. I say to my servant, 'Do this,' and he does it." When Jesus heard this, he was astonished and said to those following him, "I tell you the truth, I have not found anyone in Israel with such great faith." (Matthew 8:6–10)

The devil is always trying to keep you away from the presence and power of God.

DEFEATING WITCHCRAFT

The devil attacks our minds with the weapons of our imagination. He uses fear tactics to bully us into believing that God is not listening to our prayers and that we are going to perish. The only way we can win against his attacks is by casting down and demolishing those thoughts, doubts, and imaginations that torment us.

> We demolish arguments and every pretension that sets itself up against the knowledge of God, and we take captive every thought to make it obedient to Christ. (2 Corinthians 10:5)

Perhaps you have not felt the peace of God in a very long time. If not, you must change the way you think. Do not allow the fear that is attached to your circumstances to rob you of the promises of God. Don't fall for the devil's ploy to convince you that there is no answer to your plight; after all, God has promised that all things are under His feet. (See 1 Corinthians 15:27.)

Often, however, the carnal realities of life become exalted above your relationship with God, hindering you from coming in contact with His presence. When you become so discouraged that you even begin to give up on God, this is the place where you become most susceptible to the witchcraft of demons overtaking you. Anytime you lose the ability to enter into the shadow of God, you forfeit your privileged access to His promises and protection. When you are able to see Jesus, your life begins to change, your breakthrough becomes eminent, and healing begins to manifest supernaturally on your behalf.

The devil uses fear tactics to bully us into believing that God is not listening to our prayers.

Regardless of what you go through in life, never allow anything to make you turn away from God, exposing your life to the devil's plans. Now is the time for you to live your life in total surrender to God. Your testimony must stand in the face of adversity. Then the angels of the Lord are camped around you because He has commissioned them to strengthen you in order to fulfill His call upon your life.

Remember that Jesus did not come to condemn the world, but to set the captives free. Satan is not going to be happy about your freedom. He will use any and all of your weaknesses against you and do whatever is within his power to make you revert to your old way of thinking.

When you move out of the way, God can show forth His marvelous works in your life and propel you into your purpose and victory. Never be afraid to trust God. Realize that it's not worth missing out on life or on God simply because you are too afraid to let go of the past.

*Your testimony must stand in
the face of adversity.*

The only way to realize your true potential is to focus on the glory that's going to be revealed through the suffering you presently endure. This is why Jesus cannot simply be an afterthought when everything else fails. Instead, go to Him immediately, and He will give you an answer to meet your needs. Don't view opposition as defeat. Instead, see it as an opportunity to get closer to God while exploring your true potential in the process. Have you ever been so close to destiny that it felt as if you could reach out and touch it, but something or someone always seemed to get in the way?

It took me twenty years to recognize that I would not have been as successful in life as I am today had I not experienced the tests and trials of opposition. When God is training you, resistance is your greatest friend.

Chapter 14

SALVATION AND DELIVERANCE

An attractive, young, single woman told a minister about some of the problems she experienced since giving her life to Christ. First, because her small hometown did not offer many job opportunities, she had to leave her loving Christian family and friends in order to find work in a distant city. Once there, she couldn't find a church like the one she attended back home. Finally, she struggled with the recurring theme among so many young people today. She had not found a husband with whom to settle down.

Upon hearing the desperation in her voice, the minister asked how she was handling her sexual desires. He wanted to know if her desire to marry was based solely on her desire to be sexually intimate.

"I've abstained from sexual intercourse for a long time, but I'm not a nun," she admitted. "If the right man came along, I would probably be sexually intimate with him even though we were not married."

Her attitude is widespread among many young people today. Most people decide to serve the Lord because of a religious experience or some form of conviction. Based on these happenings, they live an exemplary life for a while.

Do these experiences and convictions constitute salvation when the person reverts back to those old habits from which he or she was supposedly delivered?

SALVATION AND DELIVERANCE

If we want to be saved, we must also understand deliverance. In the Bible, one word is translated two ways. The word *save* is *sozo* in Greek and *natssal* in Hebrew. Sometimes the word is used as *deliver*: "*You shall beat him with a rod, and deliver his soul from hell*" (Proverbs 23:14 NKJV). At other times the word is used as *saved*: "*The king saved us from the hand of our enemies, He delivered us from the hand of the Philistines*" (2 Samuel 19:9 NKJV).

Deliver means "to rescue or provide safety from something or someone." If we say we are saved, that means we have been delivered from something. If we return to that thing, however, can we truly say that we are delivered or saved?

The apostle Paul wrote, "*Now that you know God—or rather are known by God—how is it that you are turning back to those weak and miserable principles? Do you wish to be enslaved by them all over again?*" (Galatians 4:9).

Does our ability to suppress sinful desires for a season constitute salvation, or is there much more to it?

Your deliverance has not been accomplished if sin continues to reign in your mortal body.

> *Don't you know that when you offer yourselves to someone to obey him as slaves, you are slaves to the one whom you obey—whether you are slaves to sin, which leads to death, or to obedience, which leads to righteousness?*
> (Romans 6:16)

Why do we need deliverance? Satan is the ruler of this world, and he holds us captive if we have not accepted Jesus as Lord and Savior. (See Galatians 4:3–5.) This is the reason people cannot quit sinning. No matter how many counselors they have seen, or prescription drugs they have taken, true deliverance comes only through Jesus Christ. Everything else is only a lie masquerading as the truth. No lie endures forever; eventually, it will be found out. A great conflict will ultimately occur between the lie and the truth.

We cannot wage spiritual warfare successfully without Jesus Christ. Scripture says, "*The reason the Son of God appeared was to destroy the devil's work*" (1 John 3:8). If we have not received Christ Jesus as Lord and Savior, we need deliverance. If we cannot resist the temptations of the world, we need deliverance. If God's Word is not the guide for our lives, we need deliverance.

> *If we want to be saved,*
> *we must also understand deliverance.*

The nation of Israel was chosen by God. Even though they were in captivity in Egypt, their relationship to God as His chosen people did not change. On the other hand, even though the people of Israel performed their rituals and maintained their religion through worship, they were not free. They had the relationship, but they were still in bondage.

How many of us have confessed faith in Jesus Christ only to find it difficult to refrain from sin? We love God, but somehow it seems that our weakness to temptation outweighs our love for God.

Does this mean we are not saved? If an old habit creeps up on us again, have we lost our salvation?

To answer this question, we must understand that salvation is a process. If we do not understand the process, the consequences can be dire. Imagine baking a cake. If you put the eggs, butter, flour, and sugar into a hot oven without first mixing the ingredients, you will not have a cake. The ingredients for a cake which is properly mixed are the same as for a cake that has not been mixed. One has gone through the process of preparation; the other has not. Our salvation is very similar.

SPIRIT, SOUL, AND BODY

The process of salvation involves bringing the three parts of our being into agreement with one another. Before they can be brought into agreement, we must understand the role of each part.

We are tripartite beings composed of spirit, soul, and body. (See 1 Thessalonians 5:23.) Every part of our total being has a part to play in our salvation. The spirit is the part from God that gives life. *"The Spirit gives life; the flesh counts for nothing"* (John 6:63). Without the spirit there is no life to the body. The spirit does not contain your emotions and thoughts, but the soul does. *"But now, by dying to what once bound us, we have been released from the law so that we serve in the new way of the Spirit"* (Romans 7:6). Our spirits enable us to respond to God.

When Adam disobeyed God in the garden of Eden, he suffered physical and spiritual death. God told Adam, *"You must not eat from the tree of the knowledge of good and evil, for when you eat of it you will surely die"* (Genesis 2:17).

> *If God's Word is not the guide for our lives, we need deliverance.*

Eve, who had not received this direct instruction from God, was subsequently seduced by the cunning words of the serpent and ate the fruit. Not only was Eve seduced, but she also seduced Adam to eat the fruit. (See Genesis 3:5–6.) Based on Adam's disobedience, death took place. Adam and Eve did not drop dead physically that day, however. After their disobedience, God banished them from the garden of Eden. They went on to have children, and Adam lived to a very old age.

Did God lie? No! Death did take place in the garden of Eden, but it was spiritual, not physical. Spiritual death is separation from God. When Adam sinned in the Garden, he became separated from God. How could this relationship be restored? That spiritual connection had to be reestablished. When a person receives Jesus Christ as Lord and Savior, the Father accepts His perfect sacrifice as a substitute for our death. (See 1 John 2:2.) This acceptance reestablishes our relationship with God.

Because of sin, the body also dies. We know that Adam did not live forever. After the fall, God pronounced a curse upon the first couple, beginning with the man.

By the sweat of your brow you will eat your food until you return to the ground, since from it you were taken; for dust you are and to dust you will return. (Genesis 3:19)

The body's origin is earthly, while the Spirit's origin is heavenly. Upon death there is a return to the source from which part of the tripartite being originated. The apostle Paul addressed this issue: *"I declare to you, brothers, that flesh and blood cannot inherit the kingdom of God"* (1 Corinthians 15:50).

This curse upon mankind has endured from Adam until now. While we are enduring the curse, the flesh strives to please itself. It does not know anything about heaven and has no desire to go there.

THE BATTLEGROUND

The third part of the tripartite being is where the battle really takes place: the soul. God breathed the breath of life into the man created from the dust of the earth, and Adam *"became a living soul"* (Genesis 2:7 KJV). The flesh houses the soul and spirit. This is why Jesus told Nicodemus, *"I tell you the truth, no one can enter the kingdom of God unless he is born of water and the Spirit....You should not be surprised at my saying, 'You must be born again'"* (John 3:5, 7). When a person is not born again, his spirit has no active influence over the soul. How can the spirit affect the soul? The curse of Adam must be negated by the process of being born again. You cannot do the things of God if you have not been born again. A person who has not been born again is left to manipulation by the world and Satan.

A person who has not been born again is left to manipulation by the world and Satan.

When you are saved, your spirit is made alive in Jesus Christ. Your spirit rejoices in contacting the Father. When a person dies, his spirit returns to God who made it. (See Ecclesiastes 12:7.) Your flesh has no desire to be saved, however. It was made from the earth, and that's where it will return. Your flesh and spirit become enemies of each other. A great battle for your soul ensues.

You must first accept Jesus Christ as Lord and Savior to enable your spirit to respond to God the Father. Then you must bring the flesh under subjection. This is the tough part. That's why the spirit is first regenerated. *"I say then: walk in the Spirit, and you shall not fulfill the lust of the flesh"* (Galatians 5:16 NKJV).

The spirit of man communicates with the Spirit of God. This communication directs the believer in living a godly life. The Spirit of God shows us how to bring the flesh under subjugation. When we are spirit-controlled instead of flesh-controlled, we receive complete deliverance. That is why the apostle Paul wrote that their *"whole spirit, soul and body be kept blameless at the coming of our Lord Jesus Christ"* (1 Thessalonians 5:23).

IT'S A HEART ISSUE

Unfortunately, Christians often judge according to the flesh. Is a babe in Christ saved if he or she is not demonstrating a mature Christian walk? It depends on the condition of the heart. *"But God be thanked that though you were slaves of sin, yet you obeyed from the* **heart** *that form of doctrine to which you were delivered"* (Romans 6:17, emphasis added).

The word *obeyed* means "to submit without reservation." If a person purposes in his heart to serve God but falters along the way because he has not mastered the flesh, he is not lost. It is not the outward manifestation but the inward decision of the heart that determines the destination of man.

A young woman was raped by her brother at the age of nine. When her parents found out, they punished the boy severely. This girl continued on with her life with no guilt or hatred toward her brother. Later in adult life, however, the guilt and hatred stirred within her toward her brother. This guilt and hatred were stilted only when a counselor told her that an incident does not make a person. Because she had forgiven her brother from her heart, this determined who she was—not a woman who had been raped, but a woman who had chosen to forgive.

Just as the decision from her heart determined who she was, our decision of the heart determines who we are in Jesus Christ. God knows the flesh is weak, and He makes an allowance for it by providing grace. We must not deceive ourselves, however. If our hearts are not right, we cannot avail ourselves of God's grace.

This is why the church is in turmoil today. There is far too little effort within the heart to seek God. Newborn Christians are openly condemned for their failures when they have not yet gone through the process of being Christians.

Let us consider the saints in the New Testament. Peter denied the Lord. Mark deserted the work of God and the apostle Paul. Paul and Barnabas had such a bitter falling-out that they had to separate. These were all great men of God, but they were not perfect. They were quick to acknowledge their shortcomings and make amends with God. They did not justify their shortcomings, but instead confessed and repented of them.

Rather than admit that they have shortcomings, however, too many Christians today simply accommodate the presence of sin in their lives.

If our hearts are not right, we cannot avail ourselves of God's grace.

WORSHIP GOD

How then does a person gain deliverance? The demoniac whom Jesus met in the country of the Gerasenes found one way and gained his deliverance by worshipping Jesus.

They went across the lake to the region of the Gerasenes. When Jesus got out of the boat, a man with an evil spirit came from the tombs to meet him....When he saw Jesus from a distance, he ran and fell on his knees in front of him. He shouted at the top of his voice, "What do you want with me, Jesus, Son of the Most High God? Swear to God that you won't torture me!" For Jesus had said to him, "Come out of this man, you evil spirit!"....When they came to Jesus, they saw the man who had been possessed by the legion of demons, sitting there, dressed and in his right mind; and they were afraid. (Mark 5:1–2, 6–8, 15)

To understand how the demon-possessed man gained his deliverance, we must know what worship involves.

Jesus addressed the problem of worship:

*Yet a time is coming and has now come when the **true worshippers** will worship the Father in spirit and truth, for they are the kind of worshipers the Father seeks.* (John 4:23, emphasis added)

Worship means "to submit or make oneself low." This can be seen by the position taken by worshippers in biblical times. They prostrated themselves to show their humility and lowly position in relationship to God.

After we have humbled ourselves before God, we commune with God by our spirit. This can only happen, however, if we have been born again. Then, to maintain this connection, we must dwell in the truth as revealed in God's Word.

OBEY THE WORDS OF JESUS

Worship is just the beginning of deliverance. We must also obey the Word of God. Jesus once asked, *"Why do you call me, 'Lord, Lord,' and do not do what I say?"* (Luke 6:46). He also said, *"If anyone loves me, he will obey my teaching. My Father will love him, and we will come to him and make our home with him"* (John 14:23).

Your total deliverance is directly related to your obedience to God's Word. When you yield yourself to God's Word, the Father and Son come to live with you. If they are living with you, you'll have the strength you need to get and maintain your deliverance.

Your deliverance is directly related to your obedience to God's Word.

Sometimes our deliverance is gradual. In the same way that it takes an hour to bake a cake, so our deliverance may take time.

Jesus knows how to administer your healing. *"Then they brought him a demon-possessed man who was blind and mute, and Jesus healed him, so that he could both talk and see"* (Matthew 12:22). The word for *"healed"* is the Greek word *therapeuo*, from which our word *therapy* comes.

In its original form, the word meant "to serve in a menial way," such as attending to a family member during an illness. In other words, the healing is gradual, not instantaneous. At times, healing and deliverance are used interchangeably.

> *He himself bore our sins in his body on the tree, so that we might die to sins and live for righteousness; by his wounds you have been healed.*
> (1 Peter 2:24)

The healing spoken of here is not a healing from disease, but a healing from the effects of our sinful condition. Do not give up on your salvation because you are not where you desire to be. Continue striving for righteousness. In seeking God, you purify your soul.

The most important thing is that you not return to the sin from which you were delivered.

> *When an evil spirit comes out of a man, it goes through arid places seeking rest and does not find it. Then it says, "I will return to the house I left." When it arrives, it finds the house unoccupied, swept clean and put in order. Then it goes and takes with it seven other spirits more wicked than itself, and they go in and live there. And the final condition of that man is worse than the first.* (Matthew 12:43–45)

Getting free is one thing; staying free is another. Too many Christians lack the discipline to renew their minds by meditating on God's Word. They fail to avoid enticing situations and sever bad relationships that will only drag them down.

Don't be an empty vessel that attracts demonic influence. Read and meditate on Scripture and ask God to fill you with the Holy Spirit. God delights in filling us again and again. Yield your life to God, resist the enemy, and position yourself in the victory that Christ has won for you.

It is for freedom that Christ has set us free. Stand firm, then, and do not let yourselves be burdened again by a yoke of slavery.

(Galatians 5:1)

I trust that this book has opened your eyes to various deceptions that have infiltrated our society and the church. May you always seek the truth and walk in the glorious freedom that Jesus Christ has made available to everyone who believes in Him.

Now, allow me to agree with you in prayer:

Father, You said in Your Word that in the last days some will depart from the faith, giving heed to seducing spirits and doctrines of devils, speaking lies and hypocrisy, and having their conscience seared with a hot iron. Right now, I come against the satanic spirit that feeds false teaching. I pray that nothing or no one will be able to separate us from Your love, mercy, and power.

Father, I pray that those who have strayed from Your teachings will regain their focus and faith. I pray the blessings of the Lord upon the individuals now holding this book, that they would trust in You and Your Word, regardless of the circumstances they are currently facing. May Your anointing be upon their mind and heart to see with spiritual vision as never before.

Now Father, I pray that in this time and day when Satan is trying to hijack the faithful, that You would raise up men and women who will earnestly contend for the faith. I pray, dear God, that we would stop fighting with each another over issues and focus our attention on the real battle: defeating the forces of the enemy. In Jesus' name, Amen.

SPIRITUAL WARFARE

CONTENTS

FOREWORD

My friend Bishop George Bloomer knows what it is like to be stuck in hopelessness and despair, but he also knows the redemptive power of Christ to lift up, restore, and redeem. His writing does not employ gauzy symbolism or theoretical platitudes. From the crucible of his own life experiences and from the pages of the Word of God, he provides timeless principles that will not only produce freedom, but perpetuate it.

In this book, Bishop Bloomer tackles *Spiritual Warfare* and reveals to us the truth about witchcraft, which is intimidation, manipulation, and domination. The strongest prisons are made of concrete and steel, and the worst judgments are never those handed down from a courtroom judge. The impenetrable fortresses are those constructed by forces such as poverty, sickness, and sin. And the most damaging judgments are fear, false accusations, inaccurate perceptions, unfortunate assumptions, a victim mentality, a sense of shame, hopelessness, and many other like conditions.

"These signs shall follow them that believe; in my name shall they cast out devils; they shall speak with new tongues…lay hands on the sick, and they shall recover" (Mark 16:17–18). Anyone can sing a tune on a clear day at noon. Today you will hear from someone who can talk about being seated in heavenly places when the sludge of a Roman sewer is swirling around their feet.

—*Dr. Rod Parsley*
Senior pastor, World Harvest Church
Author; TV show host

INTRODUCTION

I was raised in the projects of Brooklyn, New York. We lived on the sixth floor of a government building in apartments A, B, and C, so we had a "condo in the ghetto." We were raised on welfare, food stamps, government cheese, and Buster Brown shoes. If you could wear out a pair of Buster Brown shoes, you were *bad*! I grew up in a household that at one time included twenty-four children and, therefore, constant struggles for territory. From who got the last piece of pie to whose shoes you were wearing, there always was a battle going on and a pecking order being established.

We kids employed many strategies in this battle. Sometimes a strategy was so subtle the rest of us were hardly aware that anything was happening. You could call this the "I'll manage you" maneuver. Some waged war using the "I'll scare you" maneuver, engendering fear among the other children. Occasionally those who were able used the "I'll crush you" maneuver, where only the strong survive and the mighty slay the weak. Whatever the method, the battle raged on with frequent skirmishes.

Everyone had his or her own turf—and a strategy to maintain it. I had a brother who turned the "I'll trick you" maneuver into an art form. He was younger and smaller than most, so the option of threat or brute force was not available to him. But he knew how to whine and how to push the right buttons to get what he wanted. He used his small size as a strategy: He threw tantrums. He was able to use the family members' own love against them.

My brother would show his displeasure in rages of self-destructive fury, getting red in the face and stomping his feet until my parents thought he would explode. Needless to say, he frequently got what he wanted and so maintained his turf. He was a champion *manipulator*. He was able to manage the family as if he were ten feet tall.

Unfortunately, what began as voluntary fits of self-will later became physical affliction. Satan was able to capitalize on my brother's manipulative antics and turned his tantrums into seizures, which ultimately caused him to go into a coma. And it all started through manipulation—his manipulating my mom and the rest of the family to get what he wanted.

This same war is fought on every level of humanity. It is fought in the family, on school playgrounds, in corporate headquarters, and even among nations. In each case the strategies remain the same. We of the household of God must realize that this same warfare is going on in the church. Hell-inspired maneuvers are being executed all around us. Battles are fought and demonic strategies employed from the front door to the pastor's study to the choir loft.

These attacks are the product of a deliberate, demonic strategy. There is a war being waged in us and through us, and we are all caught up in it. It is a war wrought from rebellion around the highest throne of heaven.

We are talking about spiritual warfare in this book, but we will approach it in a more personal way than you may have considered. We will discover how to unmask the strategies of the enemy and how to free ourselves from his devices—and we will learn how to live a life of power from the throne of God Himself. These are the issues we will take up in this book. It's about *you*...it's about your *family*...it's about your *church*.

This is war, but we are the victors in Christ Jesus!

And they overcame him by the blood of the Lamb and by the word of their testimony, and they did not love their lives to the death. Therefore rejoice, O heavens, and you who dwell in them! Woe to the inhabitants of the earth and the sea! For the devil has come down to you, having great wrath, because he knows that he has a short time.

(Revelation 12:11–12)

Chapter 1

REBELLION AT THE THRONE OF GOD

You were the seal of perfection, full of wisdom and perfect in beauty. You were in Eden, the garden of God; every precious stone was your covering: the sardius, topaz, and diamond, beryl, onyx, and jasper, sapphire, turquoise, and emerald with gold. The workmanship of your timbrels and pipes was prepared for you on the day you were created. You were the anointed cherub who covers; I established you; you were on the holy mountain of God; you walked back and forth in the midst of fiery stones. You were perfect in your ways from the day you were created, till iniquity was found in you.
—Ezekiel 28:12–15

SOMEWHERE BEFORE TIME

Before there was time—before there was anything—he was the brightest of the brilliant, the highest of the exalted. He stood at the throne of the Most High, consumed in its glory. All that surrounded him burned with the holy intensity of the presence of God. He was perfection; his beauty was such that it can scarcely be described by the tongues of men.

His appearance was as thousands of precious stones of every hue and color, refracting and magnifying the unapproachable light of the Creator. He was the personification of worship itself, covering the very throne of God. His worship was the reflection of God's glory.

To him was given wisdom and authority above all others. He stood at the place of ultimate influence in heaven. He was the joy of his Creator—a being created for adoration and given a place at the apex of all that there was. He was Lucifer, the morning star, the supreme servant of God.

A MOMENT'S GLANCE

Somewhere in the vastness of eternity, the anointed cherub was distracted from his worship of the Sovereign of heaven and caught a fleeting glance of his own image. His heart was filled with the wonder of his own appearance. He beheld his own beauty for an instant—and changed eternity. Though he had all wisdom and authority, it would never again be enough. He coveted the worship and honor of heaven. In that momentary deflection of adoration, the crookedness of iniquity was born in him. He said in his heart,

> *I will ascend into heaven, I will exalt my throne above the stars of God; I will also sit on the mount of the congregation on the farthest sides of the north; I will ascend above the heights of the clouds, I will be like the Most High.* (Isaiah 14:13–14, emphasis added)

Lucifer's priority shifted from reflecting the glory of God in worship to seeking glory for himself. This one who had stood at the place of ultimate influence at the throne of God perverted his position, lusting after the adoration that filled heaven. He took his eyes off his Creator and sought his own glory. He thought, *I can be just like God!* And, turning his eyes from God for an instant, he lost all.

He who was exalted was now cast down—fallen below the others whose devotion was stayed on the throne of God. Now, this son of the morning, this brilliant cherub, would be banished to lesser domains, to lesser lights.

There were others who were fascinated with Lucifer. They diverted their focus from the throne of God and became converts to mutiny.

Perhaps as many as a third of heaven's warring host joined Lucifer and was cast down with him.

> *And war broke out in heaven: Michael and his angels fought with the dragon; and the dragon and his angels fought, but they did not prevail, nor was a place found for them in heaven any longer. So the great dragon was cast out, that serpent of old, called the Devil and Satan, who deceives the whole world; he was cast to the earth, and his angels were cast out with him.* (Revelation 12:7–9)

And there was a void in heaven—a chasm of adoration to be filled.

IT'S ALL ABOUT INFLUENCE

All that happened at the throne of God, all that resulted in separation and war, was tied up in one word: *influence.* Lucifer, or Satan, was at the pinnacle of influence in heaven. The purpose of heaven was worship of God, and Lucifer was the instigator of worship. In a primordial instant, Lucifer turned away from God, and iniquity was born.

> *The purpose of heaven was worship of God.*

The Hebrew word for iniquity, *avon,* denotes a crookedness, a perversity.* It specifically indicates a turning or a deflection in another direction. In heaven everything was flowing toward the throne of God in worship. There could be no other direction, no other object worthy of praise. Then came a change in course: Lucifer deflected his worship away from God and onto himself. As a result, the peace of heaven was shattered. (Isaiah 26:3 says, *"You will keep him in perfect peace, whose mind is stayed on You."*)

This diversion, this other, less worthy self-worship, is the very definition of iniquity. It is a diversion from God or the ways of God. Iniquity has been Satan's nature and diversion his strategy since creation. He uses whatever he can to influence us away from God.

Consider the events surrounding the fall of man. Lucifer exchanged his eternal beauty for the skin of a snake and slithered into the Paradise of God. He left his place in the *adoration* to God and took up a place in the *accusation* of man, hence his name change to Satan, the accuser.

Satan saw man enjoying God's attention and fellowship as they visited in the cool of the day. Man stood in the place of intimacy that Lucifer had lost. Now Lucifer sought to bring down the new object of God's affection: man. Note Satan's words to Eve:

> *Then the serpent said to the woman, "You will not surely die. For God knows that in the day you eat of it your eyes will be opened, and you will be like God, knowing good and evil."* (Genesis 3:4–5)

Does this sound familiar? What Satan was saying to Eve was an echo of what he said to himself, that he could be "just like God." Satan told Eve, "*You will be like God,*" and for an instant Eve believed him and disobeyed God. Now man was infected with the disease of iniquity, the crookedness inspired by Satan.

The devil is all about influence. His desire is to have us take our eyes off God and put them on ourselves. Notice that he was filled with "*I will*" as he fell. The issue was not what *God* willed, but what *he* willed. Our enemy encourages and influences us to move into this same self-willed way. We are more concerned about "*I will*" than about God's will. So we spend our lives, inside and outside the church, getting what *we will*. This leads us toward all kinds of man-centered doctrines and strategies for personal gain. However, *whatever serves to enrich us at the expense of God's glory is iniquity.*

There is a war being waged in the heavenlies for our minds and hearts. The devil and his minions of fallen demonic servants are at work on us, in us, and through us. If they can, Satan's host will divert us from giving glory to God and cause us to believe that we are not as close to Him as we think we are. They assist us in getting *our wills* accomplished—in pleasing our carnality.

The result is that our personal lives, our families, and our churches have become spiritual war zones. Most of the time, however, we are ignorant of the war raging around us. In fact, we believe that conflict and sin are normal. We even jockey for position within the community of God's people and think nothing of trampling a brother or sister under the feet of our ecclesiastical ambitions. We defend our turf, and we lose sight of God in the process.

Satan lost his place and wants us to lose ours as well. He is much like a jealous woman who sees another woman enjoying an "old flame" of hers. Satan hates to see the loving relationship between God and His saints and does everything in his power to destroy it. The very thought of God's creation enjoying any part of what Satan once enjoyed himself deeply angers him, and like a jealous woman trying to rip apart a relationship that she wishes she could have, Satan seeks to destroy the love and fellowship God has with His saints.

Those who have accepted God's grace cannot be separated from Him.

The reality is that those who have accepted the grace of God through Jesus Christ cannot be separated from Him. As Paul wrote,

> Who shall separate us from the love of Christ? Shall tribulation, or distress, or persecution, or famine, or nakedness, or peril, or sword? As it is written: "For Your sake we are killed all day long; we are accounted as sheep for the slaughter." Yet in all these things we are more than conquerors through Him who loved us. For I am persuaded that neither death nor life, nor angels nor principalities nor powers, nor things present nor things to come, nor height nor depth, nor any other created thing, shall be able to separate us from the love of God which is in Christ Jesus our Lord. (Romans 8:35–39)

SATAN'S POWER SOURCE

A very basic yet important question we must ask is: Where did Satan get the power he is using to deceive and enslave mankind? The answer is: from God Almighty.

Next we might ask: Why does God allow the devil to have such power? Perhaps the best way to reach an understanding of this question is to refer to Adam and Eve's transgression in Genesis 2:16–17.

> And the LORD God commanded the man, saying, "Of every tree of the garden you may freely eat; but of the tree of the knowledge of good and evil you shall not eat, for in the day that you eat of it you shall surely die."

Of course, Adam and Eve did disobey and ate from the Tree of Knowledge of Good and Evil. Because they did, we, as their offspring, also have a knowledge of good and evil and a nature that strays toward evil. Since God is good and there is no evil in Him (see James 1:13, 17), He cannot tolerate the evil in us. He has allowed the devil to continue to exist to show us the difference between good and evil to help us make a proper choice.

> See, I have set before you today life and good, death and evil....I call heaven and earth as witnesses today against you, that I have set before you life and death, blessing and cursing; therefore choose life, that both you and your descendants may live.   (Deuteronomy 30:15, 19)

Although Satan has power, the book of Job reveals that he is under God's authority and that God can limit and prevent his attacks. (See Job 1:6–12.) This is because God has sovereignty and truly holds the reins, not Satan. Nothing can be done apart from Him.

A POWERFUL ILLUSION

Satan wants to make us believe that he has power. And he does. But his power is tied up in heaven's legal system. He can't use it any way he'd like to because he's held in check by God, who has our interests in mind.

A good example of this is a will. I could die tomorrow, leaving all my money to the benefactors of my will. But if other members of my family wanted to, they could contest my will in favor of their own interests. This would then lock up my willed money until my rightful heirs got a lawyer and straightened things out. Those wanting to alter my will would probably try to prove the unjustness of my choice. But once my heirs got a good lawyer on the case, the legality of my will would defeat their arguments.

Similarly, God has willed salvation and blessings to those who receive His saving grace. But Satan has contested the will of God. As a result, you have to petition your advocate, Jesus, to take him on. But Jesus has never lost a case! He will seal your court papers with drops of His sacrificial blood and the case will be closed.

You see, no matter how powerful Satan seems to be, he is nowhere near as powerful as our Lord. So many believers have this notion—whether they realize it or not—that Satan is equal in power to God. They have what could be called a Star Wars view of spiritual things. Just as there is a "light side" and an equally powerful "dark side" to the Force in the Star Wars movies, these Christians think there is a "light side" (God) and an equally powerful "dark side" (Satan) that make up the cosmos. This is not biblical!

Although Satan retained his intelligence and power after the Fall, his power never did and never can exceed the power of almighty God. Satan may have knowledge, but he is the greatest fool of all. No matter how powerful Satan may seem, He is under divine control and cannot do anything outside of God's permissive will.

> *Satan is not all-powerful.*
> *All dominion belongs to God.*

Satan may have caused the Fall, but he is not all-powerful. We must understand this as we engage in spiritual warfare. We must always remember that Satan is already defeated!

However, although the devil is not all-powerful, he can still influence us. He can tempt us, mislead us, and even make us believe that we are separated from God. This is his tool for robbing God of His rightful worship. And this is how he diminishes our effectiveness in the kingdom of God.

We must always remember two things when we're dealing with the topic of spiritual warfare:

1. Satan is not all-powerful. All power and dominion belongs to God and God alone.

2. Although Satan is not all-powerful, he can still influence us so that our lives are marked by disobedience and rebellion to God.

It's important that we remember both of these points. We can't give Satan too much credit, but we can't ignore him either. It's our responsibility, aided by guidance from the Holy Spirit, to keep these two in balance.

Now that we know why Satan does what he does, let's spend some time learning how he does it. It is only when we are equipped with knowledge that we will be able to fight him effectively.

Be sober, be vigilant; because your adversary the devil walks about like a roaring lion, seeking whom he may devour. Resist him, steadfast in the faith, knowing that the same sufferings are experienced by your brotherhood in the world. But may the God of all grace, who called us to His eternal glory by Christ Jesus, after you have suffered a while, perfect, establish, strengthen, and settle you. To Him be the glory and the dominion forever and ever. Amen. (1 Peter 5:8–11)

Chapter 2

LIVING UNDER
THE INFLUENCE

Several years ago, I read a book that dealt with the incredible violence that has occurred in the United States Postal Service. At regular intervals, disturbed former postal employees fired upon post offices, killing and wounding many people. The reasons given for these massacres seem to be trivial when compared to the carnage that results. Is it mere coincidence that post office massacres were so common? Apparently not.

According to the book, the events described were the result of a curse. The book revealed that, sometime in the early twentieth century, people dressed in witches' garb gathered to pronounce a curse on the United States Postal Service. What happened in these post offices was no mere coincidence. It was the result of a deliberate act of witchcraft.

WITCHCRAFT

Normally, when we think of witchcraft, we envision black cats and old hags dressed in black with pointy hats and riding on broomsticks. In reality, however, witchcraft is an attempt to influence someone by ungodly spiritual means. It is the calling forth of spiritual influences with the goal of causing someone or something to perform in a certain way. Witchcraft is bringing a person or a thing under the influence of the demonic.

> *Witchcraft operates all around us whether we are aware of it or not.*

What exactly are demons? Demons are those angels who were cast out of heaven with Lucifer. *Demonology* is the understanding of how these evil influences work and act. In short, demonic forces operate according to a deliberate satanic strategy to influence people and events, diverting worship and devotion away from God. Witchcraft was a factor in the Bible, and it is a factor that operates all around us today, though we are scarcely aware of it.

In order to deal with the reality of witchcraft, we first must understand some basic truths. The first truth is that we are not just dealing with human weakness and peculiarity. We are dealing with spiritual forces bent on our destruction.

> *For we are not fighting against people made of flesh and blood, but against persons without bodies—the evil rulers of the unseen world, those mighty satanic beings and great evil princes of darkness who rule this world; and against huge numbers of wicked spirits in the spirit world.* (Ephesians 6:12 TLB)

We are a nation living under the influence of witchcraft: the witchcraft of the occult, the witchcraft of drugs, the witchcraft of religious spirits, and the witchcraft of rebellion. Regardless of the method or the venue, evil influences stem from the same source: Satan. And all have the same motive, which is to divert people from God and His truth. Now, I am not saying that all of the evil things that happen can be ascribed to Satan; that would give him too much power and glory. Nonetheless, witchcraft influences us in many forms and guises.

THE WITCHCRAFT OF THE OCCULT

There are many gateways through which deliberate satanic influence enters into our world. One of them is the occult. For example, there are advertisements everywhere for psychic hot lines, where desperate people consult demonically controlled counselors over the telephone.

Both the Old and the New Testaments in the Bible contain examples of occult witchcraft. In fact, God was very clear about avoiding divination of any sort:

> Give no regard to mediums and familiar spirits; do not seek after them, to be defiled by them: I am the LORD your God.   (Leviticus 19:31)

and,

> And the person who turns to mediums and familiar spirits, to prostitute himself with them, I will set My face against that person and cut him off from his people.   (Leviticus 20:6)

and,

> There shall not be found among you anyone who makes his son or his daughter pass through the fire, or one who practices witchcraft, or a soothsayer, or one who interprets omens, or a sorcerer, or one who conjures spells, or a medium, or a spiritist, or one who calls up the dead. For all who do these things are an abomination to the LORD.
>   (Deuteronomy 18:10–12)

The central issue in the prohibition of sorcery in the Old Testament was that it led people away from God and attempted to control future events through spells and evil spirits. Again, the result was separation from God. God repeatedly warned Israel about taking up the gods and altars of the people they were to displace in the Promised Land.

> When the LORD your God brings you into the land which you go to possess, and has cast out many nations before you, the Hittites and the Girgashites and the Amorites and the Canaanites and the Perizzites and the Hivites and the Jebusites, seven nations greater and mightier than you, and when the LORD your God delivers them over to you,

you shall conquer them and utterly destroy them. You shall make no covenant with them nor show mercy to them. Nor shall you make marriages with them. You shall not give your daughter to their son, nor take their daughter for your son. For they will turn your sons away from following Me, to serve other gods; so the anger of the LORD will be aroused against you and destroy you suddenly. But thus you shall deal with them: you shall destroy their altars, and break down their sacred pillars, and cut down their wooden images, and burn their carved images with fire.   (Deuteronomy 7:1–5)

The people of God were warned not to get involved in any way with those who did not serve God. They were to tear down and destroy the enemy influences among them. We know from reading the rest of the Scriptures that the Israelites did not do so. The nations that God displaced served false gods of every sort, and some of their occult practices crept unnoticed into the everyday lives of God's people.

The Israelites had been desert wanderers and shepherds for many years, and slaves before that. But when they came into the land of promise, they had to become farmers. Being unfamiliar with the ways of farming, they probably picked up pagan practices by observation. Perhaps a pagan farmer placed a small idol at the end of his field to ensure a good crop. The Israelites then saw that idol as just something everybody did to get good crops, so they set up idols too. In doing so, though, they placed themselves under the legal control of demonic influence. Thus, little by little, they took up pagan practices until God became just one god among many. Second Kings 17 says, *"They feared the LORD, yet served their own gods; according to the rituals of the nations from among whom they were carried away"* (verse 33).

Occult practices have even crept into the church.

Superstition, New Age, and occult practices have crept into the church as well. Though some may be offended at what I'm about to say, I must caution some African-American churches that have taken up the celebration of Kwanza. This holiday is supposed to be a celebration of African culture and is filled with color and ritual. But it also is filled with demonic influence. Kwanza is rooted in an African religion that is polluted with spiritism. The name *Kwanza* comes from the Swahili words for "firstfruits," and it is a harvest celebration that dates back as far as ancient Egypt. Kwanza does not glorify Yahweh God in any way. Those who celebrate this holiday unknowingly serve pagan false gods. There can be no mixture in the kingdom of God. God alone is worthy to be worshipped and adored. We cannot fear the Lord and at the same time serve other gods in any form or to any extent.

Similarly, in very subtle ways, the church has taken up the gods of materialism from the world that we are supposed to be claiming for Christ. Celebrity preachers wear thousand-dollar suits and drive sixty-thousand-dollar cars. We have placed ourselves under the demonic influence of materialism and have learned to measure our success in terms of facilities and dollars. How are we different from drug dealers? Jesus set a different standard for His disciples.

> *And when Jesus saw great multitudes about Him, He gave a command to depart to the other side. Then a certain scribe came and said to Him, "Teacher, I will follow You wherever You go." And Jesus said to him, "Foxes have holes and birds of the air have nests, but the Son of Man has nowhere to lay His head."* (Matthew 8:18–20)

In the New Testament there are a few notable examples of witchcraft. In Acts 16:16 we read of a slave girl who was controlled by a spirit of divination. Not only did the spirit that oppressed her control her life, this same spirit sought to control or influence others *through* her.

> *Now it happened, as we went to prayer, that a certain slave girl possessed with a spirit of divination met us, who brought her masters much profit by fortune-telling. This girl followed Paul and us, and cried out, saying, "These men are the servants of the Most High God, who proclaim to us the way of salvation." And this she did for many days. But Paul, greatly annoyed, turned and said to the spirit, "I command you in the name of Jesus Christ to come out of her." And he came out that very hour. But when her masters saw that their hope of profit was gone,*

they seized Paul and Silas and dragged them into the marketplace to
the authorities. (Acts 16:16–19)

Notice that this spirit began its harassment as Paul and the others went to prayer, that place of fellowship with God. Divination is the counterfeit of God's truth. It involves using the stars and evil spirits to foretell or control the future. The girl followed them proclaiming the truth, but in a mocking manner. Finally Paul had had enough and "dispossessed" the demonic spirit in the name of Jesus Christ. We see in the following verse that not only did the spirit influence the girl, but it also brought her masters under the influence of a spirit of greed as they profited by her lying divination. One spirit opened the way for the other. All, however, were living under the influence of the witchcraft of the occult.

In Acts 13:8 Paul had another power encounter with a sorcerer named Elymas.

But Elymas the sorcerer (for so his name is translated) withstood them,
seeking to turn the proconsul away from the faith. Then Saul, who also is
called Paul, filled with the Holy Spirit, looked intently at him and said, "O
full of all deceit and all fraud, you son of the devil, you enemy of all righteous-
ness, will you not cease perverting the straight ways of the Lord?"
(Acts 13:8–10)

Note that the man was guilty of diverting others from *"the straight ways of the Lord."* He was employing Satan's old habit of seeking to deflect and distort the true worship of God. Paul also called him a *"son of the devil";* literally, one who does what the devil does.

> *Divination is the counterfeit*
> *of God's truth.*

In an even earlier account, Peter encountered a sorcerer named Simon who amazed a city of 70,000 people through the power of Satan. But when the people came to Christ, his powers were no longer impressive. So he became a "believer" as well. But did he really? Later, when Simon witnessed the true power of God flowing through Peter, he offered to pay the apostles so that he could have this same power.

> And when Simon saw that through the laying on of the apostles' hands the Holy Spirit was given, he offered them money, saying, "Give me this power also, that anyone on whom I lay hands may receive the Holy Spirit." (Acts 8:18–19)

What was it that Simon offered to purchase? It was power, pure and simple. He had no desire to see the Holy Spirit come upon people to empower them and set them free. It was all about control, his control. Nothing had changed in him; he still wanted to influence and impress. This time it was just through what he saw as a greater power. But the same demonic motive was in operation.

This same spirit is active in the psychic hot lines of today. In many instances, these modern soothsayers/witches are there to tell people what they think they want to hear, while their 900-number meters rack up $3.99 a minute. In all cases the callers are giving legal ground to the enemy to draw them even deeper into the influence of the demonic.

Our nation is living under the influence of the occult in many ways. It is even true that our nation's capitol was designed in the form of the Masonic symbol. The exercises and practices of the Freemasons are filled with the symbols and rites of an ancient Arabic religion, which in some cases glorified the murder of Christians. Its symbols include the inverted pentagram that is also found in witchcraft and Satanism. The Masonic Lodge has been home to many presidents, judges, members of Congress, and other government officials. Nevertheless, the Masonic Lodge, with its secret rites and orders, is an occult organization whose influence is felt throughout every part of the country—even in the church of Jesus Christ.

Whatever the source or description, we are living under the influence of the witchcraft of the occult.

THE WITCHCRAFT OF DRUGS

Drugs are another tool of the enemy to influence those who use them. Galatians, in the King James Version, lists witchcraft among the deeds of the flesh.

> *Now the works of the flesh are manifest, which are these; adultery, fornication, uncleanness, lasciviousness, idolatry, witchcraft, hatred, variance, emulations, wrath, strife, seditions, heresies, envyings, murders, drunkenness, revellings, and such like.*   (Galatians 5:19–21 KJV)

The Greek word used for *"witchcraft"* here is *pharmakeia*,* from which we get the word *pharmacy*, the place where prescription drugs are available. In ancient times the pharmacist was one who mixed potions and poisons with which to influence or kill people. Today, illegal drugs enslave us and make us dependent. They waste our lives and our money.

Illegal drugs plague our neighborhoods and families, robbing us of the next generations. At the same time, we must realize that we are also the most medicated people on earth. Never have so many people used prescription drugs. We have drugs to bring us out of depression and drugs to calm our stress. Antidepressant drugs are prescribed almost automatically today. Although in some cases prescription drugs are helpful in correcting chemical imbalances in the brain, that is not the only cause of depression. Depression also can be the result of demonic influence. Drugs may treat the symptoms, but they fail to address the source of the depression. It is comparable to seeing someone with an arrow stuck in his chest and handing him an aspirin instead of removing the arrow. In any event, drugs of any kind represent a powerful means of influence.

THE WITCHCRAFT OF RELIGION

Paul asked an interesting question in his epistle to the Galatians. Many in the Galatian church were falling back into a mind-set of works and rituals in order to please those who sought to bind them to religion again. He asked them, *"O foolish Galatians! Who has bewitched you that you should not obey the truth, before whose eyes Jesus Christ was clearly portrayed*

---

*. *Strong's Exhaustive Concordance of the Bible* (Iowa Falls: World Bible Publishers, Inc., 1980, 1986), G#5331.

among you as crucified?" (Galatians 3:1). It appears that religion itself can be an influencing factor to bring fear into the lives of believers and separate them from the true and living God.

Religion itself can become an obstacle.

What do I mean by *religion?* Religion, in the broadest sense, refers to a system of beliefs about God. But religion itself can become an obstacle if we begin to relate to our system of beliefs or doctrine and forget about our personal relationship with God. For the ancient Jewish people, religion became a mechanical following of rules, done by rote, rather than being motivated by a personal relationship with their God. God Himself told them that, while they practiced religion, their hearts were not in it.

> *Therefore the* LORD *said: "Inasmuch as these people draw near with their mouths and honor Me with their lips, but have removed their hearts far from Me, and their fear toward Me is taught by the commandment of men."* (Isaiah 29:13)

The Galatians had begun to fall back into that religious pattern. They put aside the truth of the Gospel of grace through Jesus Christ and began trying to earn their way to fellowship with God through legalistic religion. If it were possible for us to save ourselves, who would be in control? We would! Man would *"be like God"* (Genesis 3:5). It's the oldest lie in the cosmos. God is God, and He alone saves through His Son Jesus Christ.

Throughout the history of the church, various leaders have tried to exert control over the people they were called to serve. In the Middle Ages, a hierarchy of church leaders evolved that took control of every phase of the people's lives. The church became a political force with the power of life or death. The result was corruption throughout the church to the point of selling forgiveness to those with enough money. Again, those in the church assumed a place that was not theirs. They took their eyes off God and said to themselves, "We can *be like God*" and issue forgiveness.

Thankfully, Luther and other Reformers came along, and the church was redirected to its original purpose: worship of God, not a form of religion. (Unfortunately, these Reformers themselves eventually persecuted those who participated in subsequent reforms.)

It is still a fact, however, that, from time to time, movements and individuals rise up and assume a place of control. Leaders must remain diligent to examine their hearts in areas of leadership. Leaders serve the Lord by caring for, not dominating, the church. Jesus talked about this issue:

> But Jesus called them to Himself and said, "You know that the rulers of the Gentiles lord it over them, and those who are great exercise authority over them. Yet it shall not be so among you; but whoever desires to become great among you, let him be your servant."
>
> (Matthew 20:25–26)

THE WITCHCRAFT OF REBELLION

> Has the LORD as great delight in burnt offerings and sacrifices, as in obeying the voice of the LORD? Behold, to obey is better than sacrifice, and to heed than the fat of rams. For rebellion is as the sin of witchcraft, and stubbornness is as iniquity and idolatry. Because you have rejected the word of the LORD, He also has rejected you from being king.
>
> (1 Samuel 15:22–23)

Saul was anointed to be king of Israel. He was given clear instructions to destroy the Amalekites, who were a great offense to God. But Saul disobeyed. He rebelled against God and saved some of the loot for himself and the people. Saul was afraid of the murmuring of the people; thus, he disregarded God's word. Although he retained a religious appearance, he was diverted from the worship of God and took some of the glory of the conquest for himself. Does the idea of taking glory that belongs to God sound familiar? Shortly thereafter, an evil spirit came upon Saul to torment him. (See 1 Samuel 16:14.)

There is an atmosphere of rebellion in our own time. Children rebel against parents; parents rebel against their employers; people rebel against the authority God has established over them in government; and government has rebelled against God by passing laws that permit all kinds of shameful and godless activities. Those who are openly homosexual dare God to condemn them. They demand equal rights and flout the laws of God. We have become a rebellious nation of individuals who think only of ourselves.

> *We have served at a different altar and turned away from God.*

The witchcraft of rebellion in every form and flavor has overtaken our generation. Why are we surprised that children and teachers are shot down and killed when we have torn the laws of God off the walls of our schools? We permit "health organizations" to pass out condoms in public schools, giving tacit blessing to premarital sex among teens. We have served at a different altar and turned away from God. Humanism reigns in government and public schools, and God has been asked to leave. The witchcraft of rebellion has infected our nation at every level. The result will be what it always has been: separation from God.

None of this is by coincidence. Witchcraft is part of a deliberate strategy to undermine our worship and fellowship with God.

SATAN HAS A STRATEGY

Satan has a strategy. He isn't sitting around hell throwing darts at a dartboard to determine his next move. He knows exactly what he wants to do and to whom he wants to do it. *So should we.*

Satan's strategy is applied through three basic means: *intimidation, manipulation,* and *domination.* Satan tries to influence us and divert us from fellowship with God by scaring us, managing us, or overpowering us. His strategies are applied not only directly on us, but also through us. We try to intimidate or impress one another, manage what others think, or lift ourselves above them in pride. We must understand that there is an active plot against our families, the church, and every one of us individually. From the corporate CEO's office to the pastor's study, Satan employs his scheme through unwitting players. There are many "Simons" among us who are accepted and revered by many as community leaders and even representatives of God. The trappings are different, but domination and manipulative control are still the undercurrent.

THIS IS WAR

This is war! And Satan's strategy is to wage war by using terrorism, psychological warfare, and overwhelming force. Many born-again believers are robbed and rendered ineffective because they are unaware of the devices that the enemy employs for their destruction. In the next chapters we will examine Satan's strategies of *intimidation, manipulation,* and *domination.*

Chapter 3

THE TERRORIST TACTIC
OF INTIMIDATION

*Then Caleb quieted the people before Moses, and said, "Let us go
up at once and take possession, for we are well able to overcome it."
But the men who had gone up with him said, "We are not able to
go up against the people, for they are stronger than we." And they
gave the children of Israel a bad report of the land which they had
spied out, saying, "The land through which we have gone as spies
is a land that devours its inhabitants, and all the people whom
we saw in it are men of great stature. There we saw the giants
(the descendants of Anak came from the giants); and we were like
grasshoppers in our own sight, and
so we were in their sight.*
—Numbers 13:30–33

FEAR

We see the following kinds of stories all too often. A man straps
explosives to himself and detonates them on a bus, killing himself and
many others. Who will ever forget the bombing in Oklahoma City, when

hundreds were killed by a truckload of volatile chemicals parked in front of a government building? Then there were those men who blew up a 747 over the skies of Scotland, killing men, women, and children of all ages and nationalities. Most recently, the World Trade Center towers and the Pentagon were attacked, causing many deaths and the destruction of the towers. Though the methods used and the causes served may have differed, all of these acts were acts of "terrorism."

Those who commit these heinous acts are called terrorists. A terrorist is essentially a coward serving a lost cause. They do not have the power or ability to win an outright confrontation, so they resort to terrorism to prove a point and get some attention.

Their chief objective is to put terror and fear into us. The terrorist believes that if he can scare us, he can *defeat* us, *distract* us, and *deny* us. Terrorism is a way in which an enemy of inferior strength can control a vastly superior foe. Terror is the single strongest weapon that any opposing force can employ because it can defeat us before we fire a shot. Terror is the weapon of intimidation.

We must differentiate here between fear and terrorism. Fear itself is a natural response to a threat. We would be foolish not to have some fear and respect for danger, whether it be natural or man-made. But to be controlled by fear, when fear is used as a deliberate tool of the enemy, is a different matter entirely. There is a major difference between healthy fear and terrorism.

FEAR IN THE FAMILY

If you grow up in a family of five or six, one of your brothers or sisters inevitably becomes the thinker of the family pack—usually the eldest. This sibling sometimes gets the other children to do what he wants through fear. He may cause them to be afraid with his physical size, or perhaps he makes them afraid by causing them to feel stupid. This child controls the other children with terror. Of course, this is mostly learned behavior. He intimidates because someone or something else has intimidated him, whether it be parents or circumstances.

This terrorism goes on in many families, including the family of God. Preachers can intimidate the people of God from the pulpit by preaching the judgment of God without the grace of God. These leaders betray their position as the under-shepherds of God's flock. I have seen Christian leaders whose followers cower in fear when they walk into the room. They are shepherds who hold clubs over the heads of the sheep. In this way, the enemy uses fear to make God's flock afraid of their heavenly Father. Pastors and other leaders in the church must not lead by intimidation. Shepherds are to feed, guide, and protect the flock of God. The apostle Peter, who was asked by Jesus to care for the flock of God (John 21:15–17), gave instructions to other Christian leaders regarding the attitude of those who would shepherd God's flock:

Fear itself is a natural response to a threat.

The elders who are among you I exhort, I who am a fellow elder and a witness of the sufferings of Christ, and also a partaker of the glory that will be revealed: shepherd the flock of God which is among you, serving as overseers, not by compulsion but willingly, not for dishonest gain but eagerly; nor as being lords over those entrusted to you, but being examples to the flock; and when the Chief Shepherd appears, you will receive the crown of glory that does not fade away. (1 Peter 5:1–4)

FEAR AS A TOOL OF INFLUENCE

Fear is a powerful tool of influence. Satan's strategy is to make us afraid, thus preventing us from possessing the promises of God. When he makes us afraid, we take our eyes off God and focus on the object of fear the devil presents to us. Obstacles, threats, and circumstances overwhelm us. If he can distract us, we will take our eyes off God and His promises. Then Satan can effectively defeat us before we set one foot into our Promised Land. Once defeated, even born-again believers can become depressed and open to further demonic oppression that keeps them ineffective in the kingdom of God.

The enemy can cause fear to control us by various means. We can have a fear of rejection, a fear of failure, a fear of success, a fear of responsibility, a fear of loneliness, even a fear of fear itself. Whatever the guise, fear will keep us on the wrong side of the river if we allow it to.

This was the case of Israel when God led them to the front porch of the Promised Land. The faithless majority of the spies saw the obstacles and took their eyes off God, focusing instead on giants and grasshoppers. They looked at their own ability, saying, *"We are not able"* (Numbers 13:31). They were right. They were not able in their own strength to overcome the inhabitants of the land. So they saw God's abundance as a devouring beast before which they were helpless.

Whenever we are poised to enter some new and greater dimension of God, the enemy will use fear to stop us in our tracks. It was fear that prevented Israel from entering into the land of promise. We must remember, though, that fear takes many, and sometimes less obvious, forms.

We've already mentioned a few. There is the fear of rejection, the fear of loneliness, the fear of failure, the fear of embarrassment, and the list goes on. All these prevent us from effectively employing our gifts in the body of Christ. The enemy sees the power and purpose that God is bringing us into, so he plants a minefield of fear on the frontier of our inheritance.

Even the most seasoned Christian can be a victim of intimidation. It seems that the greater the anointing, the greater the enemy's effort to terrorize us and bring us to a halt. I think of the great prophet Elijah, who, after slaying hundreds of false prophets and calling down the fire of God, was threatened by an evil queen named Jezebel.

> And Ahab told Jezebel all that Elijah had done, also how he had executed all the prophets with the sword. Then Jezebel sent a messenger to Elijah, saying, "So let the gods do to me, and more also, if I do not make your life as the life of one of them by tomorrow about this time." And when he **saw** that, he arose and ran for his life, and went to Beersheba, which belongs to Judah, and left his servant there.
> (1 Kings 19:1–3, emphasis added)

First Kings 19:3 tells us that when this great man of God *"saw"* this threat from Jezebel, he ran into the desert. He took his eyes off the purpose and calling of God and he *"saw"* only fear. Later, God revealed Himself to Elijah in a powerful way, enabling him to continue in God's purpose.

God knows the enemy's tactics.

God knows the enemy's tactics as well. Whenever God was about to do something great in the Bible, He pre-handled the issue of fear.

Consider Moses and Israel on the western shores of the Red Sea. The Egyptians were behind them and the sea in front of them. That would be enough to make anyone afraid.

> *Then they said to Moses, "Because there were no graves in Egypt, have you taken us away to die in the wilderness? Why have you so dealt with us, to bring us up out of Egypt? Is this not the word that we told you in Egypt, saying, 'Let us alone that we may serve the Egyptians?' For it would have been better for us to serve the Egyptians than that we should die in the wilderness." And Moses said to the people, "Do not be afraid. Stand still, and see the salvation of the LORD, which He will accomplish for you today. For the Egyptians whom you see today, you shall see again no more forever. The LORD will fight for you, and you shall hold your peace."* (Exodus 14:11–14)

When fear comes, it causes us to turn away from promise and back to bondage. The Israelites said, *"Let us alone."* Fear made them recoil; it paralyzed them. But into this fear God spoke through Moses, saying, *"Do not be afraid. Stand still, and see the salvation of the LORD."* In other words, "Take your eyes off the Egyptians and see what I will do." How many times have we turned our backs on God's salvation and looked at the problem instead of at the Lord?

In most instances in the Bible, when God was about to do something great, He dealt with fear and put His servants at peace.

- ⋄ Think of God's words to Israel and Joshua as they entered to conquer the Promised Land.

Have I not commanded you? Be strong and of good courage; **do not be afraid,** *nor be dismayed, for the* LORD *your God is with you wherever you go.*   (Joshua 1:9, emphasis added)

+   Think of Jehoshaphat and Judah as they were about to enter into a battle with the enemies of God.

And he said, "Listen, all you of Judah and you inhabitants of Jerusalem, and you, King Jehoshaphat! Thus says the LORD *to you:* **'Do not be afraid** *nor dismayed because of this great multitude, for the battle is not yours, but God's.'"*   (2 Chronicles 20:15, emphasis added)

+   Think of the people of Jerusalem rebuilding the walls and gates under Nehemiah.

And I looked, and arose and said to the nobles, to the leaders, and to the rest of the people, **"Do not be afraid** *of them. Remember the Lord, great and awesome, and fight for your brethren, your sons, your daughters, your wives, and your houses."*
                         (Nehemiah 4:14, emphasis added)

+   Think of Mary as she was about to conceive Jesus by the Holy Spirit. This was the greatest deliverance of all.

Then the angel said to her, **"Do not be afraid,** *Mary, for you have found favor with God. And behold, you will conceive in your womb and bring forth a Son, and shall call His name* JESUS.*"*
                         (Luke 1:30–31, emphasis added)

In the Bible, God tells us, in one form or another, 365 times not to be afraid. If we focus on fear, then we will be controlled by it. But if we really understand fear and how the enemy uses it, we can *turn the tables on terrorism.*

TURNING THE TABLES ON TERRORISM

As I said before, terrorism is the weapon of a defeated foe. It will be thrown at us from every angle and every source. Whether it comes from inside or outside the church, fear will *distract* us, *deny* us, and *defeat* us if we allow it to do so. But God makes a promise to those who look to Him rather than at fear. His promise is to turn the tables on the enemy and make him *run!*

> *Terrorism is the weapon of a defeated foe.*

I will send My fear before you, I will cause confusion among all the people to whom you come, and will make all your enemies turn their backs to you.   (Exodus 23:27)

How do we turn the tables on the weapon of terrorism? How do we fight the fear that keeps us from God's best?

FIGHTING FEAR WITH FOCUS

The best defense against fear is never to take our eyes off Jesus. In dealing with fear, it is important to focus on God's purpose rather than be distracted by the terrorism of the enemy. God's supreme purpose is to save mankind, and *you* are His strategy. The devil knows this all too well, so he will throw terror in front of you to scare you out of fulfilling God's purpose.

Every time a soul is saved, a major battle has been won. Think about it for a moment. What is it that prevents us from sharing our testimony or the Gospel with a friend or a neighbor? *Fear!* We are afraid that we might be embarrassed or that we will be rejected in some way, so we clam up and watch our friend struggle and slide into hell. If we fail to share the Good News because of the terror tactics of the enemy, then we have allowed him to win.

We don't serve a God who is standing over in the corner scratching His head, trying to figure out how He will bring us out of our latest dilemma. He delivered us before He brought us into the problem. He brought us to the threshold of promise and continuous victory. But we must wake up to His deliverance. The battle has already been won! We need only to appropriate it.

You will keep him in perfect peace, whose mind is stayed [focused] on You, because he trusts in You. Trust in the LORD forever, for in YAH, the LORD, is everlasting strength. (Isaiah 26:3–4)

FIGHTING FEAR WITH FELLOWSHIP

Another antidote for the poison of fear is fellowship. The purpose of fellowship is to encourage each other, to handle the fears we each bring to the body. We come together as a body in order to *remind* one another about God. We come together to *minister* encouragement to each other. We come together to *learn* more of God and gain confidence in Him. We come together to *tell* stories of God's victory over the enemy's terror tactics.

Hear the Word of God:

I myself am confident concerning you, my brethren, that you also are full of goodness, filled with all knowledge, able also to admonish one another. (Romans 15:14)

and,

Let the peace of God rule in your hearts, to which also you were called in one body; and be thankful. Let the word of Christ dwell in you richly in all wisdom, teaching and admonishing one another in psalms and hymns and spiritual songs, singing with grace in your hearts to the Lord. (Colossians 3:15–16)

and,

Now we exhort you, brethren, warn those who are unruly, comfort the fainthearted [those who are being terrorized], *uphold the weak, be patient with all.* (1 Thessalonians 5:14)

and,

Therefore strengthen the hands which hang down, and the feeble knees, and make straight paths for your feet, so that what is lame may not be dislocated, but rather be healed. (Hebrews 12:12–13)

FIGHTING FEAR WITH FACTS

It is important to any military campaign that those on the front lines have all the facts about the enemy. An intelligence-gathering operation must take place in order to understand the position and strength of the enemy in relation to ours. The enemy always employs fear because he cannot win. Perhaps we can learn something here. When we are the most afraid, the devil is even more afraid of us. You see, whatever fight we are in, wherever God has led us, the fight belongs to God, not to us. When we read the Bible and memorize Scriptures, we are ingesting an antidote for fear. When the enemy throws his terrorist tactics before us, we must not listen to him but listen to what God says instead. And what does God tell us about the battles we fight?

> And he shall say to them, "Hear, O Israel: Today you are on the verge of battle with your enemies. Do not let your heart faint, do not be afraid, and do not tremble or be terrified because of them; for the LORD your God is He who goes with you, to fight for you against your enemies, to save you." (Deuteronomy 20:3–4)

and,

> You will chase your enemies, and they shall fall by the sword before you. Five of you shall chase a hundred, and a hundred of you shall put ten thousand to flight; your enemies shall fall by the sword before you. (Leviticus 26:7–8)

And, in Jesus' own words,

> These things I have spoken to you, that in Me you may have peace. In the world you will have tribulation; but be of good cheer [don't be afraid], I have overcome the world. (John 16:33)

When I am faced with fear, I remember that I need to get my priorities in order. The best way to drown out the word of fear is with the sounds of praise. In 2 Chronicles, Jerusalem was faced with strong enemies who wanted to ransack the city. Instead of gathering swords and spears and measuring the might of the army, King Jehoshaphat held a praise festival.

And Jehoshaphat feared, and set himself to seek the LORD, and pro-claimed a fast throughout all Judah. So Judah gathered together to ask help from the LORD; and from all the cities of Judah they came to seek the LORD....Then the Spirit of the LORD came upon Jahaziel the son of Zechariah, the son of Benaiah, the son of Jeiel, the son of Mattaniah, a Levite of the sons of Asaph, in the midst of the assembly. And he said, "Listen, all you of Judah and you inhabi-tants of Jerusalem, and you, King Jehoshaphat! Thus says the LORD to you: 'Do not be afraid nor dismayed because of this great multitude, for the battle is not yours, but God's....You will not need to fight in this battle. Position yourselves, stand still and see the salvation of the LORD, who is with you, O Judah and Jerusalem!' Do not fear or be dismayed; tomorrow go out against them, for the LORD is with you."...And when he had consulted with the people, he appointed those who should sing to the LORD, and who should praise the beauty of holiness, as they went out before the army and were saying: "Praise the LORD, for His mercy endures forever." Now when they began to sing and to praise, the LORD set ambushes against the people of Ammon, Moab, and Mount Seir, who had come against Judah; and they were defeated.

(2 Chronicles 20:3–4, 14–15, 17, 21–22)

Perhaps the real key to spiritual warfare is to remember who is fighting the battle. The people did not shout at the enemy or bind evil sprits; they lifted up the name of the Lord, and the Lord set the ambush for the enemy.

> *The key is to remember who is fighting the battle.*

Satan is focused on distracting us with fear. We must learn to recognize his plan and let God into the fight. We may be in the battle, but the battle belongs to God. God hasn't left us alone to fight Satan. Without these facts, we will lose hope, and the host of hell will keep us ineffective. Begin the process of discovery by taking the Word of God into your heart. God's Holy Word is the weapon of truth and knowledge.

When the enemy threatens us with terror, we must fight with the facts—and the main fact is that the battle belongs to the Lord.

THE FINAL WORD ON FEAR

Remember that we began this chapter with a story of defeat and distraction at the frontier of promise. We need to have the same attitude and understanding that Joshua and Caleb did if we are to defeat the enemy's terrorism. Listen:

> But Joshua the son of Nun and Caleb the son of Jephunneh, who were among those who had spied out the land, tore their clothes; and they spoke to all the congregation of the children of Israel, saying: "The land we passed through to spy out is **an exceedingly good land**. If the LORD delights in us, then **He will bring us** into this land and give it to us, 'a land which flows with milk and honey.' Only do not rebel against the LORD, nor fear the people of the land, **for they are our bread**; their protection has departed from them, and the LORD is with us. **Do not fear them.**" (Numbers 14:6–9, emphasis added)

Joshua and Caleb understood a few things that you and I need to remember as we turn the tables on terrorism. They summarize what we have been saying in this chapter.

- When the enemy is using fear, God is bringing us into *"an exceedingly good land."*
- We don't fight in our own strength. *"He will bring us."*
- The enemy is a defeated and desperate foe. *"They are our bread."*
- God alone is worthy of fear. *"Do not fear them."*

If there is anything that we can be sure of, it is that we will face the terrorism of the enemy as we move on in God. But we cannot be controlled by the terror of the enemy when we know the truth of God.

> For God has not given us a spirit of fear, but of power and of love and of a sound mind. (2 Timothy 1:7)

Chapter 4

MANIPULATION: THE PSYCHOLOGICAL WARFARE OF THE ENEMY

In the 1930s and '40s, Hitler was able to convince an entire nation that people of a particular ethnicity were inferior and should be eliminated. Of course, the Jewish people were the most frequently targeted group. The Germans instituted a program of "disinformation," which is to say, they deliberately put out the wrong facts to the German people. This was done in every phase of life, from the media, to art, to the classroom. Jews were seen as subhuman and not worthy of the air they breathed. This manipulation of the truth was so effective that by the time Hitler implemented the "Final Solution," those who murdered Jewish children thought they were doing the right thing.

In a similar vein, widespread racism in the United States resulted in the devaluation of African-Americans. Black and white children grew up believing that black children were somehow inferior. In fact, I recall reading about a particular study where little black girls were given a choice of either black or white dolls, and they chose the white ones as the more desirable. Whether we call it the "Final Solution" or "segregation" or "apartheid," the strategy and inspiration are motivated by Satan.

> *Manipulation is one of Satan's*
> *most effective weapons.*

One of Satan's most effective weapons in distracting and influencing us is *manipulation*. To manipulate means to manage people or circumstances to gain an advantage. What is being manipulated is the mind through the offering of lies and half-truths. There is a deliberate attempt to manage what people think. When nations go to war, they frequently employ tactics that seek to manipulate what the opposition thinks. This is called "psychological warfare." Satan, our enemy, also engages in a kind of manipulation in which he employs his own tactics of psychological warfare.

TACTICS OF PSYCHOLOGICAL WARFARE

Psychological warfare includes the manipulation of facts to discredit what is true. The basic idea is to create doubt in the minds of the enemy. In Paul's second epistle to the Corinthians, there is a picture of the tactics that Satan uses to distract us from God and His truth.

> *For though we walk in the flesh, we do not war according to the flesh. For the weapons of our warfare are not carnal but mighty in God for pulling down strongholds, casting down **arguments** and **every high thing** that exalts itself against the knowledge of God, bringing every thought into captivity to the obedience of Christ, and being ready to punish all disobedience when your obedience is fulfilled.*
> (2 Corinthians 10:3–6, emphasis added)

The apostle Paul preached the Gospel of grace to the Gentiles. But there were those who opposed his message. When Paul planted churches in the area of Corinth, Judaizers came from Jerusalem to preach a fleshly and legalistic kind of Christianity. They taught that the converted Gentiles should follow the Jewish Law, including circumcision and dietary regulations. The way that the Judaizers chose to wage war against Paul's Gospel was to call into question his motives and his authority. If they could not defeat the message, then they would discredit the messenger. They accused

Paul of hypocrisy, saying that he spoke one way through letters and another in person. They did not like what he preached or the manner in which it was presented. (See 2 Corinthians 10:1–2.)

The gospel that the Judaizers preached raised up high walls between man and God. It sought to keep man in control of his salvation and his relationship with God. Does this sound familiar? *"You will be like God"* (Genesis 3:5). The result was that Paul, in return, waged war against those things that were raised up *"against the knowledge of God."*

What exactly was Paul warring against? He was warring against *arguments*, *actions*, and *attitudes* that separate people from God. He referred to them as *"strongholds,"* a place of enemy control. Paul warred against a legalistic and manipulative kind of gospel that kept its hearers in bondage and separated from God.

Remember, Satan's objective is to divert and distract us from fellowship with God. The battleground of this psychological warfare is the mind. Whereas Satan's tactics of *intimidation* seek to divert us from God by fear, his tactic of *manipulation* seeks to create doubts and distractions to preoccupy our minds, thus preventing us from fellowshipping with God. The tactics of manipulation take place in every area of our lives, from the boardroom to the bedroom, but they are most destructive in the body of Christ. This demonic psychological warfare takes place among brothers and sisters in the body of Christ by several means. The first is what the Bible calls *"arguments"* (2 Corinthians 10:5).

ARGUMENTS

An argument in the biblical sense is a reasoning, an opinion, or perhaps a word. These arguments are expressed in a variety of ways, including criticism, gossip, innuendo, sarcasm, moodiness, and religious pretense, as well as others. Satan rides into our churches on the critical opinions we voice about someone or something. He launches his attack through the angry and manipulative words issued from a carnal heart.

Over the years, I have seen these kinds of arguments in the church. You see, when we come to Christ, our spirits are saved, but our minds are still in the ghetto. When we don't renew our minds according to the Word of God, they stay carnal. Some of those carnal tendencies sit in the pews of our churches. When individuals don't get their way, they begin to criticize the preacher or others in leadership. They voice their "concern" about the issues they wish to manipulate to their favor. The world calls this "pressure"; the sanctified call it "concern." What was "gossip" in the world becomes a "conversation of concern" in the church. The result and the sources are the same, whether it is inside or outside the body of Christ. They are demonic!

> *Satan rides into our churches on our complaints and criticism.*

It is amazing how a single sentence motivated by iniquity can ruin an otherwise great day. Perhaps you have experienced something like the following situation.

You get up on Sunday morning and start getting ready to go to church. There is the hum of a hymn breaking the Sabbath air, and you are feeling great! To your surprise and delight, the kids are ready on time, and everything is going smoothly. This is going to be *your* day. You jump into the car and pop a worship tape into the tape deck. You are happy and excited and worshiping God on the way to church. You are on time for the first time in a year. You look great, your spouse looks great, and your kids are the very picture of the Christian upbringing you have provided. Everything is "perfect." As you pull into the church parking lot, you see that the best parking spot is open, and you pull right in. Now, serene, you walk into the church with your head lifted up worshipfully in the clouds. But the minute you get inside the door, there's somebody with whom you had an earlier disagreement blocking the path to your seat.

"Oh, I know you aren't going to just walk by me and not speak," the person says in a rather condescending tone.

Suddenly, all of what you felt is gone. Anger and contempt have replaced your peace and power. Your head drops down from the clouds and begins to throb with stress. Where only moments ago all was "perfect" and you were ready to ascend to heaven with praise, now you are a defeated lump of flesh.

What happened to you? An argument or word from another person—inspired and produced by iniquity—just reached out and touched you. Suddenly, all the warm worshipful thoughts you had about the Lord are drowned out by the sound of your own heart pounding out a rising blood pressure level. You have been derailed, diverted, and distracted from fellowship with God. You have been the victim of an argument of Satan's psychological warfare. He has manipulated and managed your mind to distract you from God. And it worked. You couldn't worship after that even if you had angels on either arm singing into your injured ears.

The substance of what that person said to you at the back door is not the issue. Any number of arguments produces the same kinds of responses. We can get sidetracked by doctrinal disputes regarding how many angels can stand on the head of a pin, or where we should place the new piano in the sanctuary. From the color of the carpet to the mode of communion, Satan can argue us out of fellowship with God.

Perhaps the most frequent targets of our words of doubt and criticism are the pastors and other leaders in the church. There are those carnal minds that feel their "gifts" are not being used to the fullest, or perhaps their voices are not being heard and their opinions are not given the weight they deserve. Thus they begin an assault against those who lead them by whispering "concerns" expressed in terms of great passion and love of God. All the while they attack God's ordained leadership and draw other like-minded people to themselves. A demonic strategy has been employed through them, which sometimes results in church division or even a church split.

Sometimes there are legitimate reasons for concern regarding church leaders, but these are never to be processed among brothers and sisters. These problems must first be taken directly to the leader in question. As soon as we voice "concern" to a peer in the congregation, we have invited the devil into the church. Note that in the Corinthian church, the very ones who attacked Paul for speaking with two different tones never approached him directly. Instead, they allowed themselves to become tools of the enemy to separate people from God and one another.

The enemy can control us not only by what we *say*, but also by what we *do*—through our actions.

ACTIONS

How many times have you seen people stay away from fellowship with the church body because they were offended in some way? They believe that by withholding themselves from others, they somehow control them. It is not unlike what my brother used to do with his manipulative tantrums. They use our love as a weapon against us. (They do not realize that they have played right into the plan of the enemy; they are separated and isolated from other believers and the Lord.) Though they may not admit it, this isolation is a way to manipulate others in the body into agreeing with them against the one who offended them. Perhaps this is why people hop from church to church, leaving a trail of injured people in their wakes. The writer of Hebrews instructed us,

> *People sometimes use our love as a weapon against us.*

And let us consider one another in order to stir up love and good works, not forsaking the assembling of ourselves together, as is the manner of some, but exhorting one another, and so much the more as you see the Day approaching. (Hebrews 10:24–25)

There are actions of commission and omission that some employ to manage the minds of others. They seek to manage or influence other people's minds by what they do or don't do. It is probably those things that they don't do that are the most effective in their manipulation. For example, some people withhold love; others withhold their tithes and offerings.

Money should never become a weapon. Withholding your tithe invites a curse. It opens a demonic doorway into the area of your finances.

> *"Will a man rob God? Yet you have robbed Me! But you say, 'In what way have we robbed You?' In tithes and offerings. **You are cursed with a curse**, for you have robbed Me, even this whole nation. Bring all the tithes into the storehouse, that there may be food in My house, and try*

Me now in this," says the LORD *of hosts, "If I will not open for you the windows of heaven and pour out for you such blessing that there will not be room enough to receive it."* (Malachi 3:8–10, emphasis added)

Money does not belong to the one who holds it. It belongs to God. In one sense, when we withhold money from the church, we are trying to manipulate God. God will not be managed!

Any action that we take with the motive of influencing the behavior of someone else, plays into the hands of Satan. And the more we play the game, the more of a foothold he gains. We become centers of his influence.

What we say and what we do can be used by the enemy for the purposes of diverting us from God. But there is another factor, and that is the stronghold of pride. All of us live behind this stronghold to some extent. It concerns the *attitude* with which we say or do something.

ATTITUDES

The king of Tyre is a biblical type of Satan. All of his iniquity and arrogance stemmed from pride.

Son of man, say to the prince of Tyre, "Thus says the Lord GOD: *'Because your heart is lifted up, and you say, "I am a god, I sit in the seat of gods, in the midst of the seas," yet you are a man, and not a god, though you set your heart as the heart of a god.'"* (Ezekiel 28:2)

As we described in Chapter One, Satan caught a glimpse of himself and became proud. He is the originator of pride, and he imparted iniquity to us through the fall of Adam and Eve. Again, it's the old lie that we can *"be like God"* (Genesis 3:5). We begin to see ourselves as being above others.

Pride is an exalted opinion of ourselves. Pride places us on a judgment bench from which we look down on other people. We hold "lesser" people and opinions in contempt. We may not be openly hostile to those we judge, but we talk down to them. We treat them as children and give them no respect. We issue our judicial opinions about their value. If there is one common indicator as to whether or not we are prideful, it is how we value other people. If we see others as inferior to us, then pride has done its work. The result is separation and persecution of those we value less.

God warns us about pride throughout the Bible.

> *Pride is indicated by how we value other people.*

> *Do not lift up your horn on high; do not speak with a stiff neck.*
> (Psalm 75:5)

and,

> *Pride goes before destruction, and a haughty spirit before a fall. Better to be of a humble spirit with the lowly, than to divide the spoil with the proud.* (Proverbs 16:18–19)

Judgment is God's business. We are not in any position to question Him or devalue other people. The problem with pride is that, like other forms of manipulation, it invites judgment.

> *For exaltation comes neither from the east nor from the west nor from the south. But God is the Judge: He puts down one, and exalts another. For in the hand of the LORD there is a cup, and the wine is red; it is fully mixed, and He pours it out; surely its dregs shall all the wicked of the earth drain and drink down.* (Psalm 75:6–8)

and,

> *A man's pride will bring him low, but the humble in spirit will retain honor.* (Proverbs 29:23)

Jesus instructed us not to judge others because we would invite the same judgment upon ourselves (Matthew 7:1). We are to release others to the judgment of God. Whether through criticism or condescension, pride is the main flavor of iniquity. We must examine not only our words and actions, but also the attitudes with which each are generated.

TEARING DOWN STRONGHOLDS

The first step in our demolition of enemy strongholds is to realize that we all have them. Yes, even believers filled with the Holy Spirit can come under demonic influence.

One time I was in the middle of ministering against satanic curses when I realized that there was a stronghold in my own life in the area of criticism. Before then, I had believed that Christians, saved and filled with the Holy Spirit, could not be oppressed by demons. How could a blood-bought Christian be part of the plan and program of Satan in the earth? I truly believed that a fountain couldn't bring forth both bitter and sweet water. And that is absolutely true; a fountain cannot bring forth bitter and sweet water. But a human being can most definitely speak well in one sentence and absolute evil in the next. We see this truth demonstrated through Peter, who was used by the Holy Spirit to reveal Jesus as the Messiah, only to be rebuked by the Messiah a short time later because of Satan's working through him! (See Matthew 16:16, 21–23.)

What I learned was that strongholds are in the mind, not the spirit, of a believer. When we come to Christ, we are His; however, our minds have not caught up to our spirits. There is a war being waged in our minds to see who will control it, God or flesh and the devil. Paul spoke of this same thing:

> For we know that the law is spiritual, but I am carnal, sold under sin. For what I am doing, I do not understand. For what I will to do, that I do not practice; but what I hate, that I do. If, then, I do what I will not to do, I agree with the law that it is good. But now, it is no longer I who do it, but sin that dwells in me. For I know that in me (that is, in my flesh) nothing good dwells; for to will is present with me, but how to perform what is good I do not find. For the good that I will to do, I do not do; but the evil I will not to do, that I practice. Now if I do what I will not to do, it is no longer I who do it, but sin that dwells in me. I find then a law, that evil is present with me, the one who wills to do good. (Romans 7:14–21)

It is clear that Paul understood that though he belonged to God, there was still a war going on in him, seeking to distract him from the Lord.

Although we must realize that there is a war going on in us, we also must realize that God alone will win that war. Think of Joshua as he commanded Israel to march around the walls of Jericho. The walls did not fall because of Israel's military might, but because they walked out the word of the Lord to them.

We cannot win by our own ability. As Paul said,

> O wretched man that I am! Who will deliver me from this body of death? I thank God; through Jesus Christ our Lord! So then, with the mind I myself serve the law of God, but with the flesh the law of sin.
>
> (Romans 7:24–25)

We can tear down the strongholds of *arguments, actions,* and *attitudes* through which the enemy manipulates us by doing what Paul instructed the Corinthians to do. We must *"bring every thought into captivity to the obedience of Christ"* (2 Corinthians 10:5). In other words, we must say what Jesus would say and do what Jesus would do—all with the same attitude of humility He had. Humility is not groveling; it is knowing who we are in Christ Jesus.

> *Humility is knowing who we are in Christ.*

The antidote for the disinformation that the devil uses to manipulate us is the truth of God's Word. We free ourselves from the enemy's psychological warfare of manipulation when we receive the truth and then walk in it. As we continue in the truth of God's Word, we will escape the devices of the enemy.

> Then Jesus said to those Jews who believed Him, "If you abide in My word, you are My disciples indeed. And you shall know the truth, and the truth shall make you free."
> (John 8:31–32)

Chapter 5

DOMINATION: THE USE OF OVERWHELMING FORCE

Some time ago I was accorded the great privilege of speaking in a large and well-known church. I was honored by the invitation and excited at the prospect of speaking in this particular church. Imagine, George Bloomer, from the projects of Brooklyn, was coming to preach in the church of this well-known and influential pastor.

I was instructed by the pastor to arrive a little while after the service began so that I would not have to sit through all the preliminary announcements and such. When I arrived at the front entrance of this impressive facility, there was no one waiting to direct me. Walking in the front entrance, I felt awestruck. There were television cameras everywhere and the place was jam-packed. This was going to be so exciting!

My heart was filled with the prospects and possibilities of speaking from that renowned pulpit. I was rehearsing my sermon in my mind and thought it might be a good idea to go over my notes one last time. At the same time, my mind and attention were caught up in the background music and activity on the other side of the sanctuary doors. My heart was awhirl with the anticipation of this tremendous opportunity. In the midst of this impressive moment, I put my hand on the doorknob and pulled open the sanctuary door. The sound and excitement grew the farther I pulled it open.

Suddenly, I felt the jerk of someone rudely pulling the door out of my hand. I lost my grasp on the doorknob as it closed sharply before my stunned eyes and face. There I stood, outside the sanctuary, alone and deflated. My fervor was extinguished in a moment's time as if smothered by a wet blanket.

I said to myself, "Okay, maybe I shouldn't have touched the door. I'm in the wrong here." I had been in the church for a long time and should have known better than to just walk through a sanctuary door. After all, they could not have known it was I, the "Special Guest Preacher," on the other side of the door. But just as the swelling of my wounded ego was going down, insult was added to injury. The lady usher who had so rudely jerked the door out of my hand, dampening my excitement, slipped open the door and came back for more.

Focusing her widened eyes at me and wagging her head from side to side, she spoke *at* me in the most condescending of tones: *"You see this door? Do not put your hands on this door. Anytime you come to this church and you see this door closed, you just wait until I open it. They're up there praying; what's wrong with you?"* Then she again shut the door in my stunned face.

I was breathless! "Well, I know exactly what I'm preaching about tonight," I said to myself—"carnal church workers!" Now I would have my "pound of flesh"! She would be one sorry usher. How dare she insult me and treat me like some insignificant no-account nothing from the projects? I was the "Special Guest Preacher."

Just then, a young man came up and warmly greeted me. He said, "Come here with me." But I was so stunned and deflated by the lady usher that I could scarcely hear this man. I was out to get that "Jezebel." I was serious!

The young man, sent by the pastor to take care of my needs, took me down some steps and through a tunnel that came up into the pastor's office adjoining the platform. As I stood in the pastor's office, I gathered myself together. Then, after putting on my pastor's robe, I made a grand entrance onto the platform. As I strolled out onto the platform, the offending usher, with her condescending attitude, was standing at her door. When she saw me, she shriveled into the corner with her eyes turning downward so as not to catch my direct gaze. She had not realized with whom she had trifled. I was the "Preacher"—the honored guest speaker for the day. It was I who was to bring the Word of God. It was I who now stood in the holy majesty dressed in flowing ecclesiastical robes behind the pulpit. And now it was judgment day. She was toast!

How would I do it? What could I say to put her in her place? She was only an usher, while I was the preacher. Thoughts and strategies filled my mind as I sat there on the platform behind the pulpit. Then the praise broke out, and after a little while I was called up to minister. Suddenly, as I stood behind that renowned pulpit, the Holy Spirit took over. All the words set to spew forth from my wounded heart were now stuck in my throat. I wasn't able to "preach my thing" or "say my stuff." In an instant the Lord flooded me with His presence and brought me to His footstool. Without a word I was delivered of my arrogant and vengeful thinking. The Holy Spirit arrested me with His glory before I could say a word. By God's grace alone, I was able to minister.

> *We all stand equally in the grace of Jesus.*

As the Lord continued to cleanse me, I glanced at the usher. It was like looking in a spiritual mirror. I had wanted to use my position to crush and destroy this usher. I had wanted to use my holy appearance to crush tears of repentance out of her. But then the Lord changed that. Though I didn't feel delivered from my animosity completely, I realized that I had been thinking pretty highly of myself. At that moment, I realized, as Paul said, that we all stood equally in the grace of God of Jesus Christ.

> *For I say, through the grace given to me, to everyone who is among you, not to think of himself more highly than he ought to think, but to think soberly, as God has dealt to each one a measure of faith.*
>
> (Romans 12:3)

What happened there? Satan used an emotional bruise to start a war. This was part of his deliberate strategy to wound and kill another brother or sister in the Lord. Although we both should have been focusing on God, we were ambushed by pride and diverted by conflict. That is always Satan's strategy, his never-ending theme: distraction, diversion, and disharmony with God and one another. Without the intervention of the Holy Spirit and His gentle conviction, the day would have been lost.

So I ministered to the congregation (not on carnal church workers), finished up, and was going about my post-service business when this woman approached me to apologize. My heart now calmed, I was ready to hear her apology.

"I'm so sorry for the way I treated you," she said.

As she began to speak, I felt badly. But then she added, "If I had known you were the preacher, I would have never spoken to you like that."

When she said that, I realized that her apology was political, and my flesh rose up once again. After my first encounter with her, I had asked myself, "How dare she speak to me in such a manner?" I asked myself a lot in that short question. It was a clear indicator that I had placed myself above this sister somehow. When a preacher thinks that way, he is more likely serve the sheep up on a platter than serve the sheep in the love of Christ. By the wonderful grace of God, I had repented of my self-exaltation and now extended mercy to this sister.

Nevertheless, her second qualifying remark caused me to wonder how many came through that door on a weekly basis who probably didn't return to the church again because of her nasty, condescending attitude. Then again, I wondered how many times I had spoken down to people from my own pulpit. The same shoe fit both of us. Indeed, it fits most of us.

OVERWHELMING FORCE

When Satan can't scare us by terrorism or manage us with psychological warfare, he tries to crush us through the overwhelming force of domination. This is the tactic that an army uses to utterly destroy their opponent. It is a "blitzkrieg" strategy that simply overpowers an enemy through brute force. As with the other strategies of distraction, we become tools in Satan's hand to crush and dominate others, keeping them from the grace of God.

This was the strategy that Satan employed in the events at the church where I was the guest speaker. Ironically, both the usher and myself were the channels through which Satan employed the strategy of overwhelming force. Each of us tried to put the other in our respective places while at the same time guarding our own. Both of us thought we were something and that the other was nothing. We were both wrong.

We were standing in a place set aside for the worship of God, and we could not get our minds off our own positions. Both of us tried to dominate the other, looking down from our lofty positions. Both of us were operating in the flesh. This same scene is played out with different characters in different settings every day and in many different arenas of life. We try to dominate one another in the workplace, in the family, and, most appallingly, in the church. Why? Because, though we are saved, there is still a part of us that is not submitted to God. We are living or walking in the flesh rather than in the spirit as spiritual people.

> *When we try to dominate one another,*
> *we are operating in the flesh.*

I say then: Walk in the Spirit, and you shall not fulfill the lust of the flesh. For the flesh lusts against the Spirit, and the Spirit against the flesh; and these are contrary to one another, so that you do not do the things that you wish. But if you are led by the Spirit, you are not under the law. (Galatians 5:16–18)

and,

For those who live according to the flesh set their minds on the things of the flesh, but those who live according to the Spirit, the things of the Spirit. For to be carnally minded is death, but to be spiritually minded is life and peace. (Romans 8:5–6)

We could say this another way: "The flesh ignores the spirit." To live by the flesh is to live by the same things that motivated us before we were saved: *"the lust of the flesh, the lust of the eyes* [mind], *and the pride of life"* (1 John 2:16). Look at the progression: flesh, mind, and pride, of which the latter is the fuel for the use of overwhelming force.

All of these are associated with the three strategies Satan uses to distract us from God. *Intimidation* has to do with the flesh, *manipulation* with the mind, and *domination* with pride or self-exaltation. If we look carefully, we will see Satan's full array of strategies employed throughout the Bible, even in his dealings with Jesus Himself.

> *So when the woman saw that the tree was good for food, that it was pleasant to the eyes, and a tree desirable to make one wise, she took of its fruit and ate.*   (Genesis 3:6)

Do you see the enemy's arsenal? Look at this verse more closely:

+ *"So when the woman saw that the tree was good for food."* This is the flesh.

+ *"It was pleasant to the eyes."* Here's the mind.

+ *"A tree desirable to make one wise."* This is pride.

We see the same strategies in the wilderness when the enemy tempted Jesus.

+ *"The devil said to Him, 'If You are the Son of God, command this stone to become bread'"* (Luke 4:3). This appeals to the flesh.

+ *"Then the devil, taking Him up on a high mountain, showed Him all the kingdoms of the world in a moment of time"* (verse 5). This appeals to the mind.

+ *"Then he brought Him to Jerusalem, set Him on the pinnacle of the temple, and said to Him, 'If You are the Son of God, throw Yourself down from here'"* (verse 9). This appeals to pride of position.

Pride is the result of thinking that we are more than we are.

Pride is a result of thinking that we are more than we are. It is Satan's oldest weapon. Again, he tells us, "You can be like God." Part of us believes him. When we believe him, we use our position to dominate other people. We *"bite and devour one another,"* as Paul said in Galatians 5:15.

OPPORTUNITIES FOR FORCE

Pride is an important issue because, in this strategy, we rob God of worship. Pride is, in effect, self-worship. If our eyes are on ourselves, then they will not be focused on the Lord. God cannot be seated on the thrones of our hearts if we are seated there ourselves. Satan does not always try to get us to worship him right away; sometimes he leads us to worship ourselves first, and we call that *pride.*

At no time does the strategy of overwhelming force have a greater opportunity than when we have been wounded in some way. When we are wounded, we remove our saintly suits and put on judge's robes. We feel that we have a right to judge the one who has wounded us, just as I did when the usher offended me. Our *flesh* is offended, our *mind* is distracted, and our *pride* takes over. "Here comes the judge!" But we are not carnal; we are spiritual creatures. When we are wounded, we are to restore in the Spirit rather than wound in the flesh.

> *My friends, if someone is caught in any kind of wrongdoing, those of you who are spiritual should set him right; but you must do it in a gentle way. And keep an eye on yourselves, so that you will not be tempted, too. Help carry one another's burdens, and in this way you will obey the law of Christ. If you think you are something when you are really nothing, you are only deceiving yourself.*
>
> (Galatians 6:1–3 GNT)

POSITION

The dangers and opportunities to use overwhelming force lurk in the hearts of leaders in the church as well. Some leaders don't want to be held accountable. Self-exalted people don't want to be disciplined. But all leaders are "under-shepherds" of the Good Shepherd, Jesus Christ. They are therefore accountable for their personal morals and attitudes toward the sheep, whom they are given the privilege of serving.

> But Jesus called them to Himself and said to them, "You know that those who are considered rulers over the Gentiles lord it over them, and their great ones exercise authority over them. Yet it shall not be so among you; but whoever desires to become great among you shall be your servant. And whoever of you desires to be first shall be slave of all. For even the Son of Man did not come to be served, but to serve, and to give His life a ransom for many." (Mark 10:42–45)

Anyone who knows anything should be able to discern that leadership and dictatorship are two different things, just as authority and domination are two different things. My example of this church visit could be replayed in the Sunday school department or anywhere else in the church where the people of God allow prideful thinking to direct their steps. Leaders in the church must remember that they are one of the sheep as well. They need to keep in mind that the flock belongs to God. The authority belongs to God. The worship and glory all belong to God. If we succumb to pride and self-exaltation, then we are on our own. The grace of God cannot flow to us or through us until we are submitted to Him. Grace always flows from the greater to the lesser.

> Yes, all of you be submissive to one another, and be clothed with humility, for "God resists the proud, but gives grace to the humble." Therefore humble yourselves under the mighty hand of God, that He may exalt you in due time, casting all your care upon Him, for He cares for you. (1 Peter 5:5–7)

HOW IS YOUR WALK?

How do we determine the character of our walk? Are we walking with people or over them? Are we walking in such a way that demonstrates the lordship of Christ in our lives? You and I must walk (live) in such a way so as to keep our eyes on God. We must walk by the Spirit, walk in love, and walk in humility.

WALK BY THE SPIRIT

> *I say then: Walk in the Spirit, and you shall not fulfill the lust of the flesh.* (Galatians 5:16)

When we are walking by the Spirit, we are living with eyes lifted toward heaven. We are walking as Jesus did, which means we make pleasing the Father our priority. We do not walk independently, but we take each step in the footprints of God's leading.

> *Most assuredly, I say to you, the Son can do nothing of Himself, but what He sees the Father do; for whatever He does, the Son also does in like manner....I can of Myself do nothing. As I hear, I judge; and My judgment is righteous, because I do not seek My own will but the will of the Father who sent Me.* (John 5:19, 30)

When we live by the Spirit, we live in a way that pleases God. We are no longer concerned with our own plans and our own image. Walking by the Spirit is a moment-by-moment decision to believe God. Our old iniquitous nature is gone; it has been buried with Christ. We are no longer subject to fear or manipulation. *"We were buried with Him through baptism into death, that just as Christ was raised from the dead by the glory of the Father, even so we also should walk in newness of life"* (Romans 6:4).

We must also walk in love.

WALK IN LOVE

> *Then one of them, a lawyer, asked Him a question, testing Him, and saying, "Teacher, which is the great commandment in the law?" Jesus said to him, "'You shall love the LORD your God with all your heart, with all your soul, and with all your mind.' This is the first and great commandment. And the second is like it: 'You shall love your neighbor as yourself.' On these two commandments hang all the Law and the Prophets."* (Matthew 22:35–40)

Love is the greatest law and governing principle of the kingdom of God. James called it *"the royal law"* in James 2:8. But, because it is everything opposite to the carnal nature of the old man, it must be contended for. God's kind of love is not a mere emotion; it is a conscious decision. We can set out each day determined to love regardless of the events and people we encounter. We can be predisposed toward an attitude of love. But this attitude is only possible when we believe that God loves us. Love is not our idea; it is God's. Because we are loved and secure, we can risk loving other people.

> *Love is not our idea; it's God's.*

> *Love has been perfected among us in this: that we may have boldness in the day of judgment; because as He is, so are we in this world. There is no fear in love; but perfect love casts out fear, because fear involves torment. But he who fears has not been made perfect in love. We love Him because He first loved us.*　　　　　(1 John 4:17–19)

Love is the answer to the foul stench of iniquity that gives entry to the enemy's warring ways and tactics. James said that lusts of mortal flesh literally *"war in* [our] *members"* (James 4:1). When we are born again and receive the Holy Spirit, God helps us overcome our anti-love nature, but it is a daily battle that we must choose to fight. The battle lines are drawn around our families, the church, the workplace, the grocery store, the bank—wherever there is the possibility and opportunity to express the love of God.

WALK IN HUMILITY

There has been much misunderstanding about humility. To be humble does not mean that we become doormats. To walk in humility means that we have a proper concept of God and of our relationship to Him. Also remember that those sitting and working around you weekly in your New Testament church are vessels of God's Holy Spirit, just as you are. When we walk by the Spirit, in love and humility, we are able to *"overcome evil with good"* (Romans 12:21) and *"cover a multitude of sins"* (James 5:20; 1 Peter 4:8). We are able to walk in grace, both receiving and extending it to others.

But He gives more grace. Therefore He says: "God resists the proud, but gives grace to the humble." Therefore submit to God. Resist the devil and he will flee from you. Draw near to God and He will draw near to you. Cleanse your hands, you sinners; and purify your hearts, you double-minded. Lament and mourn and weep! Let your laughter be turned to mourning and your joy to gloom. Humble yourselves in the sight of the Lord, and He will lift you up. (James 4:6–10)

God gives us *"more grace"*—as much as we need. God gives us more of Himself as we resist the devil and draw near to God. God lifts us up as we humble ourselves toward His throne. As we walk by the Spirit, in love and humility, we walk in the same grace that saved us, giving glory and honor to God.

Chapter 6

TAKING OUR STAND AGAINST THE ENEMY

Finally, my brethren, be strong in the Lord and in the power of His might. Put on the whole armor of God, that you may be able to stand against the wiles of the devil.
—Ephesians 6:10–11

There is no better example for how to live our lives as Christ's followers than Christ Himself. This makes perfect sense, yet we so frequently forget it and try to be Christlike without even looking first at the life of our Lord!

This holds true in all realms, including the realm of standing against the enemy. Jesus knows firsthand what it is like to undergo temptation and we should consider how He handled temptation when we face temptation ourselves. As Hebrews 4:15 reminds us, *"We do not have a High Priest who cannot sympathize with our weaknesses, but was in all points tempted as we are, yet without sin."*

Do you remember the Lord's wilderness experience? The call of ministry was heavy upon Him as John baptized Him, and then our Lord was led by the Spirit into the wilderness, where He was to be tempted by Satan. Just as Satan is eager to attack us today, he was all too ready to take on the challenge of tempting Christ on that day as well!

After Christ had been in the wilderness fasting for quite some time, the enemy made his move. Realizing that Christ was vulnerable and weakened with hunger, Satan tried enticing the Savior to succumb to lusts of the eye, lusts of the flesh, and pridefulness.

He first sought to play upon Jesus' hunger, insisting that Jesus prove his position in the kingdom by turning stones into bread. Christ, having spent time in his Father's presence, drew the sword of the Spirit to contend with His enemy, saying, *"It is written, 'Man shall not live by bread alone, but by every word that proceeds from the mouth of God'"* (Matthew 4:4).

Satan, seeing Jesus to be a worthy opponent, hurled another temptation at Him. He took Jesus to a high pinnacle and encouraged Him to throw Himself down, using distorted Scripture to convince Christ that it was a good idea, saying,

> *If You are the Son of God, throw Yourself down. For it is written: "He shall give His angels charge over you," and, "In their hands they shall bear you up, Lest you dash your foot against a stone."* (Matthew 4:6)

Again, Jesus was ready to strike back with the Word. *"It is written again,"* He said, *"'You shall not tempt the LORD your God'"* (verse 7).

The enemy, unhappy yet still too stubborn and prideful to accept defeat, took Jesus up a high mountain and showed Him all the kingdoms of the world. In his arrogance, the enemy said to Jesus, *"All these things I will give You if You will fall down and worship me"* (verse 9).

Satan often attacks when we are most vulnerable.

Christ, tired of the enemy's games, let the devil have it once more by fighting back with Scripture. *"Away with you, Satan! For it is written, 'You shall worship the LORD your God, and Him only you shall serve'"* (verse 10). Finally, Satan left the Savior in efforts to recuperate from the battle and plan his next assault.

TAKING OUR STAND AGAINST THE ENEMY 237

What do we learn from this passage? For one, we can see that Satan often chooses to attack when we are in our most vulnerable state. With Jesus, for instance, He waited until the Savior was weak with physical hunger before tempting Him to turn stone into bread. Satan still works the same way. He frequently waits until we are worn down, tired from other challenges, temptations, and trials, before he begins his assaults.

We also learn the key to standing strong against these assaults. Notice how Christ defeated Satan: He quoted Scripture. Even in His weakened state, Jesus was able to defeat Satan because He knew where to go for strength. He turned to His Father and His Father's Word, the Scriptures.

It would have been easy for Jesus to try to fight the battle on His own. How often do we try to "go it alone" when it comes to spiritual battles? Jesus could have easily done the same, but He turned to His Father and His Father's Word to help fight the battle. If Jesus, the very Son of God, turned to His Father and to Scriptures for help, shouldn't we do the same?

The apostle Paul told us that we are to *stand against the wiles of the devil.* If we are to stand against the enemy, it will not be in our own strength. We can only be *strong in the Lord and in the power of His might.* Warring against the enemy in our own strength is like sending a bunch of toddlers against an armored division. But in God we have not only protection, but also a means by which to attack and dismantle the strongholds of the enemy.

BE STRONG IN THE LORD

The key to dealing with the schemes of the enemy is to depend on the Lord rather than our own ability to defeat or outsmart him. It is by the grace of God alone that Satan is defeated. We will not overcome him with our own might and reason; the devil will not be reasonable, and, in reality, we possess nothing in ourselves with which to dispatch him. We must respect his power and call upon the wisdom of God to defeat him. Even the mighty archangel of God respected the power of Satan. As the book of Jude says, *"Michael the archangel, in contending with the devil, when he disputed about the body of Moses, dared not bring against him a reviling accusation, but said, 'The Lord rebuke you!'"* (Jude 9). If those who stand by

238 WITCHCRAFT IN THE PEWS AND SPIRITUAL WARFARE

the throne of God allow God to deal with Satan, then we probably should as well.

The word translated as *"wiles"* in Ephesians 6:11 is *methodeia,* from which we get our word *method.* A method is a predictable pattern that leads to a specific objective. Satan uses methods, which we have referred to as terrorism, psychological warfare, and overwhelming force, that, if allowed to continue, will divert glory from God.

Though we are involved in a violent battle, we have the assurance that the enemy ultimately will not prevail. We know from the Bible that the enemy is destined for destruction. For all his methods and tactics, he will ultimately fail.

> *The devil, who deceived them, was cast into the lake of fire and brimstone where the beast and the false prophet are. And they will be tormented day and night forever and ever.* (Revelation 20:10)

In the meantime, Satan is determined to oppress and destroy as many lives as possible. So, to effectively deal with the tactics of Satan, we must first understand that our battle is not one of the flesh, but of the spirit. We cannot win a spiritual battle by carnal means (using our own strength and intelligence). We will wear ourselves out by warring with our natural minds, and we will always lose. This is why 2 Corinthians 10:4 says, *"For the weapons of our warfare are not carnal but mighty in God for pulling down strongholds."*

Our ability in spiritual warfare is by the grace of God.

We have spent the previous chapters uncovering Satan's motives and methods. But unless we take Satan's deliberate and predictable strategy into account, he will take advantage of our ignorance and make us part of his plan. (See 2 Corinthians 2:11.) So now that we know what the enemy is up to, we can respond to his tactics by using what God has provided for this purpose.

The apostle Paul told us that we must *"stand against...the devil"* (Ephesians 6:11). This seems like a contradiction. How do we defeat an enemy by standing? To say that we stand, however, is to say that we are warring in the enabling grace of God rather than by human means. Just as we can make no boast about our salvation by grace, neither can we boast of our own ability in our warfare. Both are accomplished by the grace of God through Jesus Christ.

THE ARMOR OF GOD

In Paul's instructions in Ephesians 6, he told us that as we take our stand against the enemy, we must put on the *"whole armor of God."* He further explained which things we must *"put on"* and which things we must *"take up."* There are three things we *wear* and three things with which we *war*.

> *Finally, my brethren, be strong in the Lord and in the power of His might. Put on the whole armor of God, that you may be able to stand against the wiles of the devil. For we do not wrestle against flesh and blood, but against principalities, against powers, against the rulers of the darkness of this age, against spiritual hosts of wickedness in the heavenly places. Therefore take up the whole armor of God, that you may be able to withstand in the evil day, and having done all, to stand. Stand therefore, having girded your waist with truth, having put on the breastplate of righteousness, and having shod your feet with the preparation of the gospel of peace; above all, taking the shield of faith with which you will be able to quench all the fiery darts of the wicked one. And take the helmet of salvation, and the sword of the Spirit, which is the word of God; praying always with all prayer and supplication in the Spirit, being watchful to this end with all perseverance and supplication for all the saints; and for me.* (Ephesians 6:10–19)

The epistle to the Ephesians uses the words *"in Christ"* or their equivalent more than twenty times. Being "in Christ" means that we belong to Him, that we have submitted ourselves to Him as Lord. When Paul told us to put on the whole armor of God, he was referring to aspects of our being in Christ.

Ephesians 6:10–18 refers to six different items of armor that enable us to stand against the enemy's tactics. The first three items of our armor are related to our position in Christ. We have the *"truth"* of Christ, the *"righteousness"* of Christ, and the *"peace"* of Christ. These are all things that we must *"put on"* if we are to stand against the enemy. Galatians 3:27 tells us that if we have been baptized into Christ, then we have *"put on Christ."* These are the things we wear in Christ.

THE BELT OF TRUTH

All of the enemy's tactics depend upon deception and lies. Satan sprinkles just enough truth over his poison to draw his victims. As a result, many of God's children have bought into his lies. When a small mistruth is accepted, Satan adds another and then another until only the lie remains.

Jesus said that Satan was a liar from the beginning:

> *He was a murderer from the beginning, and does not stand in the truth, because there is no truth in him. When he speaks a lie, he speaks from his own resources, for he is a liar and the father of it.* (John 8:44)

The word for truth, *aletheia*, refers to what is true versus what is not true; to what is real versus what is false.

> *To stand against the enemy, we must prepare ourselves with truth.*

When we talk about having "girded our waists with truth," we are saying that if we are to stand against the enemy, we must prepare ourselves with the truth. To be prepared with truth means to be filled with the Scriptures. When we have filled ourselves with Scriptures, we are able to detect the deception of the enemy. The enemy's tactics of intimidation, manipulation, and domination cannot take us by surprise. When he tries to intimidate us, we remind him of the truth that God is in control. When he tries to manipulate our thoughts, we take those thoughts captive to the truth in Christ Jesus. When he tries to dominate us or dominate others through us, we remind ourselves of the truth that we live under the authority of Christ.

When Satan confronted Jesus in the wilderness, Jesus defeated him with the Word of God from the Torah and the Psalms. Jesus could have brought twelve legions of angels onto the scene (Matthew 26:53), but He overcame the enemy with three words: "It is written" (Matthew 4:4, 7, 10). Each time Satan manipulated and misquoted the Scriptures (and Satan can quote the Scriptures), Jesus spoke the truth of God's Word and removed the ground upon which Satan tried to stand. Satan had to leave Him alone.

Jesus gave us the pattern to follow. Don't fight hand to hand with the devil; instead, "submit to God. Resist the devil and he will flee from you" (James 4:7). Truth can and must be appropriated from the Scriptures if we are to defeat the lies of the devil. We must gird, or prepare ourselves, with the truth that we are in Christ.

THE BREASTPLATE OF RIGHTEOUSNESS

A second item that we put on is the righteousness of Christ. We need to remember whose armor we are wearing—it belongs to Christ. So first we prepare ourselves for battle with the truth of God's Word, and then we put on the righteousness of Christ.

We cannot earn righteousness (right standing before God). One of the lies of the devil is that we must work *for* salvation. In reality, we only work *out* our salvation (Philippians 2:12). The enemy, though, tries to keep us distracted so that we don't "occupy" the world for the kingdom of God (Luke 19:13 KJV).

God gives us His own righteousness by the blood of Jesus Christ. We have been "justified [made right with God] by faith, we have peace with God through our Lord Jesus Christ" (Romans 5:1). When we wear the righteousness of Christ, we are not crippled and preoccupied by trying to work for what God has already freely given us. We are able to stand in the righteousness of Jesus Christ and pursue His purpose.

Putting on the breastplate of righteousness means that we go into battle with confidence in what Jesus Christ has done for us. Note that the breastplate covers our hearts. When we don the breastplate of Christ's righteousness, we are able to stand with confidence each time the enemy tries to keep us busy with thoughts about our own unworthiness. We stand wearing the worthiness of Jesus Christ. When the enemy tries to manipulate us by planting doubts as to our salvation and relationship with Christ, we can show him a blood-soaked cross and an empty tomb.

THE GOSPEL OF PEACE

Now, having put on the *truth* of who we are in Christ and having been clothed with the *righteousness* of Christ, we put on the *peace* of Christ. Having our feet shod with the Good News of peace in Christ means that we are able to walk, or live, a life of peace in Christ. The Hebrew word for peace, *shalom*, means wholeness. It is in Christ that we are made whole. The enemy may taunt us with plaguing fears or bring up our past sins and failures, but all of these and more are settled in Christ Jesus.

Peace comes from the presence of the Holy Spirit and allows us to live effectively in the midst of turmoil. The peace of God surpasses human understanding, allowing us to know that God has everything in hand. Peace is the bequest of Jesus Christ to all those who trust Him.

> *Peace I leave with you, My peace I give to you; not as the world gives do I give to you. Let not your heart be troubled, neither let it be afraid.*
> (John 14:27)

and,

> *These things I have spoken to you, that in Me you may have peace. In the world you will have tribulation; but be of good cheer, I have overcome the world.*
> (John 16:33)

Christ has removed all cause for fear.

In Christ we are neither in fear nor in trouble. He has removed all cause for fear. He has overcome every weapon and strategy of the enemy by His own blood. It is inevitable that we will encounter the schemes of the enemy, but Christ has made it possible for us to walk and live in the peace of our position in Christ.

So there are three things that we put on in order to stand against the enemy: the *truth* of who we are in Christ, the *righteousness* of Christ, and the *peace* of Christ. There are now three things that we must *"take up"* to war against the enemy.

THE SHIELD OF FAITH

A shield is something that we stand behind to protect us from the enemy's attack. It must be taken into the hand. Paul told us that we use this shield of faith to extinguish the fiery darts that the enemy throws at us. What are these darts? They are the very tactics and strategies of the enemy that we have discussed in this book. They are his strategies of terror, psychological warfare, and overwhelming force. Taking up the shield of faith is trusting in all the things we just spoke of: putting on truth, righteousness, and peace in Christ.

Faith is the gateway to the enabling grace of God. We are saved by grace through faith (Ephesians 2:8). We also war by grace through faith. The one who trusts or depends on the Lord trusts in what He has said in His Word.

> *As for God, His way is perfect; the word of the LORD is proven; He is a shield to all who trust in Him.* (Psalm 18:30)

and,

> *Those who trust in the LORD are like Mount Zion, which cannot be moved, but abides forever.* (Psalm 125:1)

and,

> *Every word of God is pure; He is a shield to those who put their trust in Him.* (Proverbs 30:5)

and,

You will keep him in perfect peace, whose mind is stayed on You, because he trusts in You. Trust in the LORD forever, for in YAH, the LORD, is everlasting strength. (Isaiah 26:3–4)

and,

Blessed is the man who trusts in the LORD, and whose hope is the LORD. For he shall be like a tree planted by the waters, which spreads out its roots by the river, and will not fear when heat comes; but its leaf will be green, and will not be anxious in the year of drought, nor will cease from yielding fruit. (Jeremiah 17:7–8)

If we are to stand against the enemy, we must believe in all that we have put on in Jesus Christ.

THE HELMET OF SALVATION

When Paul spoke about putting on the helmet of salvation, he was referring to protecting our minds. Hope is the anticipation of God's goodness. When we take up the helmet of salvation, we are filling our minds with the hope that it is God's intention to redeem and save all people everywhere.

The helmet of salvation is linked in Scripture with hope and deliverance.

He saw that there was no man, and wondered that there was no intercessor; therefore His own arm brought salvation for Him; and His own righteousness, it sustained Him. For He put on righteousness as a breastplate, and a helmet of salvation on His head; He put on the garments of vengeance for clothing, and was clad with zeal as a cloak. (Isaiah 59:16–17)

and,

But let us who are of the day be sober, putting on the breastplate of faith and love, and as a helmet the hope of salvation. (1 Thessalonians 5:8)

As we war against the enemy, we do so knowing that it is God's intention to redeem all of creation. Isaiah 59 refers to God's deliverance of Israel, but it also speaks prophetically of Jesus Christ in His vengeance against the enemies of God. Jesus was born to destroy the works and tactics of the enemy (1 John 3:8). We read that all of creation groans with this reality (Romans 8:22). It is with this hope that we wage war against the enemy. It is through knowing this reality that we can wage a confident war against Satan. Setbacks may come, but the war is already won, and those in Christ are on the winning side.

> *Hope is the anticipation of God's goodness.*

On D-Day, June 6, 1944, the Allied armies landed at Normandy. It took them a long time to establish a beachhead and then move into the land to rout the forces of Nazi Germany. Though the war would go on for another year, Hitler's fate was sealed on D-Day. So it is with Satan. There are battles yet to be fought; there will still be causalities; but the outcome has never been in doubt. The cross of Christ was Satan's D-Day, and the "D" in this case stands for his defeat.

If we are to stand against the enemy, we must be sure of God's heart and intention. His heart is focused on salvation and His intention is to fill the earth with His glory. When we are confident of this, we can stand unaffected by the distractions of the enemy.

> *But truly, as I live, all the earth shall be filled with the glory of the* LORD. (Numbers 14:21)

THE SWORD OF THE WORD

The last article with which we war is the Word of God. The Greek word translated as *"word"* is *rhema*. The *rhema* of God is the Spirit-activated and inspired Word. It is the declaration of Scripture to address specific situations and obstacles. Here, we are referring to the Word of God being spoken against the power and strongholds of the enemy. It is the Word, the *rhema*, that destroys those prideful things lifted up against God referred to in 2 Corinthians 10. So how do we handle this sword? Through our mouths.

> *And He has made My mouth like a sharp sword.* (Isaiah 49:2)

and,

> *For the word of God is living and powerful, and sharper than any two-edged sword, piercing even to the division of soul and spirit, and of joints and marrow, and is a discerner of the thoughts and intents of the heart.* (Hebrews 4:12)

The Word of God is called the sword of the Spirit because it can be spoken under the inspiration of the Holy Spirit to address a specific issue. When the enemy speaks fear, the Word speaks faith. When the enemy speaks failure, the Word speaks purpose. When the enemy speaks diversion, the Word speaks devotion. In all, the *rhema* of God is wielded as an offensive weapon to cut down the enemy tactics that distract and divert us from fellowship with God.

With all the articles of God's armor in place, we are able to stand against Satan. As we wear and war with all God has provided, we destroy the power of the enemy to the glory and honor of God.

DISCERNMENT

> *Praying always with all prayer and supplication in the Spirit, being watchful to this end with all perseverance and supplication for all the saints.* (Ephesians 6:18)

Now that we know what the enemy is doing and the countermeasures we have in Christ, we need to be able to recognize when Satan is prowling about. To this end, God gives us discernment, so that we might live godly lives in an antichrist world system. Worldly lust, carnality, and false teaching bombard us every day. We are virtually surrounded by enemy activity everywhere we go—and we need discernment to recognize and overcome it.

All of us exercise discernment to one degree or another. Sometimes we have a "feeling" that something is "just not right." We can't put a finger on why, but somehow an inner voice, an inner knowing, lets us know. We may reason that this feeling is only a coincidence or something from our rational minds when, in fact, what is at work is discernment.

THE BATTLE FOR THE MIND

There is a conflict going on in the battleground of our minds. It is a war between flesh and spirit, between obedience and disobedience. One leads toward death and the other toward life and peace in God. If we are in a situation and have to question our motivation, then the fact that we even had to ask ourselves the source of our thoughts or feelings may be an indication that all is not as it should be. If I have to ask myself whether or not something is true, then it may be untrue in some aspect.

Paul told us that there are two directions in which we can set our minds.

> *For those who live according to the flesh set their minds on the things of the flesh, but those who live according to the Spirit, the things of the Spirit. For to be carnally minded is death, but to be spiritually minded is life and peace. Because the carnal mind is enmity against God.*
>
> (Romans 8:5–7)

Satan, operating through the flesh, always leads us toward pleasing ourselves, while God always leads us toward pleasing Him. These two are as opposite as they can be. What is of God leads us to life and peace. What is of the flesh, motivated by iniquity, leads to separation from God, which leads to death. In John 8:44, Jesus described the devil as a *"murderer"* (one who robs us of life) and as a *"liar"* (in other words, he speaks for his own purposes of distraction and diversion from God).

Discernment is that "God part" of us that warns us when we come into a demonic setting. The children of God are able to sense the clashing of God's truth versus Satan's counterfeit. God's purpose in discernment is to allow us to participate in those things that are of God and to avoid the snares of the devil. Paul desired that we would walk in discernment and thus give no offense to God.

And this I pray, that your love may abound still more and more in knowledge and all discernment, that you may approve the things that are excellent, that you may be sincere and without offense till the day of Christ. (Philippians 1:9–10)

We can clearly differentiate between what is from God and what is from the enemy by observing the attitude or direction of the words or thoughts involved. I would suggest a few "attitude indicators" here. The following is not a complete listing, but it includes some of the most obvious ones. Note the contrasting feelings that occur depending on whether God or the enemy is at work.

The Enemy at Work	God at Work
I feel pushed.	I feel invited.
I feel panic.	I feel peace.
I feel confused.	I feel clarity.
I feel condemned.	I feel confronted.
I feel insecure.	I feel loved.
I feel powerless.	I feel confident.

In addition to feelings or emotions, we also must examine the *character* of what we think and how we act. James gave us a way to determine the origin of our thoughts. Are they from God, or do they feed carnal lust?

Who is wise and understanding among you? Let him show by good conduct that his works are done in the meekness of wisdom. But if you have bitter envy and self-seeking in your hearts, do not boast and lie against the truth. This wisdom does not descend from above, but is earthly, sensual, demonic. For where envy and self-seeking exist, confusion and every evil thing are there. But the wisdom that is from above is first pure, then peaceable, gentle, willing to yield, full of mercy and good fruits, without partiality and without hypocrisy. Now the fruit of righteousness is sown in peace by those who make peace. (James 3:13–18)

James described the wisdom or thoughts that stem from our old carnal nature (inspired by the enemy) as bitter, envious, self-seeking, lying, earthly, sensual, demonic, confusing, and evil. On the other hand, he said the wisdom from God is pure, peaceable, gentle, yielding, merciful, fruitful, impartial, and honest. The contrast and the sources are clear. We are not responsible to hold on to the thoughts and attitudes that stem from the enemy's tactics. When we encounter thoughts that are not from God, we must respond by taking those thoughts captive, referring them back to God, and giving them no further consideration. We must refuse the enemy at the door and not let him into our houses.

We must examine the character of what we think and how we act.

> *Now we have received, not the spirit of the world, but the Spirit who is from God, that we might know the things that have been freely given to us by God. These things we also speak, not in words which man's wisdom teaches but which the Holy Spirit teaches, comparing spiritual things with spiritual.* (1 Corinthians 2:12–13)

STAND FIRM

Take your stand against the enemy. Wrap yourself in the truth, righteousness, and peace of Jesus Christ. Speak the Word of God incisively in the face of the enemy. Remind him whose armor you are wearing while you stand firm against him.

> *Now to Him who is able to keep you from stumbling, and to present you faultless before the presence of His glory with exceeding joy, to God our Savior, who alone is wise, be glory and majesty, dominion and power, both now and forever. Amen.* (Jude 24–25)

Chapter 7

THE LAST WORD ON WAR

Spiritual warrior, understand this. When we are in the heat of battle, God isn't scratching His head trying to figure how He will bring us victory. He knows the war we are in; He brought us into the fray, and we are standing in His power and anointing. Even though we will encounter the devil everywhere we go, he is no match for the truth of God's Word. Remember, too, that as we grow and learn new levels in God, we also will encounter new resistance. It goes, according to a saying I've heard, "New level, new devil."

Despite this resistance, you can oppose evil with confidence because God's faithfulness and ability in battle have been proven throughout the millennia. Scripture is full of God's victories over Satan, as well as the victories of His followers.

These stories of victory can encourage us as we battle against unseen forces. They can build us up when we feel that defeat is imminent. Most importantly, they can show us where our power comes from and how unlimited that source, God, is.

Battle by battle, throughout Scripture and throughout the history of His church, God has shown and continues to show His true might. Even with all His victories, these battles are but a foretaste of the final victory at the end of the age, when Satan will be defeated one final time.

MOSES VERSUS PHARAOH

When the Israelites were enslaved in Egypt, God sent Moses to deliver them. He had Moses perform various signs to convince Pharaoh of God's power and authenticity. At first, Pharaoh's magicians and astrologers performed similar signs, but God always showed Himself more powerful.

> *So Moses and Aaron went in to Pharaoh, and they did so, just as the* *LORD* *commanded. And Aaron cast down his rod before Pharaoh and before his servants, and it became a serpent. But Pharaoh also called the wise men and the sorcerers; so the magicians of Egypt, they also did in like manner with their enchantments. For every man threw down his rod, and they became serpents. But Aaron's rod swallowed up their rods.* (Exodus 7:10–12)

When this did not convince Pharaoh, God took things up a notch and sent ten plagues. The magicians felt they were equal to the plagues of blood and of frogs, but when God sent lice, even the magicians had to admit that the power working through Moses was greater than any trick of theirs.

Battle by battle, God has shown His true might.

> *Now the magicians so worked with their enchantments to bring forth lice, but they could not. So there were lice on man and beast. Then the magicians said to Pharaoh, "This is the finger of God."* (Exodus 8:18–19)

From this point on, the magicians are not mentioned again. They were no longer able to duplicate the plagues God sent, and perhaps they even stopped trying.

When Moses took on Pharaoh's astrologers and magicians, the power of God humiliated them with an utter defeat.

ELIJAH VERSUS BAAL

In the great showdown between Elijah and the prophets of Baal on Mount Carmel, God sent fire from heaven to show His power in Israel. The prophets of Baal called on their god for hours, shouting and cutting themselves with swords, with no results. But when Elijah called on the true God, things went differently.

First Elijah repaired the ruined altar of the Lord, rebuilding it with twelve stones—one for each of the Israelite tribes. Then he placed the wood and his sacrifice on the altar. At this point, he was expected to call on God to burn the sacrifice, but he wasn't done yet. He ordered four large jars of water to be poured on the sacrifice and on the wood. When this was done, he asked for four more jars, and then again for four more. Scripture says that the water ran down around the altar, even filling the trench around it. Then Elijah prayed a simple prayer.

> Elijah the prophet came near and said, "LORD God of Abraham, Isaac, and Israel, let it be known this day that You are God in Israel and I am Your servant, and that I have done all these things at Your word. Hear me, O LORD, hear me, that this people may know that You are the LORD God, and that You have turned their hearts back to You again." Then the fire of the LORD fell and consumed the burnt sacrifice, and the wood and the stones and the dust, and it licked up the water that was in the trench. (1 Kings 18:36–38)

God answered Elijah's prayer. He made it known that He was God, and that day the people fell on their faces, saying, "The LORD, He is God! The LORD, He is God" (verse 39).

THE HEBREW CHILDREN VERSUS NEBUCHADNEZZAR'S COURT

After Nebuchadnezzar, the king of Babylon, overthrew Jerusalem, he asked for any promising young men who were strong and intelligent to be brought to the king's palace to serve at his court and be assimilated into Babylonian culture. Daniel and his friends Hananiah, Mishael, and Azariah were some of these promising men. However, not only were they strong and intelligent, as Nebuchadnezzar had required, they were also determined to continue living by God's laws rather than the laws of their new home. When they were brought food from the king's table, they refused to be defiled (the first portion of the king's food was offered to idols and therefore contaminated) and instead chose to eat vegetables. Because of their continual obedience, God blessed them with wisdom and knowledge.

When they were brought to Nebuchadnezzar's court so that Nebuchadnezzar could interview them, God demonstrated to the king that His power was ten times greater than the power of his magicians and astrologers, who used power from Satan.

> *Then the king interviewed them, and among them all none was found like Daniel, Hananiah, Mishael, and Azariah; therefore they served before the king. And in all matters of wisdom and understanding about which the king examined them, he found them ten times better than all the magicians and astrologers who were in all his realm.*
>
> (Daniel 1:19–20)

PHILIP, PETER, AND JOHN VERSUS SIMON

In the earliest days of the church, Christians were persecuted harshly. As a result, the apostles and followers of Christ were often scattered throughout Roman territory and beyond. During such a time of scattering, Philip started a crusade in the city of Samaria.

Samaria was the city where the wicked queen Jezebel instituted Baal worship in Israel. (See 1 Kings 16:29–32.) Elijah destroyed her prophets and mocked Satan's worship nine hundred years before Philip brought the Gospel into the city. But by the time Philip arrived, Satan's witchcraft had re-rooted and many of its inhabitants were under curses or spells. That is, until Philip entered, and later John and Peter.

> *Then Philip went down to the city of Samaria and preached Christ to them. And the multitudes with one accord heeded the things spoken by Philip, hearing and seeing the miracles which he did. For unclean spirits, crying with a loud voice, came out of many who were possessed; and many who were paralyzed and lame were healed. And there was great joy in that city.*
>
> (Acts 8:5–8)

Now, there was a great sorcerer named Simon living in Samaria at the time (the same one we discussed earlier). After he heard that the Spirit of God had delivered many from demon possession and physical sickness, he wanted to find out about and obtain this power that was greater than his.

Simon had seen the demonstration of God's power and received the Gospel; he had believed and was baptized. However, when Peter and John came down from Jerusalem to minister to Samaria's converts, Simon sought to buy God's power.

Peter rebuked Simon's gall and iniquity, driving the new convert in prayer to his knees, saying, *"Pray to the Lord for me, that none of the things which you have spoken may come upon me"* (Acts 8:24).

Judging from Simon's fear and from his strong desire to buy the power of the Holy Spirit, we can only assume that God's power was greater than any he had seen before.

PAUL VERSUS ELYMAS

God will let His Word be heard by those who desire to hear it, no matter what evil forces stand in the way. When Elymas the sorcerer opposed Paul on the island of Paphos, trying to prevent Paul from sharing the Gospel with his fellow sorcerer, the Spirit of God struck Elymas blind.

Now when they had gone through the island to Paphos, they found a certain sorcerer, a false prophet, a Jew whose name was Bar-Jesus, who was with the proconsul, Sergius Paulus, an intelligent man. This man called for Barnabas and Saul and sought to hear the word of God. But Elymas the sorcerer (for so his name is translated) withstood them, seeking to turn the proconsul away from the faith. Then Saul, who also is called Paul, filled with the Holy Spirit, looked intently at him and said, "O full of all deceit and all fraud, you son of the devil, you enemy of all righteousness, will you not cease perverting the straight ways of the Lord? And now, indeed, the hand of the Lord is upon you, and you shall be blind, not seeing the sun for a time." And immediately a dark mist fell on him, and he went around seeking someone to lead him by the hand. Then the proconsul believed, when he saw what had been done, being astonished at the teaching of the Lord. (Acts 13:6–12)

Paul was doing God's will when he encountered this practitioner of witchcraft. When the sorcerer came against him, the Holy Spirit empowered Paul's words and he was the victor.

> *God will let His Word be heard by those who desire to hear it.*

PAUL AND SILAS VERSUS THE CRAFT

When Paul and Silas ministered in Philipi, they met a slave girl possessed with a spirit of divination. Remember, divination is the practice of using the stars and evil spirits to foretell the future.

> *Now it happened, as we went to prayer, that a certain slave girl possessed with a spirit of divination met us, who brought her masters much profit by fortune-telling. This girl followed Paul and us, and cried out, saying, "These men are the servants of the Most High God, who proclaim to us the way of salvation." And this she did for many days. But Paul, greatly annoyed, turned and said to the spirit, "I command you in the name of Jesus Christ to come out of her." And he came out that very hour. But when her masters saw that their hope of profit was gone, they seized Paul and Silas and dragged them into the marketplace to the authorities.* (Acts 16:16–19)

This fortune-teller, as we would call her today, worked for a group of men who marketed her services. But when Paul cast out the evil spirits from this girl, she could no longer see the future. Once he detected the girl's demonic disturbance, he declared, *"I command you in the name of Jesus Christ to come out of her!"* And the girl was free. That's power.

THE BATTLE IS WON

These accounts serve to show us the power God has invested in His church to destroy Satan's works. They also show us what happens when the demonic hosts of witchcraft are confronted by the power of God. As you continue to study the Scriptures closely, you can see how God's power has been resident throughout history to destroy Satan's power.

As saints of the Most High God, we should know that the hand of God is always with us. We must allow our prayers to ascend into heaven as incense every day. And we should pray for, support, and exhort others who stand up against Satan and his demonic kingdom.

As Christians, we have the gift and ability—through Christ—to cast out devils and destroy Satan's works. It's time to use it.

Chapter 8

BEFORE THE THRONE
OF GOD

We began Chapter One by describing a scene at the throne of God. Lucifer, the anointed cherub, was distracted by his own beauty and turned away from God. In that moment, the crookedness of iniquity was born. The serpent then infected man with this same diversionary crookedness at the Fall. Man believed Satan's lie that he could *"be like God"* (Genesis 5:3).

Lucifer, now Satan the accuser, uses strategies of *intimidation, manipulation,* and *domination* to draw us away from God. He works these strategies in us and sometimes through us to rob God of our fellowship and worship. Regardless of the particular strategy he uses, the enemy's objective is to shift our attention from God to ourselves. It is important to note, once again, that all sin is not the result of direct satanic involvement. Some of it is the influence of our iniquitous old nature, which is innately prone to sin. To ascribe all sin to Satan is to give him too much glory.

We have seen how the enemy's strategies work. We have learned how to stand against him by putting on the armor of God in Christ Jesus. As we conclude this study, we bring the issues of iniquity and warfare full circle, back to the throne where it all began. Why? We must understand that the war we fight is ultimately won at the throne of God. Our victory is by God's sovereign grace. Regardless of our efforts or obedience, our restoration is the product of God's love and compassion.

> *Our restoration is the product of*
> *God's love and compassion.*

CHANGING CLOTHES IN HEAVEN'S COURT

The prophet Zechariah described a scene that demonstrates a change in our nature from one of uncleanness to one of holiness by God's own design. The throne room where iniquity was born now becomes a court-room where it is removed.

> *Then he showed me Joshua the high priest standing before the Angel of the LORD, and Satan standing at his right hand to oppose him. And the LORD said to Satan, "The LORD rebuke you, Satan! The LORD who has chosen Jerusalem rebuke you! Is this not a brand plucked from the fire?" Now Joshua was clothed with filthy garments, and was stand-ing before the Angel. Then He answered and spoke to those who stood before Him, saying, "Take away the filthy garments from him." And to him He said, "See, I have removed your iniquity from you, and I will clothe you with rich robes." And I said, "Let them put a clean turban on his head." So they put a clean turban on his head, and they put the clothes on him. And the Angel of the LORD stood by.*
> (Zechariah 3:1–5)

As we enter the scene, we see Joshua standing before the throne of God. He stands as a priest in proxy for the nation of Israel, which had departed from God. In another sense, Joshua represents all of us who draw near to God by the blood of Jesus Christ. He stands before the throne in clothes stained as with dung. These stains represent the iniquity that sep-arates man from God. Each stain represents a step off the path of God's ways.

WE ARE CHARGED

The accuser stands by us to bring charges against us. Satan is a legal-ist; he's the prosecuting attorney in heaven's courtroom. He knows the law well. It is he who roams the earth looking for those he might accuse before God, as he did with Job. (See Job 1:6–11; 2:1–5.) He loves to whisper the record of our sin in our ears to bring shame and cause us to hide from God. Ironically, he inspires the very deeds that he now presents as evidence against us. He points to each stain on our robes, reminding us that we listened to him. *"Adultery, fornication, uncleanness, lewdness, idolatry, sorcery, hatred, contentions, jealousies, outbursts of wrath, selfish ambitions, dissensions, heresies, envy, murders, drunkenness, revelries"* (Galatians 5:19–21)—these are the charges that the accuser brings against us. And what is worse, he is telling the truth! We are all guilty before the bench of heaven's court.

We stand before God as *"unclean...and all our righteousnesses are like filthy rags"* (Isaiah 64:6). Just as his praise filled the halls of heaven in eternity past, now the accuser spews forth the fruit of his own treason before God. As Satan drones his list of infractions, the Lord stops him with a sudden rebuke. The Lord declares to the accuser, "Enough! Enough! God has chosen man to abide with Him." God has seen our deeds of the flesh and has chosen to be gracious to us. He has seen our dung-spattered rags, yet, in His mercy, He smothers Satan's railing account. "Enough!"

WE ARE CHANGED

As we stand before the throne, the Lord issues His decree: "Take off those filthy rags and put royal robes on him." In an instant, our contemptible clothing is removed from us at God's command. This is more than a temporary change of wardrobe; it is the permanent removal of the iniquity that has controlled us since that moment in the Garden, thousands of years ago. Our filth is removed to the trash heap, and we stand before God restored.

We do not stand naked in heaven, however. God orders the attendants of heaven's court to place a priestly crown on our heads. God begins the process of renewing our minds so that we might live holy in this new state of glory. Instead of our thoughts being filled with self, they are now focused on God and His glory. Then God orders that royal, festive robes be put on us—robes of celebration and praise. Note that it is not we who clothe ourselves, but it is the Lord who covers us. It is not by our effort or perfection that we stand in God's presence; it is by His decision alone. We are clothed with His righteousness simply because He loves us and wants us there.

> *God takes off our filthy rags and dresses*
> *us in royal robes.*

We no longer live according to the spattered rags that we wore. We are no longer bound to walk that crooked trail blazed by our fathers. We *"have no obligation whatever to [our] old sinful nature to do what it begs [us] to do"* (Romans 8:12 TLB). Instead, we have access to the throne of God in the Spirit. We are free to be devoted to God, to worship without distraction at His throne. We are restored to that place of fellowship that Adam enjoyed with God at first. Satan's rebellion has been crushed!

Now restored to God, we can turn aside the tactics of Satan and refuse to be employed in his designs. When that desire of our old nature wells up to attack another, we can say "No!" Now, when we are given a door to watch (like the lady usher I spoke of), we no longer guard it as our own possession, but keep it as an act of worship to the Lord.

PEACE DECLARED

How can this be? Zechariah told us that it is by the *"Branch."* *"For behold, I am bringing forth My Servant the Branch"* (Zechariah 3:8). The *"Branch"* is the Lord Jesus Himself, who was cast into the bitter waters of our iniquity to sweeten them.

God is a holy God, and He cannot abide defilement of any sort. His holiness demands perfection—a perfection that we are unable to supply. God says, *"By those who come near Me I must be regarded as holy; and before all the people I must be glorified"* (Leviticus 10:3). Since we are incapable of being holy or providing holiness, God has provided His own righteousness and holiness for us. The prophet Isaiah said, *"His own arm brought salvation for Him; and His own righteousness, it sustained Him"* (Isaiah 59:16).

Jesus hung on the tree, suspended between earth and glory. By the Cross He removed the curse of our iniquity and paid for each stain of our sin. We enter into His finished work through repentance and faith toward God. The curse of iniquity is removed by confessing and believing in God's provision in Christ Jesus.

> *That if you confess with your mouth the Lord Jesus and believe in your heart that God has raised Him from the dead, you will be saved. For with the heart one believes unto righteousness, and with the mouth confession is made unto salvation.*   (Romans 10:9–10)

and,

> *Christ has redeemed us from the curse of the law, having become a curse for us (for it is written, "Cursed is everyone who hangs on a tree"), that the blessing of Abraham might come upon the Gentiles in Christ Jesus, that we might receive the promise of the Spirit through faith.*
> (Galatians 3:13–14)

Jesus became a curse on the cross so we could evict the devil from our lives and destroy iniquity. He was wounded so we could be healed. He took upon Himself all the sins of the world with us in mind. He has brought healing to our hearts and enabled us to live a God-pleasing life before the throne of God.

> *Beloved, if our heart does not condemn us, we have confidence toward God. And whatever we ask we receive from Him, because we keep His commandments and do those things that are pleasing in His sight.*
> (1 John 3:21–22)

Whatever we were, Jesus became our exchange. When we accept the fact that Jesus is Lord to the glory of God the Father, and when we take captive the devil's lies to the truth of God, Satan must scamper out of the courtroom in Jesus' name!

LIVING BEFORE THE THRONE

The Lord tells us that there are two facets to our living before the throne of God in this restored state. He said, *"If you will walk in My ways,"* and *"If you will keep My command"* (Zechariah 3:7).

WALKING IN HIS WAYS

Even we believers have walked in our own ways. In other words, we have lived to please ourselves. You may say, "Wait a minute. I've done good things for God. I've gone to church and given of my money. I've served the Lord on this or that committee, and I handed out food to the needy." These and all the other things we do are good things. But *for whom* did we do them? Did we do them to appear righteous? Who has gotten the glory for all that we have done? Do we call attention to ourselves, even in a small way, as we do these good things? Do we ever look in the mirror to approve some new level of righteousness we have attained? Do we ever criticize anyone else for not doing the good things we have done? Do we delight in the recognition and status of titles we have attained in the church? Do we ever do these good things anonymously? These are some hard questions, but the answers will determine the actual motivation behind our lives and ministries.

> *God should not be a sentimental afterthought, but rather the focus of all we do.*

When God tells us to walk in His ways, He is telling us that we are to live a "throne-ward" life. We are to live to please and glorify God. He is not a sentimental afterthought; rather, He is the focus of all that we do.

When a farmer plows a field, he fixes his eyes on a point at the end of the row. Then, as he plows, he moves straight toward that point. If he were to take his eyes off that distant point, he would plow a crooked line and end up planting crooked rows. Similarly, when we walk in the ways of God, we say that He is the point at which we are aiming. We are focused on God and His glory. We do not turn aside to grab a little recognition for ourselves. Each time we do walk in our own way, or live for ourselves, we plow in the crookedness of iniquity. When we are secure in Christ, however, we no longer have to grab anything for ourselves. We can walk straight toward Him in everything we do.

Jesus told us,

When you do a charitable deed, do not let your left hand know what
your right hand is doing, that your charitable deed may be in secret;
and your Father who sees in secret will Himself reward you openly.
(Matthew 6:3–4)

To walk in the way of God is to fix our eyes upon Jesus and the throne of God. Remember that the basis for Satan's strategies is pleasing ourselves, admiring ourselves, and focusing on ourselves. But now, through Christ Jesus, we are free to center our lives on God, as before the Fall.

KEEPING HIS COMMAND

To *"keep the command of the Lord"* (2 Chronicles 13:11) refers to living a life of listening to God. A command is something God has spoken to us. The lives of all who followed God in the Bible and in history were characterized by their listening to or hearing God and then responding in obedience. Abraham heard the voice of God and founded a family. Moses heard the voice of God and delivered a nation. Jesus heard the voice of the Father and redeemed the world. Keeping the command of God also requires that we realize we live in a dynamic relationship with God. God is always speaking and always moving, so we must always be listening and responding to what we hear.

When the Lord spoke to Joshua, the high priest, about keeping His command, He also was referring to the conduct of His house. God has established each of us in a ministry of His house. To follow the command of God, we must be faithful to and minister in the place where the Lord has established us. Many try to assume a place that God has not given them. The motivation for such ministry is not grounded in devotion to God and is not the result of hearing God but, rather, of following their own whims. This is perhaps one of the greatest areas of opportunity for Satan to influence the church. Even the great apostle Paul ministered in a particular *"sphere"* that God granted to him.

For we are not overextending ourselves (as though our authority did
not extend to you), for it was to you that we came with the gospel of
Christ; not boasting of things beyond measure, that is, in other men's
labors, but having hope, that as your faith is increased, we shall be

greatly enlarged by you in our sphere, to preach the gospel in the regions beyond you, and not to boast in another man's sphere of accomplishment. But "he who glories, let him glory in the LORD." For not he who commends himself is approved, but whom the Lord commends.

(2 Corinthians 10:14–18)

We must ask ourselves, "Where would God have us minister in the body of Christ?" God is calling and equipping us to minister in whatever true burdens He has put before us. Jesus did not go around ministering wherever and whatever He wanted. No, He spoke only the words of His Father and did only what He saw the Father doing. If we are living a "throne-ward" life, then the burdens of God will become ours as well, and we will minister in His enabling grace rather than from our own ability. Jesus spoke of the correlation between relationship with God and ministry:

God is calling and equipping us to minister in whatever burdens He has put before us.

Then Jesus answered and said to them, "Most assuredly, I say to you, the Son can do nothing of Himself, but what He sees the Father do; for whatever He does, the Son also does in like manner. For the Father loves the Son, and shows Him all things that He Himself does; and He will show Him greater works than these, that you may marvel."

(John 5:19–20)

and,

Do you not believe that I am in the Father, and the Father in Me? The words that I speak to you I do not speak on My own authority; but the Father who dwells in Me does the works.   (John 14:10)

How will we know when we minister beyond our sphere—when we have not kept the command of the Lord? We will know it if we find ourselves pushing someone else aside to gain a position. We will know it when we begin to yearn for the titles men give to us rather than to please God.

We will know it when we have no peace and no fruit born of our ministry. We will know it when we catch ourselves telling others in the body how important we are and calling ourselves by official titles. It is enough to serve the Lord. Jesus taught His disciples that we should wait to be asked to move up to another position at the table. He said,

> When you are invited, go and sit down in the lowest place, so that when he who invited you comes he may say to you, "Friend, go up higher." Then you will have glory in the presence of those who sit at the table with you. For whoever exalts himself will be humbled, and he who humbles himself will be exalted.　　　　(Luke 14:10–11)

The same applies to positions in the body of Christ. Bear in mind that, regardless of position, we are all still at the same table with the Lord—and who is above Him?

When we have begun to live a "throne-ward," listening life before God, the Lord promises that there will be a positive result.

THE RESULTS OF LIVING BEFORE THE THRONE OF GOD

When we live a "throne-ward" and listening life, the Lord says, "*Then you shall also judge My house, and likewise have charge of My courts; I will give you places to walk among these who stand here*" (Zechariah 3:7).

All three things mentioned in this verse can be summed up in one word: *access*. The verse says that we walk among those who stand before the throne of heaven. This is another way of saying that we live a life in the Spirit. This is not a future event; it is available to us now. We also have access to God, walking in His very presence. We go from glory to glory, our lives becoming a reflection of whose we are. Just as Lucifer reflected the glory of God before time, so we stand before the throne of God mirroring His glory. Thus every act of our lives becomes an act of worship to God. This is as it was before the beginning, and it is now again in Christ Jesus.

The truth changes things only when it is applied.

LIVING BEFORE THE THRONE

It is not enough to know the truth, however. The truth changes things only when it is applied. We must make it our total purpose to equip God's church with the truth. Only the truth brings freedom, and it does so when we continue in it (John 8:32). We cannot send the church into battle unarmed and ill equipped; we must know and walk in the truth.

No, the war is not ended. There will yet be violent confrontations with a powerful enemy. Jesus said that *"the kingdom of heaven suffers violence, and the violent take it by force"* (Matthew 11:12). The enemy will still try to divert us from fellowship with God.

But, *you are destined to live before the throne of God.* The victory has been won and the enemy's strategies uncovered! In Christ you are back where you belong—at the throne of God with nothing to separate you from His love. I pray that the Lord will enliven His Word to you and that you will join in the overwhelming victory in Christ Jesus (John 16:33). In the words of the apostle Paul,

> *Yet in all these things we are more than conquerors through Him who loved us. For I am persuaded that neither death nor life, nor angels nor principalities nor powers, nor things present nor things to come, nor height nor depth, nor any other created thing, shall be able to separate us from the love of God which is in Christ Jesus our Lord.*
>
> (Romans 8:37–39)

Appendix A

SATAN'S DEVICES

The Bible teaches us the complete story of eternity, from creation and man's fall to the redemption of man by the blood of Jesus Christ and the final defeat of the enemy. We, as believers, are familiar with how the story ends. Unfortunately, however, many of us don't know where the pitfalls are. We don't know where to be wary of booby traps set by Satan to keep us from our purpose and destiny.

Because we often do not realize the degree of Satan's cunning ingenuity, we are frequently unprepared for the battle we are called to fight against him and his dark forces. Consequently, we end up living defeated lives, thereby not fulfilling the ministry to which God has called us.

This is why it is so important to identify the devices of Satan. It is only when we are aware of his tactics that we can effectively wage war against him. In this section, we will take a look at several common devices of the enemy. As a pastor, I have seen these tactics being employed over and over again by Satan in Christian's lives. I encourage you to carefully examine these devices and prayerfully consider if Satan is waging war against you on these fronts.

DEVICE #1: UNFORGIVENESS

Unforgiveness is a big hindrance to our relationship with God. Some of us cannot forgive ourselves because Satan reminds us of our past mistakes. Or maybe we hold grudges against those who are responsible for hurts in our past. Whatever the case, unforgiveness is a tool that Satan uses to keep us separated from ourselves, others, and, most importantly, God.

You see, if we do not forgive ourselves, then we will most likely not reach full repentance; and if we do not repent, then God cannot forgive us. At the same time, if we do not forgive our brother's trespasses, we are not in a position to receive full forgiveness and healing from God. (See Matthew 18:35.)

God gives us authority to release ourselves and others from the bondage of unforgiveness. *"Whatever you bind on earth will be bound in heaven, and whatever you loose on earth will be loosed in heaven"* (Matthew 18:18). It is crucial, as God's children, that we take steps to break these bonds of unforgiveness!

When we don't forgive, we give Satan an "in" to our lives. This "in" provides him with new opportunities to cause strife and dissension between ourselves and other Christians.

> *Now whom you forgive anything, I also forgive. For if indeed I have forgiven anything, I have forgiven that one for your sakes in the presence of Christ, lest Satan should take advantage of us; for we are not ignorant of his devices.* (2 Corinthians 2:10–11)

This is why it is crucial for us to forgive. Do not let the device of unforgiveness creep into your life. Be on the lookout!

DEVICE #2: PRIDE OF LIFE

What is pride? Pride is puffed-up, all-knowing, self-righteous, and governed by the flesh. Pride is when we are confident that we have everything all figured out when, in reality, we are following foolish human "wisdom." *"There is a way that seems right to a man, but its end is the way of death"* (Proverbs 14:12).

Pride almost always comes before a fall. Many civilizations have collapsed because of pride. Many homes have been broken because of pride. Many souls have been lost because of pride. As Proverbs 16:18 explains, *"Pride goes before destruction, And a haughty spirit before a fall."*

Are you living in pride? Pride can be difficult to identify in our own lives, especially since pride, by its very nature, makes us susceptible to overlooking our faults. One way to check your pride-level, however, is to ask yourself the following questions. Answer them honestly and prayerfully!

1.   Can I be corrected or admonished?

2.   Can I listen and learn from someone else?

3.   Do I look down on people of low estate?

4.   Do I try to keep up with the Joneses?

5.   Do I do whatever it takes to have fame, fortune, or popularity?

Pride doesn't have to be a bad thing. There is such a thing as good pride. Where many have fallen, however, is in the vanity of their minds. Their understanding has been darkened so that their pride is entirely self-centered. When they take pride in their families, their talents, and their accomplishments, for instance, they forget to give credit to the Lord, the One who has provided them with their families, talents, and accomplishments!

If you're struggling with pride, pray about it. Take time to pinpoint the areas of your life in which you are susceptible to pride. As you identify these areas, start chiseling away at your pride by returning thanks to the Lord, the One who provided all your blessings in the first place.

DEVICE #3: LUST OF THE FLESH

Just because it sounds good, feels good, and tastes good doesn't mean it's right. Just because everyone else is doing it doesn't mean you should. It is very easy to succumb to the ways of the world, to compromise our standards until our lives are characterized by the lusts of the flesh. As Christians, however, we are called to something higher.

What is lust of the flesh? I like to define it as those things that satisfy our natural man but bring sickness to our spirit man. Galatians 5:19–21 provides several examples of lustful, fleshly behavior:

Now the works of the flesh are evident, which are: adultery, fornication, uncleanness, lewdness, idolatry, sorcery, hatred, contentions, jealousies, outbursts of wrath, selfish ambitions, dissensions, heresies, envy,

murders, drunkenness, revelries, and the like; of which I tell you before-
hand, just as I also told you in time past, that those who practice such
things will not inherit the kingdom of God.   (Galatians 5:19–20)

Are you walking in the flesh? Look through the following list. If the
following attitudes or behaviors characterize your life, you may be walking
in the flesh.

1. I don't have a clear conscience. I feel regretful, ashamed, and/or
    guilty.

2. I rationalize, justify, and make excuses.

3. I cover up, hide, pretend, and remain in a state of denial.

4. I pilfer, lie, and deceive.

How do we escape the flesh? The truth is that we cannot fully do so
until the Lord perfects us completely when we pass from this life to the
next. In the meantime, though, we are called to fight against the flesh by
walking in the spirit:

For though we walk in the flesh, we do not war according to the flesh.
For the weapons of our warfare are not carnal but mighty in God for
pulling down strongholds, casting down arguments and every high
thing that exalts itself against the knowledge of God, bringing every
thought into captivity to the obedience of Christ, and being ready to
punish all disobedience when your obedience is fulfilled.
                                              (2 Corinthians 10:3–6)

Appendix B

SCRIPTURES ON SATAN

Second Timothy 2:15 says, *"Be diligent to present yourself approved to God, a worker who does not need to be ashamed, rightly dividing the word of truth."* It is sad but true that, these days, we have are often "too busy" to study God's Word on a daily basis. *"The cares of this world and the deceitfulness of riches choke the word"* (Matthew 13:22), so that when affliction or persecution arises, we are easily knocked down and left defenseless against Satan's craftiness.

As believers, it is essential that we equip ourselves with knowledge for defeating Satan and his armies. The source of such knowledge is found only in our Lord's precious Word, the Bible. I encourage you to daily seek God out through prayer and careful study of His Word. You will find it truly rewarding, as well as absolutely crucial, if you are to have spiritual victory over Satan.

Below, I have provided a few Scripture passages to get you started. These passages are specifically on Satan and on how to overcome his wiles. I encourage you, however, to be well-read in all areas of Scripture. Read on many different topics, familiarizing yourself with all of Scripture.

WHAT SCRIPTURE SAYS ABOUT SATAN

He was once a great angel:

Thus says the Lord GOD: "You were the seal of perfection, full of wisdom and perfect in beauty. You were in Eden, the garden of God; every precious stone was your covering: the sardius, topaz, and diamond, beryl, onyx, and jasper, sapphire, turquoise, and emerald with gold. The workmanship of your timbrels and pipes was prepared for you on the day you were created. You were the anointed cherub who covers; I established you; you were on the holy mountain of God; you walked back and forth in the midst of fiery stones."

(Ezekiel 28:12–14)

He was separated from God because of pride:

You were perfect in your ways from the day you were created, till iniquity was found in you. By the abundance of your trading you became filled with violence within, and you sinned; therefore I cast you as a profane thing out of the mountain of God; and I destroyed you, O covering cherub, from the midst of the fiery stones. Your heart was lifted up because of your beauty; you corrupted your wisdom for the sake of your splendor; I cast you to the ground, I laid you before kings, that they might gaze at you. You defiled your sanctuaries by the multitude of your iniquities, by the iniquity of your trading; therefore I brought fire from your midst; it devoured you, and I turned you to ashes upon the earth in the sight of all who saw you. All who knew you among the peoples are astonished at you; you have become a horror, and shall be no more forever.

(Ezekiel 28:15–19)

Your pomp is brought down to Sheol, and the sound of your stringed instruments; the maggot is spread under you, and worms cover you. How you are fallen from heaven, O Lucifer, son of the morning! How you are cut down to the ground, you who weakened the nations! For you have said in your heart: "I will ascend into heaven, I will exalt my throne above the stars of God; I will also sit on the mount of the congregation on the farthest sides of the north; I will ascend above the heights of the clouds, I will be like the Most High." Yet you shall be brought down to Sheol, to the lowest depths of the Pit.   (Isaiah 14:11–15)

He has a host of fallen angels, or demons, who assist him:

And war broke out in heaven: Michael and his angels fought with the dragon; and the dragon and his angels fought, but they did not prevail, nor was a place found for them in heaven any longer. So the great dragon was cast out, that serpent of old, called the Devil and Satan, who deceives the whole world; he was cast to the earth, and his angels were cast out with him. (Revelation 12:7–9)

He works to deceive God's people:

Satan himself transforms himself into an angel of light.
(2 Corinthians 11:14)

For false christs and false prophets will rise and show great signs and wonders to deceive, if possible, even the elect. (Matthew 24:24)

Now the serpent was more cunning than any beast of the field which the LORD *God had made. And he said to the woman, "Has God indeed said, 'You shall not eat of every tree of the garden'?...For God knows that in the day you eat of it your eyes will be opened, and you will be like God, knowing good and evil."* (Genesis 3:1, 5)

He can perform signs:

He performs great signs, so that he even makes fire come down from heaven on the earth in the sight of men. (Revelation 13:13)

He is a liar:

He was a murderer from the beginning, and does not stand in the truth, because there is no truth in him. When he speaks a lie, he speaks from his own resources, for he is a liar and the father of it. (John 8:44)

He is an accuser:

Then I heard a loud voice saying in heaven, "Now salvation, and strength, and the kingdom of our God, and the power of His Christ have come, for the accuser of our brethren, who accused them before our God day and night, has been cast down." (Revelation 12:10)

276 WITCHCRAFT IN THE PEWS AND SPIRITUAL WARFARE

He brings death:

The thief does not come except to steal, and to kill, and to destroy. I have come that they may have life, and that they may have it more abundantly. (John 10:10)

He wages war against God's servants:

It was granted to him to make war with the saints and to overcome them. And authority was given him over every tribe, tongue, and nation. (Revelation 13:7)

He will not conquer us when the Spirit is our strength:

Behold, I give you the authority to trample on serpents and scorpions, and over all the power of the enemy, and nothing shall by any means hurt you. (Luke 10:19)

He will be defeated by God once and for all:

Then He will also say to those on the left hand, "Depart from Me, you cursed, into the everlasting fire prepared for the devil and his angels." (Matthew 25:41)

Then the seventy returned with joy, saying, "Lord, even the demons are subject to us in Your name." And He said to them, "I saw Satan fall like lightning from heaven. Behold, I give you the authority to trample on serpents and scorpions, and over all the power of the enemy, and nothing shall by any means hurt you. Nevertheless do not rejoice in this, that the spirits are subject to you, but rather rejoice because your names are written in heaven." (Luke 10:17–20)

Inasmuch then as the children have partaken of flesh and blood, He Himself likewise shared in the same, that through death He might destroy him who had the power of death, that is, the devil, and release those who through fear of death were all their lifetime subject to bondage. (Hebrews 2:14–15)

Then I saw an angel coming down from heaven, having the key to the bottomless pit and a great chain in his hand. He laid hold of the dragon, that serpent of old, who is the Devil and Satan, and bound him for a thousand years; and he cast him into the bottomless pit, and shut him up, and set a seal on him, so that he should deceive the nations no more till the thousand years were finished. But after these things he must be released for a little while. (Revelation 20:1–3)

WHAT SCRIPTURE SAYS ABOUT RESISTING SATAN

We must be wary of deception:

Beloved, do not believe every spirit, but test the spirits, whether they are of God; because many false prophets have gone out into the world. (1 John 4:1)

We must forgive, so as not to give Satan a foothold:

For if indeed I have forgiven anything, I have forgiven that one for your sakes in the presence of Christ, lest Satan should take advantage of us; for we are not ignorant of his devices. (2 Corinthians 2:10–11)

"Be angry, and do not sin": do not let the sun go down on your wrath, nor give place to the devil. (Ephesians 4:26–27)

We must be on the lookout for attacks:

Be sober, be vigilant; because your adversary the devil walks about like a roaring lion, seeking whom he may devour. Resist him, steadfast in the faith, knowing that the same sufferings are experienced by your brotherhood in the world. (1 Peter 5:8–9)

We are to fight by the Spirit, not in the flesh:

For though we walk in the flesh, we do not war according to the flesh. For the weapons of our warfare are not carnal but mighty in God for pulling down strongholds, casting down arguments and every high thing that exalts itself against the knowledge of God, bringing every thought into captivity to the obedience of Christ, and being ready to punish all disobedience when your obedience is fulfilled.

(2 Corinthians 10:3–6)

Finally, my brethren, be strong in the Lord and in the power of His might. Put on the whole armor of God, that you may be able to stand against the wiles of the devil. For we do not wrestle against flesh and blood, but against principalities, against powers, against the rulers of the darkness of this age, against spiritual hosts of wickedness in the heavenly places. (Ephesians 6:10–12)

We are to resist the devil through Scripture:

Then Jesus was led up by the Spirit into the wilderness to be tempted by the devil. And when He had fasted forty days and forty nights, afterward He was hungry. Now when the tempter came to Him, he said, "If You are the Son of God, command that these stones become bread." But He answered and said, "It is written, 'Man shall not live by bread alone, but by every word that proceeds from the mouth of God.'"

(Matthew 4:1–4; see also verses 5–11)

We are to put on the armor of God:

Therefore take up the whole armor of God, that you may be able to withstand in the evil day, and having done all, to stand. Stand therefore, having girded your waist with truth, having put on the breastplate of righteousness, and having shod your feet with the preparation of the gospel of peace; above all, taking the shield of faith with which you will be able to quench all the fiery darts of the wicked one. And take the helmet of salvation, and the sword of the Spirit, which is the word of God; praying always with all prayer and supplication in the Spirit, being watchful to this end with all perseverance and supplication for all the saints. (Ephesians 6:13–18)

We must remember that the Lord has already won the battle and defeated Satan:

You are of God, little children, and have overcome them, because He who is in you is greater than he who is in the world. (1 John 4:4)

SCRIPTURES ON SATAN 279

We must remember that Satan is subject to the Lord and His commands:

> *...which He worked in Christ when He raised Him from the dead and seated Him at His right hand in the heavenly places, far above all principality and power and might and dominion, and every name that is named, not only in this age but also in that which is to come.*
>
> (Ephesians 1:20–21)

> *For I am persuaded that neither death nor life, nor angels nor principalities nor powers, nor things present nor things to come, nor height nor depth, nor any other created thing, shall be able to separate us from the love of God which is in Christ Jesus our Lord.*
>
> (Romans 8:38–39)

BONUS CHAPTER: OVERCOMING THE PYTHON SPIRIT

OVERCOMING THE PYTHON SPIRIT

This chapter is designed to bring deliverance to those who find themselves in the death grip of authority abuse.

Reading and applying its message will cause you to walk in freedom from the suffocating spirit of authority abuse that squeezes the life out of its victims, consuming the remains of their collapsed and weary frames.

The attributes and behavior of this spirit is similar to an animal in the natural realm: the python snake. This reptile wraps itself around its prey and squeezes the life out of it to satisfy its appetite.

As we consider the essence of authority abuse and discuss the process of deliverance, it will be useful to think of this analogy in the natural realm. The python snake provides a fitting parallel that evokes the very first authority abuser: Satan.

SCRIPTURAL PRECEDENT FOR THE SERPENT ANALOGY

From my studies, I know that in the book of Genesis, Satan took control of a serpent and used it as an instrument in his work of temptation.

He indwelled the serpent in the garden of Eden, where Adam and Eve lived in harmony. Satan's plan was to be the driving temptation to get

Adam and Eve out of the garden, where they had been protected from all of the satanic devices that would be perpetrated and perpetuated by the human race.

Although Satan's plan intended to bring about humankind's utter demise, God used Satan's evil schemes to bring redemption to humankind. For we know that *"all things work together for good to them that love God, to them who are the called according to his purpose"* (Romans 8:28).

> ## God used Satan's evil schemes to redeem humankind.

One of the questions that we may ask until Jesus returns is, Why did God operate that way? Why did He allow Adam and Eve to be tempted and subsequently evicted from the garden of Eden?

People have been asking this question for ages, and yet no one has received an answer—at least, no one has received an answer that we can authenticate as coming from God.

We think, *He could have just made us perfect,* yet are left wondering why He didn't. God is never without a plan or a purpose, however; His plan is for us to be perfect.

> *Now the God of peace, that brought again from the dead our Lord Jesus, that great shepherd of the sheep, through the blood of the everlasting covenant, Make you perfect in every good work to do his will, working in you that which is wellpleasing in his sight, through Jesus Christ; to whom be glory for ever and ever. Amen.*
>
> (Hebrews 13:20–21 KJV)

The serpent was Lucifer's agent to lure Adam and Eve into doing his will, which was to push them out of the garden of Eden.

Thus, God gave us His Son Jesus in order to restore us to Himself and make us perfect *"to do His will."*

Because we are dealing continually with this ever-present evil force, God allows us to go through a process in order to perfect His divine will within us.

The apostle Paul put it this way:

> *For I know that in me (that is, in my flesh,) dwelleth no good thing: for to will is present with me; but how to perform that which is good I find not. For the good that I would I do not: but the evil which I would not, that I do. Now if I do that I would not, it is no more I that do it, but sin that dwelleth in me. I find then a law, that, when I would do good, evil is present with me. For I delight in the law of God after the inward man: But I see another law in my members, warring against the law of my mind, and bringing me into captivity to the law of sin which is in my members. O wretched man that I am! who shall deliver me from the body of this death? I thank God through Jesus Christ our Lord. So then with the mind I myself serve the law of God; but with the flesh the law of sin.* (Romans 7:18–25 KJV)

HOW THE PYTHON SPIRIT OPERATES

The reptile known as a *python* is "a large, non-venomous snake that crushes its prey." It kills its prey not by biting it or injecting venom but by squeezing, crushing, and suffocating it so it can swallow and digest it.

When I discuss the *python spirit*, I am not referring to a demon. Rather, I am referring to the spirit of individuals whose character and behavior—and the influence of these traits on other people—mimic those of a python in the wild.

This type of spirit woos you into danger, becomes intimate with you, and finally kills you spiritually. It is the spirit that inspires all authority abusers.

Authority abusers are inspired by the python spirit.

When you are deceived by this false spirit, you begin telling yourself, "Nobody loves me like this person. This person makes me feel good about myself." But this person with a python spirit is forcing the life out of you. It is as if your spirit weighed 200 pounds but the python spirit has squeezed it down to 100 pounds in record time.

You may feel you're doing God's will seven days a week, but you are depriving your body of the spiritual nutrients necessary for a healthy, Christian life. Then, as you become spiritually incapacitated, the python suddenly begins sucking you in completely.

You can no longer think for yourself because you now live in the belly of a satanic spirit whose intention was always to consume you, thereby satisfying his greedy appetite.

He knew that he had to operate through deception, because if you had seen him as he truly was, you would have evaded him.

This spirit became your "friend" in order to inoculate your mind with its demonic agenda before drawing you in to crush you.

When an individual with the python spirit is finished with you, he leaves you spiritually crippled and in despair—you are actually lying in the belly of a predator.

This is a determined spirit that is not easily deterred. It is also completely confusing because it is a spirit that may attach itself to someone you love dearly or trust completely.

Often, this person is a pastor. We discussed in Chapter Six how pastors often abuse authority, but let's briefly revisit this issue as it relates to the python spirit.

PASTORS PREY ON CONGREGATIONS

I come from a Seventh-day Adventist background. One of the blessings of being raised as an Adventist was our strong, scriptural diet.

In the Adventist church I attended in my youth, the teachers and ministers didn't just come up with ideas; their teachings were full of scriptural authenticity.

Today, I often hear preachers in the pulpit make up their own doctrine on the spot, attempting to justify it by saying something like, "This is the Greek definition."

When asked to substantiate their teachings, however, they come up short and cannot qualify their philosophies with biblical accuracy.

As a pastor, I have had to overturn erroneous teachings that former pastors instilled in the minds of gullible church members. Their understanding of the Word of God had been shaped by family traditions, religious rituals, and, yes, sometimes even doctrines of devils; challenging those beliefs sometimes caused offenses to arise.

My job, however, is to continue preaching the truth, for with truth comes freedom (see John 8:32).

No one is exempt from the python spirit's influence.

We all have an agenda, a purpose, and a point that we are trying to convey when we minister or speak to others. What better way is there to convince Christians of something (which may or may not be true) than to say, "God said"?

If an individual is using this method to prove a point, then what he or she says must be confirmed, qualified, or validated by scriptural truths before you allow a false idea to slither its way into your mind, and especially into your spirit.

An unfortunate thing about the python spirit is that none of us is exempt from its influence.

All too often, we act upon things that are drummed up from the enemy whose tendency is to add just enough truth to draw his victims close enough to squeeze the life out of them.

You must be able to move on without allowing the things you hear to ruin your life or cause it to stagnate. You must receive the Word of God and allow it to transform your life. The Word of the Lord is life, and it is powerful by itself.

> *For the word of God is quick, and powerful, and sharper than any twoedged sword, piercing even to the dividing asunder of soul and spirit, and of the joints and marrow, and is a discerner of the thoughts and intents of the heart.* (Hebrews 4:12 KJV)

The truth of God is not one-sided; it cuts in both directions. It is designed to cut off things that hinder your progress.

SOOTHSAYERS AND OTHER SOURCES OF COUNSEL

I often refer to the python spirit when ministering to individuals who tend to seek the counsel of soothsayers for spiritual guidance.

A *soothsayer* is "a person who foretells events," and *soothsaying* is "prophecy or prediction; a practice or art of foretelling events."

Although the word *prophecy* is mentioned in this definition, it does not mean biblical prophecy but foretelling of events by studying and interpreting the alignment of the stars, astrology, birthstones, dates, and other natural forces.

The sixteenth chapter of the book of Acts talks about a young girl who has the spirit of divination. Obviously, many people flocked to hear her direction; she *"brought her masters much gain by soothsaying"* (Acts 16:16 KJV).

Divination is "the act or art of foretelling the unknown; the practice of seeking to tell future events."

How does one practice foretelling events? Through stargazing, birthstones, crystal-gazing, or incense reading, a diviner practices until he or she learns the art.

Throughout the 1980s and 1990s, an overwhelming number of infomercials advertised psychics and their services. The popularity of psychics and psychic readings had waned, but today it is making a comeback; its credibility is increasing as well.

This next level of divination and sorcery that we are going to encounter is so powerful because it will encompass much truth with just a few lies attached. This means that you will find those who work the principles of satanic literature appearing to be blessed by their practices.

For example, the "law of attraction," which holds that individuals possess the power to draw to themselves what they believe and articulate, sounds similar to many of our scriptural teachings, such as:

> *For verily I say unto you, that whosoever shall say unto this mountain,*
> *Be thou removed, and be thou cast into the sea; and shall not doubt in*
> *his heart, but shall believe that those things which he saith shall come to*
> *pass; he shall have whatsoever he saith.*   (Mark 11:23 KJV)

> *For with the heart man believeth unto righteousness; and with the*
> *mouth confession is made unto salvation.*   (Romans 10:10 KJV)

But where does this teaching originate? Does it come from God, or does it come from bookshelves and mystical teachings?

It is the same brand of teaching, but something is horribly wrong.

It seems that more and more people are consulting mediums, psychics, therapists, or pastors for direction. Almost everyone is searching for enlightenment, understanding, a higher power, or a greater knowledge.

The python spirit is taking advantage of this trend, which brings to light the prophetic message found in Luke 10:2: "*The harvest truly is great, but the labourers are few.*"

Psychics' predictions end with spiritual death.

There is a great harvest of individuals who desire a greater understanding of God, but the laborers are being corrupted by false doctrinal beliefs.

The python is lying in wait; he has us surrounded. But instead of rebuking him, we pet him as we would a harmless animal, thus promoting his demonic propaganda.

We are fascinated by the mystique of the pattern of his coat, blind to the fact that he is wrapping himself around our legs and preparing to pull us to our knees.

Soothsayers' practices and methods lead back to the python spirit. This practice or art of foretelling events by soothsayers is associated with a python because the predictions that you receive from soothsayers will ultimately end with spiritual death. (See, for example, Deuteronomy 18:14; Jeremiah 50:36; Micah 5:12.)

No matter how sweet, wonderful, or well-wishing a prediction may seem, it is earthly, sensual, and demonic (see James 3:15).

Although it may feel good to have your hand read by a palm reader, doing so opens the door to the *python spirit*.

You may get so caught up in wanting to know your future that you spend your fortune to find out your fortune. Charlatans will prey upon your vulnerabilities, promising to give you foresight about the future. In return, you will forfeit your enjoyment of the present.

This particular spirit preys on its victims by crushing and suffocating them after enticing them to learn about the unknown.

Many of us focus on the physical characteristics of individuals who make predictions, but our focus should be on the character of the spirit that is being used to deliver the message.

This spirit has to woo you, wrap itself around you, and squeeze you as if providing comfort. As it continues to tighten its grip, you realize that your life is actually being drained from you.

GOSSIP AND THE PYTHON SPIRIT

The true essence of the python spirit can be summed up in one word: *gossip*.

Gossipers exhibit this same type of behavior. They fill their bellies with information regarding the lives of others, and when confronted, they will regurgitate all types of disgusting propaganda to save their own hides.

There is nothing so savory, delicious, and appetizing as a good piece of gossip—as long as it's not about you, of course. The Bible tells us, however, to avoid the sin of gossip. (See, for example, Proverbs 16:28, 20:19 NIV.)

Whether we admit it, all of us are prone to gossiping and likely to formulate opinions concerning others—especially today in the age of E-mail. At certain intervals, God has to come and whisper, "That's enough. Don't allow yourself to become caught up in those types of conversations."

> *Gossipers regurgitate*
> *disgusting propaganda.*

When you start to deal with God, it's never about another person. It's God showing you yourself. You are not going to change the inherent pattern of the world; you can only make a difference, and the difference must start with you.

Ask yourself, *Why is it that when I fall, 'God knows my heart,' but when others fall, 'they should be ashamed of themselves'?*

If God's mercy can carry you through your trials, then it can surely carry others through theirs.

DEAL, DON'T DENY

After a python has swallowed its prey, it just lies there and waits for the digestion process to be completed.

Movement could mean death for the snake—the prey might penetrate its skin, stretched and weakened to allow passage of its prey.

Similarly, after it has killed something large, the python spirit just lies in silence. You can sense that something is amiss, however, because it appears to have grown strangely fat and complacent overnight.

When are real pythons caught, killed, and skinned for their skin to make beautiful shoes and bags?

When they have just consumed some of their prey, because this is when they are too fat and too delirious to move or defend themselves.

They lie still as if everything is normal, but somewhere in the midst of all that is going on, truth and deliverance show up. Attack a python suddenly, and it will regurgitate its prey in order to escape and save its own life.

When you determine to believe God, you will often come under attack.

When we are dealing with the ever-present evil forces of the python spirit, we must make a decisive effort to do what is good rather than giving in to evil.

Why is it often easier to do what is wrong than to do what is right? Because we reside in a world where it seems as if evil is always present, and if you are not careful, your flesh will tend to adapt to the present-day environment.

When the desires and inclinations of your flesh war against your mind or your spirit, you must immediately cast down every thought that might attempt to squeeze the life out of you and exalt itself above the knowledge of God (see 2 Corinthians 10:5).

Often when you determine to believe God, you will come under attack.

Should this occur, you will have to deal with the attack; denying it will not cause it to go away. The more you make it out to be something that it is not, the longer it will take for you to be delivered from it.

We leaders in ministry are called to minister with a word to set the captives free, but is it possible for us to deliver and set people free from something from which we ourselves have not been set free or delivered?

The answer is, *Sometimes…but not in every instance.* The more time you spend in private communion with God, the more God will reveal to you your flaws and any idiosyncrasies from which you need deliverance.

This could explain why many people avoid spending private time with God: spending private time with Him is self-reflective.

When you avoid God, however, the scales of injustice become unequally balanced, favoring the side of evil. If you refuse to listen to God concerning your weaknesses, you do little to strengthen your defenses or even to become delivered from many of the frailties that are keeping you bound.

This bondage makes the perfect opportunity for the python spirit to find you in the darkness and prey upon your weakened state of mind.

My deliverance started more than a decade ago, before I began pastoring and preaching to others about being set free.

I am now able to identify other people who are dealing with those same stubborn spirits and position myself to be used by God to bless them.

Two of the most vital components to deliverance are the ability to confront ourselves and the act of forgiveness.

Your identity as a Christian has much to do with how you deal with offenses and forgiveness. Forgiveness is one way in which God imparts and conveys His nature. Forgiveness is the essence of the nature and spirit of God. So when conflicts occur, we must determine to work them out and forgive our adversaries, because that is how we grow in God.

> *Forgiveness is one way in which God imparts His nature.*

Some people make up their minds not to work out misunderstandings and transgressions; instead, they say, "I'm just going to turn it over to the Lord."

These people are not following God's commands or His instructions for deliverance. Because they maintain their irate disposition, their health gradually succumbs to the grudge from which they refuse to be delivered.

When you refuse to follow the plan that God has established, you begin to backslide—you blame everyone else for your problems and spread the negative aura of your bad mood.

Many of the flaws that you now see in others are nothing new. In most cases, these individuals have long been as they are, but now you notice their apparent flaws because you have allowed yourself to stoop to their level.

It's not a newer revelation that you are receiving about others; rather, you are receiving a revelation about yourself.

The healing process almost always hurts, but as your wounds heal, you grow stronger and better.

When no one is in the house to pray for you or to help you to work your way to your next miracle, you must take the initiative to invoke your own deliverance.

Deliverance comes when you decide to be set free.

Deliverance comes when you decide to be set free. If you don't make that decision, you will remain bound. At some point, you must stop and say to yourself, "Enough is enough....This is the end of this....Now is the time for me to be set free!"

I found out that many people are dying for their right to hold on to the anger they harbor for a wound they received. They want to own the right to be upset. They see the car coming toward them, but because they have the right-of-way, they refuse to stop—even though their precious little ones are riding in the backseat of the car!

You could be holding on to something that you have the right to hold on to, but in the process, it's killing you on the inside.

You have the right to be upset, angry, and mad—you're right because you were wronged, but the person who wronged you is going on with his or her life, while yours has taken an abrupt halt.

WAIT PATIENTLY AND QUIETLY FOR DELIVERANCE

Jesus cast out demons and delivered people in three different postures: 1) *"immediately"* (see, for example, Matthew 8:3; 14:31 and Mark 1:31; 1:42), 2) *"that same hour"* (Matthew 8:13) or *"that very hour"* (Matthew 15:28; 17:18), and 3) *"not many days from now"* (Acts 1:5).

Many people will be set free immediately; some will have to travail with intercessors at the altar, and others will experience deliverance over a period of several years.

In fact, these people will grow into their deliverance, becoming individuals with an extraordinary knowledge of revelation and wisdom regarding demonic forces.

Silence often damages Satan's plans.

When you are under attack, the worst thing you can do is to keep talking, because this foils your strategy.

There is always *"a time to keep silence, and a time to speak"* (Ecclesiastes 3:7), and it is your responsibility to discern the times to preserve your spiritual health and well-being.

You will find that in many instances, silence will enable the greatest damage to the enemy's plans, for the spirit that is out to destroy you wants you to talk yourself into a spiritual grave. The more you talk, the more leeway Satan has to trip you up with your own words.

The more you hold your peace, the more the power of God arises within you to show you how to win the battle.

In our anger, we often spew things from our mouth and do more harm than good.

That is why, in the midst of the Israelites' complaints, Moses commanded them to hold their peace; God would fight the battle (see Exodus 14:14).

296 WITCHCRAFT IN THE PEWS AND SPIRITUAL WARFARE

Being quiet takes practice and requires spiritual schooling, as 1 Thessalonians 4:11 says: *"ye study to be quiet, and to do your own business, and to work with your own hands"* (KJV).

There is a campaign going on in glory on behalf of your imminent victory. That is why being quiet is so difficult that the Bible says it requires training—a course in Silence 101 as a requirement to reaching your next level.

Although this is the type of attack that we will all encounter at some point, it is also one that we all have the power to overcome—with wisdom. *Wisdom* is the ability to execute properly the knowledge you already have.

How spiritual or spirited are you? "Spirited" individuals are those who are easily knocked out of the race because they make decisions based on their emotions.

When the music stops and the song has ended, the most important question is whether you know Jesus. Does He live in your heart? Can you navigate your way through life, even when there is no song?

> *A spiritual individual can hear God's voice even when the music stops.*

Without a musician directing the band or dabbling with the synthesizer to let you know when something evil is about to take place, can you still discern the times?

This ability is what separates a "spiritual" individual from one who is simply "spirited." When the music stops playing, a spiritual individual can still hear the voice of God.

When you have conversations with people, you must be able to discern when their metaphorical horns (indicative of evil inclinations) are about to grow.

I can usually tell when an individual's conversation is about to go too far, and when I make this determination, I immediately say to him or her, "That wasn't right."

Without the ability to listen with discernment, you will get drawn in; only when it's too late will you find out that things were really not as they seemed.

You will begin to murmur regrets: "I was under an attack and I didn't even know it. I was speaking in tongues, fellowshipping with God but God never told me!"

That, of course, is a lie. God *did* tell you, but because your focus had shifted to something that was much more appealing to your flesh, you refused to listen to what God had to say.

Consequently, what you are now receiving is causing you to lose what you had. You have lost your sensitivity, your insight, and your ability to reason.

The same spirit caused an entire nation to rise up against one man: Jesus. What could a loving Savior have possibly done to incite an entire nation to rise up in outrage and kill Him?

It wasn't because He had tax problems; He paid his taxes faithfully and punctually. Instead, it was for His good deeds that He was killed—healing the sick, raising the dead, feeding the hungry on the Sabbath day, comforting a woman caught in the act of adultery, raising Lazarus from the dead, and so forth.

It was because of Jesus' good deeds that many of the people rose up against Him.

That spirit of excellence, good character, godly essence, and charismatic personality is always found in pacesetters.

What you must understand about yourself is that there are things happening in your life that do not yet have corresponding explanatory entries in the encyclopedia of life.

Why? Because you are a pacesetter, and after you have completely overcome whatever is trying to overtake you, your name and crisis are going to show up in the encyclopedia of life. You will be the one to whom others look for answers.

I know that I am called to fulfill some things that other people are not equipped to carry out. This is why I do not have to frequently go through the ritual of casting out demons.

Remaining in bondage results from a personal choice.

Instead, the Word that the Lord gives is so powerful that as I am preaching, the masses are delivered simply by hearing the Word of God as they are sitting in their seats.

Remaining in bondage comes as the result of a personal choice. The reason that pastors endure extreme hardships is often that while they are looking at the present, the devil has his eyes on the future; he will make any and every attempt to squeeze the life out of the future before it comes to pass.

Satan knows that after pastors emerge from a trial or tribulation, their example will provide answers to others regarding their own life crises.

Therefore, your job is to pray for your leaders and to avoid gossip at all costs.

In the next chapter, we will discuss how proper authority should be restored after victims of authority abuse have been delivered.

Pray that your leaders will emerge from their trials with victory and that complete healing will take place.

Prayer: *I pray in the name of Jesus for your complete freedom today from every controlling and forceful spirit that may have wrapped itself around your finances, family, marriage, relationships, health, or any other area of your life. I release you into the abundance of God's grace and pray that you will prosper and be in health, even as your soul shall* prosper. I release the prosperity of your soul so that it will be manifest in your daily life. May you be set free by the power of God! In Jesus' name, amen.

ABOUT THE AUTHOR

Bishop George Bloomer is the longtime host of *Rejoice in the Word* on The Word Network and host of *The Battleground* on Total Christian Television. He is an internationally known conference speaker, pastor of Bethel Life Family Worship Center in Durham, North Carolina, and presiding bishop of C.L.U.R.T. (Come Let Us Reason Together) International Assemblies.

Bishop Bloomer has been preaching for more than forty years in more than twenty-seven countries around the world. He is a best-selling author, having written more than seventy books, despite not being able to read until well into his adult years.

Well-known for his unique approach to Scripture and affectionately known as "General Spiritual Warfare," he is also host of his own weekly television program, *Spiritual Authority*.